50% OFF Online PERT Prep Cou~~rse!~~

Dear Customer,

We consider it an honor and a privilege that you chose our PERT Study Guide. As a way of showing our appreciation and to help us better serve you, we have partnered with Mometrix Test Preparation to offer you **50% off their online PERT Prep Course**. Many PERT courses are needlessly expensive and don't deliver enough value. With their course, you get access to the best PERT prep material, and **you only pay half price**.

Mometrix has structured their online course to perfectly complement your printed study guide. The PERT Prep Course contains **in-depth lessons** that cover all the most important topics, **170+ video reviews** that explain difficult concepts, over **350 practice questions** to ensure you feel prepared, and **434 digital flashcards**, so you can study while you're on the go.

Online PERT Prep Course

Topics Included:
- Mathematics
  - Numbers and Operations
  - Proportions and Ratios
  - Polynomial Algebra
- Reading
  - Arguments and Logical Errors
  - Vocabulary and Word Relationships
- Writing
  - Parts of Speech
  - Agreement and Sentence Structure
  - Writing Style and Form

Course Features:
- PERT Study Guide
  - Get content that complements our best-selling study guide.
- Full-Length Practice Tests
  - With over 350 practice questions, you can test yourself again and again.
- Mobile Friendly
  - If you need to study on the go, the course is easily accessible from your mobile device.
- 434 Flashcards
  - Their course includes a flashcard mode with 434 content cards to help you study.

To receive this discount, visit them at mometrix.com/university/pert/ or simply scan this QR code with your smartphone. At the checkout page, enter the discount code: **TPBPERT50**

If you have any questions or concerns, please contact them at support@mometrix.com.

SCAN HERE

 in partnership with

FREE Test Taking Tips Video/DVD Offer

To better serve you, we created videos covering test taking tips that we want to give you for FREE. **These videos cover world-class tips that will help you succeed on your test.**

We just ask that you send us feedback about this product. Please let us know what you thought about it—whether good, bad, or indifferent.

To get your **FREE videos**, you can use the QR code below or email freevideos@studyguideteam.com with "Free Videos" in the subject line and the following information in the body of the email:

    a. The title of your product

    b. Your product rating on a scale of 1-5, with 5 being the highest

    c. Your feedback about the product

If you have any questions or concerns, please don't hesitate to contact us at info@studyguideteam.com.

Thank you!

PERT Study Guide

PERT Test Prep Review with Practice Exam
Questions for the Florida Certification [3rd Edition]

Joshua Rueda

Written and edited by TPB Publishing.

TPB Publishing is not associated with or endorsed by any official testing organization. TPB Publishing is a publisher of unofficial educational products. All test and organization names are trademarks of their respective owners. Content in this book is included for utilitarian purposes only and does not constitute an endorsement by TPB Publishing of any particular point of view.

Interested in buying more than 10 copies of our product? Contact us about bulk discounts:
bulkorders@studyguideteam.com

ISBN 13: 9781637754009
ISBN 10: 1637754000

Table of Contents

Quick Overview

As you draw closer to taking your exam, effective preparation becomes more and more important. Thankfully, you have this study guide to help you get ready. Use this guide to help keep your studying on track and refer to it often.

This study guide contains several key sections that will help you be successful on your exam. The guide contains tips for what you should do the night before and the day of the test. Also included are test-taking tips. Knowing the right information is not always enough. Many well-prepared test takers struggle with exams. These tips will help equip you to accurately read, assess, and answer test questions.

A large part of the guide is devoted to showing you what content to expect on the exam and to helping you better understand that content. In this guide are practice test questions so that you can see how well you have grasped the content. Then, answer explanations are provided so that you can understand why you missed certain questions.

Don't try to cram the night before you take your exam. This is not a wise strategy for a few reasons. First, your retention of the information will be low. Your time would be better used by reviewing information you already know rather than trying to learn a lot of new information. Second, you will likely become stressed as you try to gain a large amount of knowledge in a short amount of time. Third, you will be depriving yourself of sleep. So be sure to go to bed at a reasonable time the night before. Being well-rested helps you focus and remain calm.

Be sure to eat a substantial breakfast the morning of the exam. If you are taking the exam in the afternoon, be sure to have a good lunch as well. Being hungry is distracting and can make it difficult to focus. You have hopefully spent lots of time preparing for the exam. Don't let an empty stomach get in the way of success!

When travelling to the testing center, leave earlier than needed. That way, you have a buffer in case you experience any delays. This will help you remain calm and will keep you from missing your appointment time at the testing center.

Be sure to pace yourself during the exam. Don't try to rush through the exam. There is no need to risk performing poorly on the exam just so you can leave the testing center early. Allow yourself to use all of the allotted time if needed.

Remain positive while taking the exam even if you feel like you are performing poorly. Thinking about the content you should have mastered will not help you perform better on the exam.

Once the exam is complete, take some time to relax. Even if you feel that you need to take the exam again, you will be well served by some down time before you begin studying again. It's often easier to convince yourself to study if you know that it will come with a reward!

Test-Taking Strategies

1. Predicting the Answer

When you feel confident in your preparation for a multiple-choice test, try predicting the answer before reading the answer choices. This is especially useful on questions that test objective factual knowledge. By predicting the answer before reading the available choices, you eliminate the possibility that you will be distracted or led astray by an incorrect answer choice. You will feel more confident in your selection if you read the question, predict the answer, and then find your prediction among the answer choices. After using this strategy, be sure to still read all of the answer choices carefully and completely. If you feel unprepared, you should not attempt to predict the answers. This would be a waste of time and an opportunity for your mind to wander in the wrong direction.

2. Reading the Whole Question

Too often, test takers scan a multiple-choice question, recognize a few familiar words, and immediately jump to the answer choices. Test authors are aware of this common impatience, and they will sometimes prey upon it. For instance, a test author might subtly turn the question into a negative, or he or she might redirect the focus of the question right at the end. The only way to avoid falling into these traps is to read the entirety of the question carefully before reading the answer choices.

3. Looking for Wrong Answers

Long and complicated multiple-choice questions can be intimidating. One way to simplify a difficult multiple-choice question is to eliminate all of the answer choices that are clearly wrong. In most sets of answers, there will be at least one selection that can be dismissed right away. If the test is administered on paper, the test taker could draw a line through it to indicate that it may be ignored; otherwise, the test taker will have to perform this operation mentally or on scratch paper. In either case, once the obviously incorrect answers have been eliminated, the remaining choices may be considered. Sometimes identifying the clearly wrong answers will give the test taker some information about the correct answer. For instance, if one of the remaining answer choices is a direct opposite of one of the eliminated answer choices, it may well be the correct answer. The opposite of obviously wrong is obviously right! Of course, this is not always the case. Some answers are obviously incorrect simply because they are irrelevant to the question being asked. Still, identifying and eliminating some incorrect answer choices is a good way to simplify a multiple-choice question.

4. Don't Overanalyze

Anxious test takers often overanalyze questions. When you are nervous, your brain will often run wild, causing you to make associations and discover clues that don't actually exist. If you feel that this may be a problem for you, do whatever you can to slow down during the test. Try taking a deep breath or counting to ten. As you read and consider the question, restrict yourself to the particular words used by the author. Avoid thought tangents about what the author *really* meant, or what he or she was *trying* to say. The only things that matter on a multiple-choice test are the words that are actually in the question. You must avoid reading too much into a multiple-choice question, or supposing that the writer meant something other than what he or she wrote.

2

5. No Need for Panic

It is wise to learn as many strategies as possible before taking a multiple-choice test, but it is likely that you will come across a few questions for which you simply don't know the answer. In this situation, avoid panicking. Because most multiple-choice tests include dozens of questions, the relative value of a single wrong answer is small. As much as possible, you should compartmentalize each question on a multiple-choice test. In other words, you should not allow your feelings about one question to affect your success on the others. When you find a question that you either don't understand or don't know how to answer, just take a deep breath and do your best. Read the entire question slowly and carefully. Try rephrasing the question a couple of different ways. Then, read all of the answer choices carefully. After eliminating obviously wrong answers, make a selection and move on to the next question.

6. Confusing Answer Choices

When working on a difficult multiple-choice question, there may be a tendency to focus on the answer choices that are the easiest to understand. Many people, whether consciously or not, gravitate to the answer choices that require the least concentration, knowledge, and memory. This is a mistake. When you come across an answer choice that is confusing, you should give it extra attention. A question might be confusing because you do not know the subject matter to which it refers. If this is the case, don't eliminate the answer before you have affirmatively settled on another. When you come across an answer choice of this type, set it aside as you look at the remaining choices. If you can confidently assert that one of the other choices is correct, you can leave the confusing answer aside. Otherwise, you will need to take a moment to try to better understand the confusing answer choice. Rephrasing is one way to tease out the sense of a confusing answer choice.

7. Your First Instinct

Many people struggle with multiple-choice tests because they overthink the questions. If you have studied sufficiently for the test, you should be prepared to trust your first instinct once you have carefully and completely read the question and all of the answer choices. There is a great deal of research suggesting that the mind can come to the correct conclusion very quickly once it has obtained all of the relevant information. At times, it may seem to you as if your intuition is working faster even than your reasoning mind. This may in fact be true. The knowledge you obtain while studying may be retrieved from your subconscious before you have a chance to work out the associations that support it. Verify your instinct by working out the reasons that it should be trusted.

8. Key Words

Many test takers struggle with multiple-choice questions because they have poor reading comprehension skills. Quickly reading and understanding a multiple-choice question requires a mixture of skill and experience. To help with this, try jotting down a few key words and phrases on a piece of scrap paper. Doing this concentrates the process of reading and forces the mind to weigh the relative importance of the question's parts. In selecting words and phrases to write down, the test taker thinks about the question more deeply and carefully. This is especially true for multiple-choice questions that are preceded by a long prompt.

9. Subtle Negatives

One of the oldest tricks in the multiple-choice test writer's book is to subtly reverse the meaning of a question with a word like *not* or *except*. If you are not paying attention to each word in the question, you can easily be led astray by this trick. For instance, a common question format is, "Which of the following is...?" Obviously, if the question instead is, "Which of the following is not...?," then the answer will be quite different. Even worse, the test makers are aware of the potential for this mistake and will include one answer choice that would be correct if the question were not negated or reversed. A test taker who misses the reversal will find what he or she believes to be a correct answer and will be so confident that he or she will fail to reread the question and discover the original error. The only way to avoid this is to practice a wide variety of multiple-choice questions and to pay close attention to each and every word.

10. Reading Every Answer Choice

It may seem obvious, but you should always read every one of the answer choices! Too many test takers fall into the habit of scanning the question and assuming that they understand the question because they recognize a few key words. From there, they pick the first answer choice that answers the question they believe they have read. Test takers who read all of the answer choices might discover that one of the latter answer choices is actually *more* correct. Moreover, reading all of the answer choices can remind you of facts related to the question that can help you arrive at the correct answer. Sometimes, a misstatement or incorrect detail in one of the latter answer choices will trigger your memory of the subject and will enable you to find the right answer. Failing to read all of the answer choices is like not reading all of the items on a restaurant menu: you might miss out on the perfect choice.

11. Spot the Hedges

One of the keys to success on multiple-choice tests is paying close attention to every word. This is never truer than with words like almost, most, some, and sometimes. These words are called "hedges" because they indicate that a statement is not totally true or not true in every place and time. An absolute statement will contain no hedges, but in many subjects, the answers are not always straightforward or absolute. There are always exceptions to the rules in these subjects. For this reason, you should favor those multiple-choice questions that contain hedging language. The presence of qualifying words indicates that the author is taking special care with their words, which is certainly important when composing the right answer. After all, there are many ways to be wrong, but there is only one way to be right! For this reason, it is wise to avoid answers that are absolute when taking a multiple-choice test. An absolute answer is one that says things are either all one way or all another. They often include words like *every*, *always*, *best*, and *never*. If you are taking a multiple-choice test in a subject that doesn't lend itself to absolute answers, be on your guard if you see any of these words.

12. Long Answers

In many subject areas, the answers are not simple. As already mentioned, the right answer often requires hedges. Another common feature of the answers to a complex or subjective question are qualifying clauses, which are groups of words that subtly modify the meaning of the sentence. If the question or answer choice describes a rule to which there are exceptions or the subject matter is complicated, ambiguous, or confusing, the correct answer will require many words in order to be expressed clearly and accurately. In essence, you should not be deterred by answer choices that seem excessively long. Oftentimes, the author of the text will not be able to write the correct answer without offering some qualifications and modifications. Your job is to read the answer choices thoroughly and completely and to select the one that most accurately and precisely answers the question.

13. Restating to Understand

Sometimes, a question on a multiple-choice test is difficult not because of what it asks but because of how it is written. If this is the case, restate the question or answer choice in different words. This process serves a couple of important purposes. First, it forces you to concentrate on the core of the question. In order to rephrase the question accurately, you have to understand it well. Rephrasing the question will concentrate your mind on the key words and ideas. Second, it will present the information to your mind in a fresh way. This process may trigger your memory and render some useful scrap of information picked up while studying.

14. True Statements

Sometimes an answer choice will be true in itself, but it does not answer the question. This is one of the main reasons why it is essential to read the question carefully and completely before proceeding to the answer choices. Too often, test takers skip ahead to the answer choices and look for true statements. Having found one of these, they are content to select it without reference to the question above. Obviously, this provides an easy way for test makers to play tricks. The savvy test taker will always read the entire question before turning to the answer choices. Then, having settled on a correct answer choice, he or she will refer to the original question and ensure that the selected answer is relevant. The mistake of choosing a correct-but-irrelevant answer choice is especially common on questions related to specific pieces of objective knowledge. A prepared test taker will have a wealth of factual knowledge at their disposal, and should not be careless in its application.

15. No Patterns

One of the more dangerous ideas that circulates about multiple-choice tests is that the correct answers tend to fall into patterns. These erroneous ideas range from a belief that B and C are the most common right answers, to the idea that an unprepared test-taker should answer "A-B-A-C-A-D-A-B-A." It cannot be emphasized enough that pattern-seeking of this type is exactly the WRONG way to approach a multiple-choice test. To begin with, it is highly unlikely that the test maker will plot the correct answers according to some predetermined pattern. The questions are scrambled and delivered in a random order. Furthermore, even if the test maker was following a pattern in the assignation of correct answers, there is no reason why the test taker would know which pattern he or she was using. Any attempt to discern a pattern in the answer choices is a waste of time and a distraction from the real work of taking the test. A test taker would be much better served by extra preparation before the test than by reliance on a pattern in the answers.

FREE Videos/DVD OFFER

Doing well on your exam requires both knowing the test content and understanding how to use that knowledge to do well on the test. We offer completely FREE test taking tip videos. **These videos cover world-class tips that you can use to succeed on your test.**

To get your **FREE videos**, you can use the QR code below or email freevideos@studyguideteam.com with "Free Videos" in the subject line and the following information in the body of the email:

   a. The title of your product

   b. Your product rating on a scale of 1-5, with 5 being the highest

   c. Your feedback about the product

If you have any questions or concerns, please don't hesitate to contact us at info@studyguideteam.com.

Thanks again!

Introduction to the PERT

Function of the Test

Florida's Postsecondary Education Readiness Test (PERT) is a placement test used by Florida public colleges and universities for placement of students entering degree programs at those schools. It is also taken by eleventh grade students in Florida to evaluate their readiness for college-level coursework. The PERT is similar to other college placement tests such as the College Board's Accuplacer and ACT's COMPASS test, but is distinct in that it was created for and is used exclusively within the state of Florida.

The test is customized to Florida's Postsecondary Readiness Competencies and was developed to Florida Department of Education standards. Specifically, the test is designed to determine students' readiness for two entry-level college courses: Intermediate Algebra, MAT 1033, and Freshman Composition I, ENC 1101.

Test Administration

The cost of taking the PERT is generally covered by the high school or college administering the test, although some institutions will charge a moderate fee, especially for retests or tests administered to students from other institutions. State rules permit high school students to retake the test, but local school boards may set their own policies to restrict retesting.

The test is administered by computer. Students are asked to select one of four multiple-choice answers for each question. It is generally offered at times and locations determined by the institution offering the exam.

Students with disabilities may seek accommodations for the PERT. Available accommodations include an accessibility wizard that allows students taking the test to adjust the font size, font color, and background color on the computer screen for improved visibility. There are also pencil/paper, Braille, large print, and audio versions of the exam. English Language Learners may use native heritage language dictionaries.

Test Format

There are thirty questions on each of the three sub-tests: mathematics, reading, and writing. Twenty-five of the questions are "operational" and five are used to evaluate the test itself, but students are not told which of the thirty are operational. The test is untimed, but the average length of the sub-tests is thirty minutes for mathematics, thirty minutes for writing, and sixty minutes for reading. The test is a computer adaptive test (C.A.T.), meaning that the computer adjusts the difficulty of questions based on the test taker's performance on the preceding questions.

Scoring

Scaled scores on the PERT range from 50 to 150. There is no "passing" score on the PERT. Instead, there is a "cut score" in each of the three categories (Mathematics, Reading, and Writing). Students entering college who score at or above the cut score are deemed qualified for placement in regular (or advanced) college courses, while students who score below the cut score are designated for remedial coursework. High school students below the cut score are offered postsecondary preparatory coursework.

PERT Scoring Tiers	
Placement	**Score**
Mathematics	
Lower Level Developmental Education	50-95
Higher Level Developmental Education	96-113
Intermediate Algebra (MAT 1033)	114-122
College Algebra or higher (MAC 1105)	123-150
Reading	
Lower Level Developmental Education	50-83
Higher Level Developmental Education	84-105
Freshman Composition Skills I (ENC 1101)	106-150
Writing	
Lower Level Developmental Education	50-89
Higher Level Developmental Education	90-102
Freshman Composition Skills I (ENC 1101)	103-150

Recent/Future Developments

As of 2015, the PERT is no longer mandatory for Florida 11th grade students. However, most 11th graders have continued to take the test and high schools continue to place students in 12th grade classes based on PERT results.

8

Study Prep Plan for the PERT

1	**Schedule** - Use one of our study schedules below or come up with one of your own.
2	**Relax -** Test anxiety can hurt even the best students. There are many ways to reduce stress. Find the one that works best for you.
3	**Execute** - Once you have a good plan in place, be sure to stick to it.

One Week Study Schedule

Day 1	Math
Day 2	Reading
Day 3	Writing
Day 4	Practice Test #1
Day 5	Practice Test #2
Day 6	Practice Test #3
Day 7	Take Your Exam!

Two Week Study Schedule

Day 1	Math	Day 8	Practice Test #1
Day 2	Standard Algorithms and Concepts	Day 9	Answer Explanations #1
Day 3	Reading	Day 10	Practice Test #2
Day 4	The Author's Purpose and the Relation...	Day 11	Answer Explanations #2
Day 5	Writing	Day 12	Practice Test #3
Day 6	Synthesizing Information from...	Day 13	Answer Explanations #3
Day 7	Sentence Structure Skills	Day 14	Take Your Exam!

One Month Study Schedule					
Day 1	Math	Day 11	Relationships Within and Between Sentences	Day 21	Sentence Structure Skills
Day 2	Algebra	Day 12	The Author's Purpose and the Relation...	Day 22	Grammar, Spelling, Capitalization and...
Day 3	Monomials, Binomials, and Polynomials	Day 13	The Traits, Motivations, and Thoughts of...	Day 23	Practice Questions
Day 4	Standard Algorithms and Concepts	Day 14	Practice Questions	Day 24	Practice Test #1
Day 5	Functions	Day 15	Writing	Day 25	Answer Explanations #1
Day 6	Coordinate Plane	Day 16	Grammar, Usage, Syntax, and...	Day 26	Practice Test #2
Day 7	Simultaneous Equations	Day 17	Understanding the Use of Affixes, Context...	Day 27	Answer Explanations #2
Day 8	Practice Questions	Day 18	Synthesizing Information from Multiple Sources	Day 28	Practice Test #3
Day 9	Reading	Day 19	Citing Data, Conclusions, and...	Day 29	Answer Explanations #3
Day 10	Meaning, Word Choices, Tone, and...	Day 20	Word Choice Skills	Day 30	Take Your Exam!

Build your own prep plan by visiting:

testprepbooks.com/prep

Math Reference Sheet

Symbol	Phrase
+	added to, increased by, sum of, more than
-	decreased by, difference between, less than, take away
×	multiplied by, 3 (4, 5 . . .) times as large, product of
÷	divided by, quotient of, half (third, etc.) of
=	is, the same as, results in, as much as
x, t, n, etc.	a variable which is an unknown value or quantity
<	is under, is below, smaller than, beneath
>	is above, is over, bigger than, exceeds
≤	no more than, at most, maximum; less than or equal to
≥	no less than, at least, minimum; greater than or equal to
√	square root of, exponent divided by 2

Geometry	Description
$P = 2l + 2w$	for perimeter of a rectangle
$P = 4 \times s$	for perimeter of a square
$P = a + b + c$	for perimeter of a triangle
$A = \frac{1}{2} \times b \times h = \frac{bh}{2}$	for area of a triangle
$A = b \times h$	for area of a parallelogram
$A = \frac{1}{2} \times h(b_1 + b_2)$	for area of a trapezoid
$A = \frac{1}{2} \times a \times P$	for area of a regular polygon
$C = 2 \times \pi \times r$	for circumference (perimeter) of a circle
$A = \pi \times r^2$	for area of a circle
$c^2 = a^2 + b^2; c = \sqrt{a^2 + b^2}$	for finding the hypotenuse of a right triangle
$SA = 2xy + 2yz + 2xz$	for finding surface area
$V = \frac{1}{3}xyh$	for finding volume of a rectangular pyramid
$V = \frac{4}{3}\pi r^3, \frac{1}{3}\pi r^2 h; \pi r^2 h$	for volume of a sphere; a cone; and a cylinder

Radical Expressions	Description
$\sqrt[n]{a} = a^{\frac{1}{n}}; \sqrt[n]{a^m} = (\sqrt[n]{a})^m = a^{\frac{m}{n}}$	a is the radicand, n is the index, m is the exponent
$\sqrt{x^2} = (x^2)^{\frac{1}{2}} = x$	to convert square root to exponent
$a^m \times a^n = a^{m+n}$	multiplying radicands with exponents
$(a^m)^n = a^{m \times n}$	multiplying exponents
$(a \times b)^m = a^m \times b^m$	parentheses with exponents

Property	Addition	Multiplication
Commutative	$a + b = b + a$	$a \times b = b \times a$
Associative	$(a + b) + c = a + (b + c)$	$(a \times b) \times c = a \times (b \times c)$
Identity	$a + 0 = a; 0 + a = a$	$a \times 1 = a; 1 \times a = a$
Inverse	$a + (-a) = 0$	$a \times \frac{1}{a} = 1; a \neq 0$
Distributive		$a(b + c) = ab + ac$

Data	Description
Mean	equal to the total of the values of a data set, divided by the number of elements in the data set
Median	middle value in an odd number of ordered values of a data set, or the mean of the two middle values in an even number of ordered values in a data set
Mode	the value that appears most often
Range	the difference between the highest and the lowest values in the set

Graphing	Description
(x, y)	ordered pair, plot points in a graph
$y = mx + b$	slope-intercept form; m represents the slope of the line and b represents the y-intercept
$f(x)$	read as f of x, which means it is a function of x
(x_2, y_2) and (x_2, y_2)	two ordered pairs used to determine the slope of a line
$m = \frac{y_2 - y_1}{x_2 - x_1}$	to find the slope of the line, m, for ordered pairs
$Ax + By = C$	standard form of an equation, also for solving a system of equations through the elimination method
$M = (\frac{x_1 + x_2}{2}, \frac{y_1 + y_2}{2})$	for finding the midpoint of an ordered pair
$y = ax^2 + bx + c$	quadratic function for a parabola
$y = a(x - h)^2 + k$	quadratic function for a parabola with vertex
$y = ab^x; y = a \times b^x$	function for exponential curve
$y = ax^2 + bx + c$	standard form of a quadratic function
$x = \frac{-b}{2a}$	for finding axis of symmetry in a parabola; given quadratic formula in standard form
$f = \sqrt{\frac{\Sigma(x - \bar{x})^2}{n - 1}}$	function for standard deviation of the sample; where $\bar{x}$ = sample mean and n = sample size

Proportions and Percentage	Description
$\frac{gallons}{cost} = \frac{gallons}{cost} : \frac{7\ gallons}{\$14.70} = \frac{x}{\$20}$	written as equal ratios with a variable representing the missing quantity
$\frac{y_1}{x_1} = \frac{y_2}{x_2}$	for direct proportions
$(y_1)(x_1) = (y_2)(x_2)$	for indirect proportions
$\frac{change}{original\ value} \times 100 = percent\ change$	for finding percentage change in value
$\frac{new\ quantity - old\ quantity}{old\ quantity} \times 100$	for calculating the increase or decrease in percentage

11

Equations

Equations and Inequalities

The sum of a number and 5 is equal to -8 times the number. To find this unknown number, a simple **equation** can be written to represent the problem. Key words such as difference, equal, and times are used to form the following equation with one variable:

$$n + 5 = -8n$$

When solving for n, opposite operations are used. First, n is subtracted from $-8n$ across the equals sign, resulting in $5 = -9n$. Then, -9 is divided on both sides, leaving $n = -\frac{5}{9}$. This solution can be graphed on the number line with a dot as shown below:

If the problem were changed to say, "The sum of a number and 5 is greater than -8 times the number," then an **inequality** would be used instead of an equation. Using key words again, **greater than** is represented by the symbol >. The inequality $n + 5 > -8n$ can be solved using the same techniques, resulting in $n < -\frac{5}{9}$. The only time solving an inequality differs from solving an equation is when a negative number is either multiplied times or divided by each side of the inequality. The sign must be switched in this case. For this example, the graph of the solution changes to the following graph because the solution represents all real numbers less than $-\frac{5}{9}$. Not included in this solution is $-\frac{5}{9}$ because it is a **less than** symbol, not *equal to*.

Equations and inequalities in two variables represent a relationship. Jim owns a car wash and charges $40 per car. The rent for the facility is $350 per month. An equation can be written to relate the number of cars Jim cleans to the money he makes per month. Let x represent the number of cars and y represent the profit Jim makes each month from the car wash. The equation $y = 40x - 350$ can be used to show Jim's profit or loss. Since this equation has two variables, the coordinate plane can be used to show the relationship and predict profit or loss for Jim. The following graph shows that Jim must wash at least nine cars to pay the rent, where $x = 9$. Anything nine cars and above yield a profit shown in the value on the y-axis.

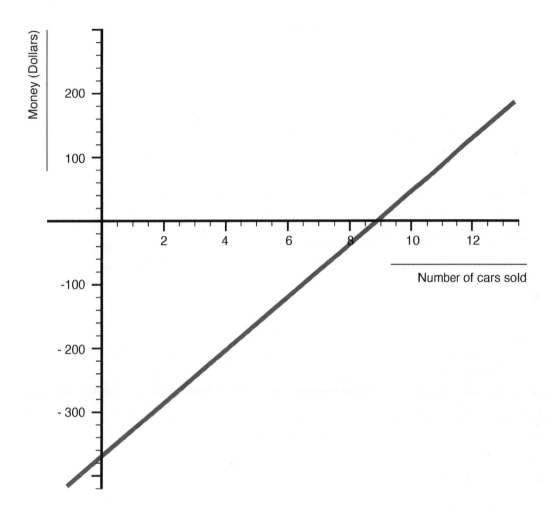

With a single equation in two variables, the solutions are limited only by the situation the equation represents. When two equations or inequalities are used, more constraints are added. For example, in a system of linear equations, there is often—although not always—only one answer. The point of intersection of two lines is the solution. For a system of inequalities, there are infinitely many answers.

The intersection of two solution sets gives the solution set of the system of inequalities. In the following graph, the darker shaded region is where two inequalities overlap. Any set of x and y found in that region satisfies both inequalities. The line with the positive slope is solid, meaning the values on that line

13

are included in the solution. The line with the negative slope is dotted, so the coordinates on that line are not included.

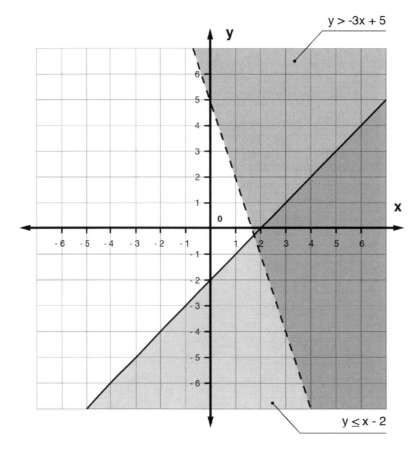

Formulas with two variables are equations used to represent a specific relationship. For example, the formula $d = rt$ represents the relationship between distance, rate, and time. If Bob travels at a rate of 35 miles per hour on his road trip from Westminster to Seneca, the formula $d = 35t$ can be used to represent his distance traveled in a specific length of time. Formulas can also be used to show different roles of the variables, transformed without any given numbers. Solving for r, the formula becomes $\frac{d}{t} = r$. The t is moved over by division so that *rate* is a function of distance and time.

Solving Linear Equations and Inequalities

The simplest equations to solve are **linear equations**, which have the form $ax + b = 0$. These have the solution $x = -\frac{b}{a}$.

For instance, in the equation $\frac{1}{3}x - 4 = 0$, it can be determined that $\frac{1}{3}x = 4$ by adding 4 on each side. Next, both sides of the equation are multiplied by 3 to get $x = 12$.

Solving an inequality is very similar to solving equations, with one important issue to keep track of: if multiplying or dividing both sides of an inequality by a negative number, the direction of the inequality *flips*.

For example, consider the inequality $-4x < 12$. Solving this inequality requires the division of -4. When the negative four is divided, the less-than sign changes to a greater-than sign. The solution becomes $x > -3$.

Example
$-4x - 3 \leq -2x + 1$

$2x$ is added to both sides, and 3 is added to both sides, leaving $-2x \leq 4$.

$-2x \leq 4$ is multiplied by $-\frac{1}{2}$, which means flipping the direction of the inequality.

This gives $x \geq -2$.

An **absolute inequality** is an inequality that is true for all real numbers. An inequality that is only true for some real numbers is called **conditional**.

In addition to the inequalities above, there are also **double inequalities** where three quantities are compared to one another, such as $3 \leq x + 4 < 5$. The rules for double inequalities include always performing any operations to every part of the inequality and reversing the direction of the inequality when multiplying or dividing by a negative number.

When solving equations and inequalities, the solutions can be checked by plugging the answer back in to the original problem. If the solution makes a true statement, the solution is correct.

Solving Quadratic Equations by Factoring

Solving **quadratic equations** is a little trickier. If they take the form $ax^2 - b = 0$, then the equation can be solved by adding b to both sides and dividing by a to get $x^2 = \frac{b}{a}$.

Using the sixth rule above, the solution is $x = \pm\sqrt{\frac{b}{a}}$. Note that this is actually two separate solutions, unless b happens to be 0.

If a quadratic equation has no constant—so that it takes the form $ax^2 + bx = 0$—then the x can be factored out to get $x(ax + b) = 0$. Then, the solutions are $x = 0$, together with the solutions to $ax + b = 0$. Both factors x and $(ax + b)$ can be set equal to zero to solve for x because one of those values must be zero for their product to equal zero. For an equation $ab = 0$ to be true, either $a = 0$, or $b = 0$.

A given quadratic equation $x^2 + bx + c$ can be factored into $(x + A)(x + B)$, where $A + B = b$, and $AB = c$. Finding the values of A and B can take time, but such a pair of numbers can be found by guessing and checking. Looking at the positive and negative factors for c offers a good starting point.

For example, in $x^2 - 5x + 6$, the factors of 6 are 1, 2, and 3. Now, $(-2)(-3) = 6$, and $-2 - 3 = -5$. In general, however, this may not work, in which case another approach may need to be used.

A quadratic equation of the form $x^2 + 2xb + b^2 = 0$ can be factored into $(x + b)^2 = 0$. Similarly, $x^2 - 2xy + y^2 = 0$ factors into $(x - y)^2 = 0$.

Math

In general, the constant term may not be the right value to be factored this way. A more general method for solving these quadratic equations must then be found. The following two methods will work in any situation.

Solving Linear and Quadratic Equations and Inequalities

An **equation** is an expression that uses an equals sign to demonstrate that two quantities are equal to one another, such as the expression $x^2 - x = -4x + 3$. **Solving** an equation means to find all possible values that x can take which make the equation true.

Given an equation where one side is a polynomial in the variable x and the other side is zero, the solutions are also called the **roots** or **zeros** of the equation.

To solve an equation, the equation needs to be modified to determine the solution. Starting with an equation $a = b$, the following are also true equations:

$$a + c = b + c$$

$$a - c = b - c$$

$$ac = bc$$

$$\frac{a}{c} = \frac{b}{c} \text{ (provided that } c \text{ is not 0)}$$

$$a^c = b^c$$

$$\sqrt{a} = \pm\sqrt{b}$$

The following rule is important to remember when solving equations:

If $ab = 0$, then $a = 0$ or $b = 0$.

Sometimes, instead of an equation, an **inequality** is used to indicate that one quantity is less than another (or greater than another). They may specify that the two quantities might also be equal to each other. If the quantities are not allowed to equal one another, the expression is a **strict inequality**. For example, $x + 3 \leq 5$ is an inequality, while $7 - 2x > 1$ is a strict inequality.

A **solution set** is a collection of all values of a variable that solve an equation or an inequality. For inequalities, this can be illustrated on a number line by shading in the part of the number line that satisfies the inequality. An open circle on the number line indicates that one gets arbitrarily close to that point, but cannot actually touch that point while remaining in the solution set. For example, to graph the solution set for the inequality $x > 2$, it would look like the following:

Solution Set x>2

Completing the Square

The first method is called **completing the square**. The idea here is that in any equation $x^2 + 2xb + c = 0$, something could be added to both sides of the equation to get the left side to look like $x^2 + 2xb + b^2$, meaning it could be factored into:

$$(x + b)^2 = 0$$

Example
$x^2 + 6x - 1 = 0$

The left-hand side could be factored if the constant were equal to 9, since:

$$x^2 + 6x + 9 = (x + 3)^2$$

To get a constant of 9 on the left, 10 needs to be added to both sides.

That changes the equation to $x^2 + 6x + 9 = 10$.

Factoring the left gives $(x + 3)^2 = 10$.

Then, the square root of both sides can be taken (remembering that this introduces a $\pm$): $x + 3 = \pm\sqrt{10}$.

Finally, 3 is subtracted from both sides to get two solutions: $x = -3 \pm \sqrt{10}$.

The Quadratic Formula

The first method of completing the square can be used in finding the second method, the quadratic formula. It can be used to solve any quadratic equation. This formula may be the longest method for solving quadratic equations and is commonly used as a last resort after other methods are ruled out.

It can be helpful in memorizing the formula to see where it comes from, so here are the steps involved.

The most general form for a quadratic equation is:

$$ax^2 + bx + c = 0$$

17

First, dividing both sides by a leaves us with:

$$x^2 + \frac{b}{a}x + \frac{c}{a} = 0$$

To complete the square on the left-hand side, $\frac{c}{a}$ can be subtracted on both sides to get:

$$x^2 + \frac{b}{a}x = -\frac{c}{a}$$

$(\frac{b}{2a})^2$ is then added to both sides.

This gives $x^2 + \frac{b}{a}x + (\frac{b}{2a})^2 = (\frac{b}{2a})^2 - \frac{c}{a}$.

The left can now be factored and the right-hand side simplified to give:

$$(x + \frac{b}{2a})^2 = \frac{b^2 - 4ac}{4a}$$

Taking the square roots gives:

$$x + \frac{b}{2a} = \pm\frac{\sqrt{b^2 - 4ac}}{2a}$$

Solving for x yields the quadratic formula:

$$x = \frac{-b \pm \sqrt{b^2 - 4ac}}{2a}$$

It isn't necessary to remember how to get this formula, but memorizing the formula itself is the goal.

If an equation involves taking a root, then the first step is to move the root to one side of the equation and everything else to the other side. That way, both sides can be raised to the index of the radical in order to remove it, and solving the equation can continue.

Complex Numbers

Some types of equations can be solved to find real answers, but this is not the case for all equations. For example, $x^2 = k$ can be solved when k is non-negative, but it has no real solutions when k is negative. Equations do have solutions if complex numbers are allowed.

Complex numbers are defined in the following manner: every complex number can be written as $a + bi$, where $i^2 = -1$. Thus, the solutions to the equation $x^2 = -1$ are $\pm i$.

In order to find roots of negative numbers more generally, the properties of roots (or of exponents) are used. For example:

$$\sqrt{-4} = \sqrt{-1}\sqrt{4} = \pm 2i$$

All arithmetic operations can be performed with complex numbers, where i is like any other constant. The value of i^2 can replace -1.

Strategies and Algorithms to Perform Operations on Rational Numbers

A **rational number** is any number that can be written in the form of a ratio or fraction. Integers can be written as fractions with a denominator of 1 ($5 = \frac{5}{1}$; $-342 = \frac{-342}{1}$; etc.). Decimals that terminate and/or repeat can also be written as fractions ($47 = \frac{47}{100}$; $.\overline{33} = \frac{1}{3}$).

When adding or subtracting fractions, the numbers must have the same denominators. In these cases, numerators are added or subtracted, and denominators are kept the same. For example, $\frac{2}{7} + \frac{3}{7} = \frac{5}{7}$ and $\frac{4}{5} - \frac{3}{5} = \frac{1}{5}$. If the fractions to be added or subtracted do not have the same denominator, a common denominator must be found. This is accomplished by changing one or both fractions to a different but equivalent fraction. Consider the example $\frac{1}{6} + \frac{4}{9}$. First, a common denominator must be found. One method is to find the **least common multiple (LCM)** of the denominators 6 and 9.

This is the lowest number that both 6 and 9 will divide into evenly. In this case the LCM is 18. Both fractions should be changed to equivalent fractions with a denominator of 18. To obtain the numerator of the new fraction, the old numerator is multiplied by the same number by which the old denominator is multiplied. For the fraction $\frac{1}{6}$, 6 multiplied by 3 will produce a denominator of 18. Therefore, the numerator is multiplied by 3 to produce the new numerator $\left(\frac{1\times3}{6\times3} = \frac{3}{18}\right)$. For the fraction $\frac{4}{9}$, multiplying both the numerator and denominator by 2 produces $\frac{8}{18}$. Since the two new fractions have common denominators, they can be added $\left(\frac{3}{18} + \frac{8}{18} = \frac{11}{18}\right)$.

When multiplying or dividing rational numbers, these numbers may be converted to fractions and multiplied or divided accordingly. When multiplying fractions, all numerators are multiplied by each other and all denominators are multiplied by each other.

For example,

$$\frac{1}{3} \times \frac{6}{5} = \frac{1 \times 6}{3 \times 5} = \frac{6}{15}$$

and

$$\frac{-1}{2} \times \frac{3}{1} \times \frac{11}{100} = \frac{-1 \times 3 \times 11}{2 \times 1 \times 100} = \frac{-33}{200}$$

When dividing fractions, the problem is converted by multiplying by the reciprocal of the divisor. This is done by changing division to multiplication and "flipping" the second fraction, or divisor. For example, $\frac{1}{2} \div \frac{3}{5} \rightarrow \frac{1}{2} \times \frac{5}{3}$ and $\frac{5}{1} \div \frac{1}{3} \rightarrow \frac{5}{1} \times \frac{3}{1}$. To complete the problem, the rules for multiplying fractions should be followed.

Note that when adding, subtracting, multiplying, and dividing mixed numbers (ex. $4\frac{1}{2}$), it is easiest to convert these to improper fractions (larger numerator than denominator). To do so, the denominator is

19

kept the same. To obtain the numerator, the whole number is multiplied by the denominator and added to the numerator. For example, $4\frac{1}{2} = \frac{9}{2}$ and $7\frac{2}{3} = \frac{23}{3}$. Also, note that answers involving fractions should be converted to the simplest form.

Solving Equations

Solving equations in one variable is the process of isolating a variable on one side of the equation. For example, in $3x - 7 = 20$, the variable x needs to be isolated. Using opposite operations, the -7 is moved to the right side of the equation by adding seven to both sides: $3x - 7 + 7 = 20 + 7$, resulting in $3x = 27$. Dividing by three on each side, $\frac{3x}{3} = \frac{27}{3}$, results in isolation of the variable. It is important to note that if an operation is performed on one side of the equals sign, it has to be performed on the other side to maintain equality. The solution is found to be $x = 9$. This solution can be checked for accuracy by plugging $x = 7$ in the original equation. After simplifying the equation, $20 = 20$ is found, which is a true statement.

When solving radical and rational equations, extraneous solutions must be accounted for when finding the answers. For example, the equation $\frac{x}{x-5} = \frac{3x}{x+3}$ has two values that create a 0 denominator: $x \neq 5, -3$. When solving for x, these values must be considered because they cannot be solutions. In the given equation, solving for x can be done using cross-multiplication, yielding the equation:

$$x(x + 3) = 3x(x - 5)$$

Distributing results in the quadratic equation $x^2 + 3x = 3x^2 - 15x$; therefore, all terms must be moved to one side of the equals sign. This results in $2x^2 - 18x = 0$, which in factored form is:

$$2x(x - 9) = 0$$

Setting each factor equal to zero, the apparent solutions are $x = 0$ and $x = 9$. These two solutions are neither 5 nor -3, so they are viable solutions. Neither 0 nor 9 create a 0 denominator in the original equation.

A similar process exists when solving radical equations. One must check to make sure the solutions are defined in the original equations. Solving an equation containing a square root involves isolating the root and then squaring both sides of the equals sign. Solving a cube root equation involves isolating the radical and then cubing both sides. In either case, the variable can then be solved for because there are no longer radicals in the equation.

Methods for Solving Equations

Equations with one variable can be solved using the **addition principle** and **multiplication principle**. If $a = b$, then $a + c = b + c$, and $ac = bc$. Given the equation $2x - 3 = 5x + 7$, the first step is to combine the variable terms and the constant terms. Using the principles, expressions can be added and subtracted onto and off both sides of the equals sign, so the equation turns into $-10 = 3x$. Dividing by 3 on both sides through the multiplication principle with $c = \frac{1}{3}$ results in the final answer of $x = \frac{-10}{3}$.

Some equations have a higher degree and are not solved by simply using opposite operations. When an equation has a degree of 2, completing the square is an option. For example, the quadratic equation

20

$x^2 - 6x + 2 = 0$ can be rewritten by completing the square. The goal of completing the square is to get the equation into the form:

$$(x - p)^2 = q$$

Using the example, the constant term 2 first needs to be moved over to the opposite side by subtracting. Then, the square can be completed by adding 9 to both sides, which is the square of half of the coefficient of the middle term $-6x$. The current equation is:

$$x^2 - 6x + 9 = 7$$

The left side can be factored into a square of a binomial, resulting in $(x - 3)^2 = 7$. To solve for x, the square root of both sides should be taken, resulting in $(x - 3) = \pm\sqrt{7}$, and $x = 3 \pm \sqrt{7}$.

Other ways of solving quadratic equations include graphing, factoring, and using the quadratic formula. The equation $y = x^2 - 4x + 3$ can be graphed on the coordinate plane, and the solutions can be observed where it crosses the x-axis. The graph will be a parabola that opens up with two solutions at 1 and 3.

The equation can also be factored to find the solutions. The original equation, $y = x^2 - 4x + 3$ can be factored into $y = (x - 1)(x - 3)$. Setting this equal to zero, the x-values are found to be 1 and 3, just as on the graph. Solving by factoring and graphing are not always possible. The quadratic formula is a method of solving quadratic equations that always results in exact solutions. The formula is:

$$x = \frac{-b \pm \sqrt{b^2 - 4ac}}{2a}$$

a, b, and c are the coefficients in the original equation in standard form $y = ax^2 + bx + c$. For this example,

$$x = \frac{4 \pm \sqrt{(-4)^2 - 4(1)(3)}}{2(1)}$$

$$\frac{4 \pm \sqrt{16 - 12}}{2} = \frac{4 \pm 2}{2} = 1, 3$$

The expression underneath the radical is called the *discriminant*. Without working out the entire formula, the value of the discriminant can reveal the nature of the solutions. If the value of the discriminant $b^2 - 4ac$ is positive, then there will be two real solutions. If the value is zero, there will be one real solution. If the value is negative, the two solutions will be imaginary or complex. If the solutions are complex, it means that the parabola never touches the x-axis. An example of a complex solution can be found by solving the following quadratic: $y = x^2 - 4x + 8$. By using the quadratic formula, the solutions are found to be:

$$x = \frac{4 \pm \sqrt{(-4)^2 - 4(1)(8)}}{2(1)}$$

$$\frac{4 \pm \sqrt{16 - 32}}{2} = \frac{4 \pm \sqrt{-16}}{2} = 2 \pm 2i$$

The solutions both have a real part, 2, and an imaginary part, $2i$.

Algebra

Algebraic Expressions and Equations

Algebraic expressions look similar to equations, but they do not include the equal sign. **Algebraic expressions** are comprised of numbers, variables, and mathematical operations. Some examples of algebraic expressions are $8x + 7y - 12z$, $3a^2$, and $5x^3 - 4y^4$.

Algebraic expressions and equations can be used to represent real-life situations and model the behavior of different variables. For example, $2x + 5$ could represent the cost to play games at an arcade. In this case, 5 represents the price of admission to the arcade, and 2 represents the cost of each game played. To calculate the total cost, use the number of games played for x, multiply it by 2, and add 5.

Solving for a Variable

Similar to order of operation rules, **algebraic rules** must be obeyed to ensure a correct answer. Begin by locating all parentheses and brackets, and then solving the equations within them. Then, perform the operations necessary to remove all parentheses and brackets. Next, convert all fractions into whole numbers and combine common terms on each side of the equation.

Beginning on the left side of the expression, solve operations involving multiplication and division. Then, work left to right solving operations involving addition and subtraction. Finally, cross-multiply if necessary to reach the final solution.

Example 1

$$4a - 10 = 10$$

Constants are the numbers in equations that do not change. The variable in this equation is a. Variables are most commonly presented as either x or y, but they can be any letter. Every variable is equal to a number; one must solve the equation to determine what that number is. In an algebraic expression, the answer will usually be the number represented by the variable. In order to solve this equation, keep in mind that what is done to one side must be done to the other side as well. The first step will be to remove 10 from the left side by adding 10 to both sides. This will be expressed as $4a - 10 + 10 = 10 + 10$, which simplifies to $4a = 20$. Next, remove the 4 by dividing both sides by 4. This step will be expressed as $4a \div 4 = 20 \div 4$. The expression now becomes $a = 5$.

Since variables are the letters that represent an unknown number, you must solve for that unknown number in single variable problems. The main thing to remember is that you can do anything to one side of an equation as long as you do it to the other.

Example 2
Solve for x in the equation $2x + 3 = 5$.

Answer: First you want to get the "$2x$" isolated by itself on one side. To do that, first get rid of the 3. Subtract 3 from both sides of the equation $2x + 3 - 3 = 5 - 3$ or $2x = 2$. Now since the x is being

22

multiplied by the 2 in "$2x$," you must divide by 2 to get rid of it. So, divide both sides by 2, which gives $\frac{2x}{2} = \frac{2}{2}$ or $x = 1$.

Solving for X in Proportions

Proportions are commonly used to solve word problems to find unknown values such as x that are some percent or fraction of a known number. Proportions are solved by cross-multiplying and then dividing to arrive at x. The following examples show how this is done:

1) $\frac{75\%}{90\%} = \frac{25\%}{x}$

To solve for x, the fractions must be cross multiplied: ($75\%x = 90\% \times 25\%$). To make things easier, let's convert the percentages to decimals: ($0.9 \times 0.25 = 0.225 = 0.75x$). To get rid of x's coefficient, each side must be divided by that same coefficient to get the answer $x = 0.3$. The question could ask for the answer as a percentage or fraction in lowest terms, which are 30% and $\frac{3}{10}$, respectively.

2) $\frac{x}{12} = \frac{30}{96}$

Cross-multiply: $96x = 30 \times 12$
Multiply: $96x = 360$
Divide: $x = 360 \div 96$
Answer: $x = 3.75$

3) $\frac{0.5}{3} = \frac{x}{6}$

Cross-multiply: $3x = 0.5 \times 6$
Multiply: $3x = 3$
Divide: $x = 3 \div 3$
Answer: $x = 1$

You may have noticed there's a faster way to arrive at the answer. If there is an obvious operation being performed on the proportion, the same operation can be used on the other side of the proportion to solve for x. For example, in the first practice problem, 75% became 25% when divided by 3, and upon doing the same to 90%, the correct answer of 30% would have been found with much less legwork. However, these questions aren't always so intuitive, so it's a good idea to work through the steps, even if the answer seems apparent from the outset.

Simplifying Rational Algebraic Expressions

A **rational expression** is a ratio or fraction of two polynomials. An expression is in **lowest terms** when the numerator and denominator have no common factors. The rational expression $\frac{7}{4x+3}$ is in lowest terms because there are no common factors between the numerator and denominator. The rational expression $\frac{x^2+2x+1}{x^2-1}$ can be simplified to $\frac{(x+1)(x+1)}{(x-1)(x+1)} = \frac{x+1}{x-1}$ because there is a common factor of $x + 1$.

Math

Evaluation of Simple Formulas and Expressions

To evaluate simple formulas and expressions, the first step is to substitute the given values in for the variable(s). Then, the order of operations is used to simplify.

<u>Example 1</u>
Evaluate $\frac{1}{2}x^2 - 3, x = 4$.

The first step is to substitute in 4 for x in the expression: $\frac{1}{2}(4)^2 - 3$.

Then, the order of operations is used to simplify.

The exponent comes first, $\frac{1}{2}(16) - 3$, then the multiplication $8 - 3$, and then, after subtraction, the solution is 5.

<u>Example 2</u>
Evaluate $4|5 - x| + 2y, x = 4, y = -3$.

The first step is to substitute 4 in for x and -3 in for y in the expression: $4|5 - 4| + 2(-3)$.

Then, the absolute value expression is simplified, which is $|5 - 4| = |1| = 1$.

The expression is $4(1) + 2(-3)$ which can be simplified using the order of operations.

First is the multiplication, $4 + (-6)$; then addition yields an answer of -2.

<u>Example 3</u>
Find the perimeter of a rectangle with a length of 6 inches and a width of 9 inches.

The first step is substituting in 6 for the length and 9 for the width in the perimeter of a rectangle formula, $P = 2(6) + 2(9)$.

Then, the order of operations is used to simplify.

First is multiplication (resulting in $12 + 18$) and then addition for a solution of 30 inches.

Graphs of Algebraic Functions

A graph can shift in many ways. To shift it horizontally, a constant can be added to all the x variables. Replacing x with $(x + a)$ will shift the graph to the left by a. If a is negative, this shifts the graph to the right. Similarly, vertical shifts occur by adding a constant to each of the y variables. Replacing y by $(y + a)$ will shift the graph up by a. If a is negative, then it shifts the graph down.

A graph can also stretch and shrink the graph in the horizontal and vertical directions. To stretch by a (positive) factor of k horizontally, all instances of x are replaced with $\frac{x}{k}$. To stretch vertically by k, all instances of y are replaced with $\frac{y}{k}$.

The graph can be reflected over the y-axis by replacing all instances of x with $(-x)$. The graph can also be reflected over the x-axis by replacing all instances of y with $(-y)$.

24

Other Algebraic Functions

A **function** $f(x)$ is a mathematical object which takes one number, x, as an input and gives a number in return. The input is called the **independent variable**. If the variable is set equal to the output, as in $y = f(x)$, then this is called the **dependent variable**. To indicate the dependent value a function, y, gives for a specific independent variable, x, the notation $y = f(x)$ is used.

The **domain** of a function is the set of values that the independent variable is allowed to take. Unless otherwise specified, the domain is any value for which the function is well defined. The **range** of the function is the set of possible outputs for the function.

In many cases, a function can be defined by giving an equation. For instance, $f(x) = x^2$ indicates that given a value for x, the output of f is found by squaring x.

Not all equations in x and y can be written in the form $y = f(x)$. An equation can be written in such a form if it satisfies the **vertical line test**: no vertical line meets the graph of the equation at more than a single point. In this case, y is said to be a *function of* x. If a vertical line meets the graph in two places, then this equation cannot be written in the form $y = f(x)$.

The **graph of a function** $f(x)$ is the graph of the equation $y = f(x)$. Thus, it is the set of all pairs (x, y) where $y = f(x)$. In other words, it is all pairs $(x, f(x))$. The x-intercepts are called the *zeros* of the function. The y-intercept is given by $f(0)$.

If, for a given function f, the only way to get $f(a) = f(b)$ is for $a = b$, then f is *one-to-one*. Often, even if a function is not one-to-one on its entire domain, it is one-to-one by considering a restricted portion of the domain.

A function $f(x) = k$ for some number k is called a **constant function**. The graph of a constant function is a horizontal line.

The function $f(x) = x$ is called the **identity function**. The graph of the identity function is the diagonal line pointing to the upper right at 45 degrees, $y = x$.

Given two functions, $f(x)$ and $g(x)$, new functions can be formed by adding, subtracting, multiplying, or dividing the functions. Any algebraic combination of the two functions can be performed, including one function being the exponent of the other. If there are expressions for f and g, then the result can be found by performing the desired operation between the expressions. So, if $f(x) = x^2$ and $g(x) = 3x$, then:

$$f \times g(x) = x^2 \times 3x = 3x^3$$

Given two functions, $f(x)$ and $g(x)$, where the domain of g contains the range of f, the two functions can be combined together in a process called **composition**. The function—"g composed of f"—is written:

$$(g \circ f)(x) = g(f(x))$$

This requires the input of x into f, then taking that result and plugging it in to the function g.

Math

If f is one-to-one, then there is also the option to find the function $f^{-1}(x)$, called the *inverse* of f. Algebraically, the inverse function can be found by writing y in place of $f(x)$, and then solving for x. The inverse function also makes this statement true: $f^{-1}(f(x)) = x$.

Computing the inverse of a function f entails the following procedure:

Given $f(x) = x^2$, with a domain of $x \geq 0$

$x = y^2$ is written down to find the inverse

The square root of both sides is determined to solve for y.

Normally, this would mean $\pm\sqrt{x} = y$. However, the domain of f does not include the negative numbers, so the negative option needs to be eliminated.

The result is $y = \sqrt{x}$, so $f^{-1}(x) = \sqrt{x}$, with a domain of $x \geq 0$.

A function is called **monotone** if it is either always increasing or always decreasing. For example, the functions $f(x) = 3x$ and $f(x) = -x^5$ are monotone.

An **even function** looks the same when flipped over the y-axis:

$$f(x) = f(-x)$$

The following image shows a graphic representation of an even function.

An **odd function** looks the same when flipped over the y-axis and then flipped over the x-axis: $f(x) = -f(-x)$. The following image shows an example of an odd function.

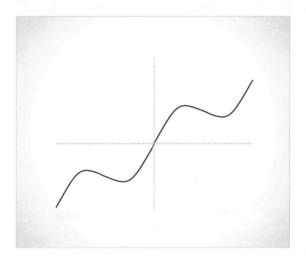

Rewriting Expressions

Algebraic expressions are made up of numbers, variables, and combinations of the two, using mathematical operations. Expressions can be rewritten based on their factors. For example, the expression $6x + 4$ can be rewritten as $2(3x + 2)$ because 2 is a factor of both $6x$ and 4. More complex expressions can also be rewritten based on their factors. The expression $x^4 - 16$ can be rewritten as $(x^2 - 4)(x^2 + 4)$. This is a different type of factoring, where a difference of squares is factored into a sum and difference of the same two terms. With some expressions, the factoring process is simple and only leads to a different way to represent the expression. With others, factoring and rewriting the expression leads to more information about the given problem.

In the following quadratic equation, factoring the binomial leads to finding the zeros of the function:

$$x^2 - 5x + 6 = y$$

This equations factors into $(x - 3)(x - 2) = y$, where 2 and 3 are found to be the zeros of the function when y is set equal to zero. The zeros of any function are the x-values where the graph of the function on the coordinate plane crosses the x-axis.

Factoring an equation is a simple way to rewrite the equation and find the zeros, but factoring is not possible for every quadratic. Completing the square is one way to find zeros when factoring is not an option. The following equation cannot be factored:

$$x^2 + 10x - 9 = 0$$

The first step in this method is to move the constant to the right side of the equation, making it $x^2 + 10x = 9$. Then, the coefficient of x is divided by 2 and squared. This number is then added to both sides of the equation, to make the equation still true. For this example, $\left(\frac{10}{2}\right)^2 = 25$ is added to both sides of the equation to obtain:

$$x^2 + 10x + 25 = 9 + 25$$

27

This expression simplifies to $x^2 + 10x + 25 = 34$, which can then be factored into $(x + 5)^2 = 34$. Solving for x then involves taking the square root of both sides and subtracting 5. This leads to two zeros of the function: $x = \pm\sqrt{34} - 5$. Depending on the type of answer the question seeks, a calculator may be used to find exact numbers.

Given a quadratic equation in standard form— $ax^2 + bx + c = 0$—the sign of a tells whether the function has a minimum value or a maximum value. If $a > 0$, the graph opens up and has a minimum value. If $a < 0$, the graph opens down and has a maximum value. Depending on the way the quadratic equation is written, multiplication may need to occur before a max/min value is determined.

Exponential expressions can also be rewritten, just as quadratic equations. Properties of exponents must be understood. Multiplying two exponential expressions with the same base involves adding the exponents:

$$a^m a^n = a^{m+n}$$

Dividing two exponential expressions with the same base involves subtracting the exponents:

$$\frac{a^m}{a^n} = a^{m-n}$$

Raising an exponential expression to another exponent includes multiplying the exponents:

$$(a^m)^n = a^{mn}$$

The zero power always gives a value of 1: $a^0 = 1$. Raising either a product or a fraction to a power involves distributing that power: $(ab)^m = a^m b^m$ and $\left(\frac{a}{b}\right)^m = \frac{a^m}{b^m}$. Finally, raising a number to a negative exponent is equivalent to the reciprocal including the positive exponent:

$$a^{-m} = \frac{1}{a^m}$$

Simplifying Algebraic Fractions

A **rational expression** is a fraction with a polynomial in the numerator and denominator. The denominator polynomial cannot be zero. An example of a rational expression is:

$$\frac{3x^4 - 2}{-x + 1}$$

The same rules for working with addition, subtraction, multiplication, and division with rational expressions apply as when working with regular fractions.

The first step is to find a common denominator when adding or subtracting. This can be done just as with regular fractions. For example, if $\frac{a}{b} + \frac{c}{d}$, then a common denominator can be found by multiplying to find the following fractions: $\frac{ad}{bd}, \frac{cb}{db}$.

A **complex fraction** is a fraction in which the numerator and denominator are themselves fractions, of the form $\frac{\left(\frac{a}{b}\right)}{\left(\frac{c}{d}\right)}$. These can be simplified by following the usual rules for the order of operations, or by remembering that dividing one fraction by another is the same as multiplying by the reciprocal of the divisor. This means that any complex fraction can be rewritten using the following form:

$$\frac{\left(\frac{a}{b}\right)}{\left(\frac{c}{d}\right)} = \frac{a}{b} \times \frac{d}{c}$$

The following problem is an example of solving a complex fraction:

$$\frac{\left(\frac{5}{4}\right)}{\left(\frac{3}{8}\right)} = \frac{5}{4} \times \frac{8}{3} = \frac{40}{12} = \frac{10}{3}$$

Solving Verbal Problems Presented in an Algebraic Context

There is a four-step process in problem-solving that can be used as a guide:

- Understand the problem and determine the unknown information.

- Translate the verbal problem into an algebraic equation.

- Solve the equation by using inverse operations.

- Check the work and answer the given question.

Example
Three times the sum of a number plus 4 equals the number plus 8. What is the number?

The first step is to determine the unknown, which is the number, or x.

The second step is to translate the problem into the equation, which is $3(x + 4) = x + 8$.

The equation can be solved as follows:

$3x + 12 = x + 8$	Apply the distributive property
$3x = x - 4$	Subtract 12 from both sides of the equation
$2x = -4$	Subtract x from both sides of the equation
$x = -2$	Divide both sides of the equation by 2

The final step is checking the solution. Plugging the value for x back into the equation yields the following problem:

$$3(-2) + 12 = -2 + 8$$

Using the order of operations shows that a true statement is made: $6 = 6$.

Translation of Written Phases into Algebraic Expressions

An *algebraic expression* contains one or more operations and one or more variables. To convert written phrases into algebraic expression, there are some key terms to recognize:

- Key terms with addition are sum, increase, plus, add, more than, and total.
- Key terms with subtraction are difference, decrease, minus, subtract, and less than.
- Key terms with multiplication are product, times, and multiplied.
- Key terms with division are quotient, divided, and ratio.
- Key terms with exponent are squares, cubed, and raised to a power.

To write a phrase as an algebraic expression, it's necessary to identify the unknown(s) where variables will be used and the words for the correct operation.

Example 1

Write an expression for three times the sum of twice the number n plus five.

Three times means $3 \times$, twice a number and five means $2n + 5$, and the final expression is $3(2n + 5)$.

Example 2

Write an expression for the total price of $2 per pound for grapes and $3 per pound for strawberries.

The total means the sum. The price for grapes is $2g$, and the price for strawberries is $3s$. The expression is $2g + 3s$.

Monomials, Binomials, and Polynomials

Polynomials

Algebraic expressions are built out of monomials. A **monomial** is a variable raised to some power multiplied by a constant: ax^n, where a is any constant and n is a whole number. A constant is also a monomial.

A **polynomial** is a sum of monomials. Examples of polynomials include $3x^4 + 2x^2 - x - 3$ and $\frac{4}{5}x^3$. The latter is also a monomial. If the highest power of x is 1, the polynomial is called **linear**. If the highest power of x is 2, it is called **quadratic**.

Adding and Subtracting Monomials and Polynomials

To add or subtract polynomials, add the coefficients of terms with the same exponent. For instance,

$$(-2x^2 + 3x + 1) + (4x^2 - x)$$

$$(-2 + 4)x^2 + (3 - 1)x + 1 = 2x^2 + 2x + 1$$

Multiplying and Dividing Monomials and Polynomials

To multiply polynomials each term of the first polynomial multiplies each term of the second polynomial, and adds up the results. Here's an example:

$$(3x^4 + 2x^2)(2x^2 + 3)$$

$$3x^4 \cdot 2x^2 + 3x^4 \cdot 3 + 2x^2 \cdot 2x^2 + 2x^2 \cdot 3$$

Then, add like terms with a result of:

$$6x^6 + 9x^4 + 4x^4 + 6x^2 = 6x^6 + 13x^4 + 6x^2$$

A polynomial with two terms is called a **binomial**. Another way of remember the rule for multiplying two binomials is to use the acronym **FOIL**: multiply the *First* terms together, then the *Outside* terms (terms on the far left and far right), then the *Inner* terms, and finally the *Last* two terms. For longer polynomials, there is no such convenient mnemonic, so remember to multiply each term of the first polynomial by each term of the second, and add the results.

To divide one polynomial by another, the procedure is similar to long division. At each step, one needs to figure out how to get the term of the dividend with the highest exponent as a multiple of the divisor. The divisor is multiplied by the multiple to get that term, which goes in the quotient. Then, the product of this term is subtracted with the dividend from the divisor and repeat the process. This sounds rather abstract, so it may be easiest to see the procedure by describing it while looking at an example.

Example

$$(4x^3 + x^2 - x + 4) \div (2x - 1)$$

The first step is to set up the problem for long division:

$$2x - 1 \overline{\smash{\big)}\ 4x^3 + x^2 - x + 4}$$

Divide the first term of the divisor on the left by the first term of the numerator under the bar and place the result over the bar:

$$\begin{array}{r} 2x^2 \\ 2x - 1 \overline{\smash{\big)}\ 4x^3 + x^2 - x + 4} \end{array}$$

Next, multiply that new term by the divisor and place it beneath the numerator:

$$\begin{array}{r} 2x^2 \\ 2x - 1 \overline{\smash{\big)}\ 4x^3 + x^2 - x + 4} \\ 4x^3 - 2x^2 \end{array}$$

Subtract it from the numerator to find the difference, a new polynomial:

31

$$2x^2$$

$$2x - 1 \overline{\smash{\big)}\ 4x^3 + x^2 - x + 4}$$
$$-\ \ 4x^3 - 2x^2$$
$$\overline{3x^2 - x + 4}$$

The same steps are repeated until there are no more x-terms in the quotient above the bar or the subtraction step leaves no remainder.

Divide the first term of the new polynomial by the first term of the divisor, multiply that by divisor, and subtract from the new polynomial:

$$2x^2 + \frac{3}{2}x + \frac{1}{4}$$

$$2x - 1 \overline{\smash{\big)}\ 4x^3 + x^2 - x + 4}$$
$$-\ \ 4x^3 - 2x^2$$
$$\overline{3x^2 - x + 4}$$
$$-\ \ 3x^2 - \frac{3}{2}x$$
$$\overline{\frac{1}{2}x + 4}$$
$$-\ \ \frac{1}{2}x - \frac{1}{4}$$
$$\overline{\frac{17}{4}}$$

In this case, the problem doesn't divide evenly, so the answer is the quotient, plus the remainder divided by the divisor $(2x - 1)$:

$$2x^2 + \frac{3}{2}x + \frac{1}{4} + \frac{17}{4(2x - 1)}$$

Factoring

Factors for polynomials are similar to factors for integers—they are numbers, variables, or polynomials that, when multiplied together, give a product equal to the polynomial in question. One polynomial is a factor of a second polynomial if the second polynomial can be obtained from the first by multiplying by a third polynomial.

$6x^6 + 13x^4 + 6x^2$ can be obtained by multiplying together $(3x^4 + 2x^2)(2x^2 + 3)$. This means $2x^2 + 3$ and $3x^4 + 2x^2$ are factors of $6x^6 + 13x^4 + 6x^2$.

32

In general, finding the factors of a polynomial can be tricky. However, there are a few types of polynomials that can be factored in a straightforward way.

If a certain monomial is in each term of a polynomial, it can be factored out. There are several common forms polynomials take, which if you recognize, you can solve. The first example is a perfect square trinomial. To factor this polynomial, first expand the middle term of the expression:

$$x^2 + 2xy + y^2$$

$$x^2 + xy + xy + y^2$$

Factor out a common term in each half of the expression (in this case x from the left and y from the right):

$$x(x + y) + y(x + y)$$

Then the same can be done again, treating $(x + y)$ as the common factor:

$$(x + y)(x + y) = (x + y)^2$$

Therefore, the formula for this polynomial is:

$$x^2 + 2xy + y^2 = (x + y)^2$$

Next is another example of a perfect square trinomial. The process is the similar, but notice the difference in sign:

$$x^2 - 2xy + y^2$$

$$x^2 - xy - xy + y^2$$

Factor out the common term on each side:

$$x(x - y) - y(x - y)$$

Factoring out the common term again:

$$(x - y)(x - y) = (x - y)^2$$

Thus,

$$x^2 - 2xy + y^2 = (x - y)^2$$

The next is known as a difference of squares. This process is effectively the reverse of binomial multiplication:

$$x^2 - y^2$$

$$x^2 - xy + xy - y^2$$

$$x(x - y) + y(x - y)$$

$$(x + y)(x - y)$$

33

Therefore,

$$x^2 - y^2 = (x + y)(x - y)$$

The following two polynomials are known as the sum or difference of cubes. These are special polynomials that take the form of $x^3 + y^3$ or $x^3 - y^3$. The following formula factors the sum of cubes:

$$x^3 + y^3 = (x + y)(x^2 - xy + y^2)$$

Next is the difference of cubes, but note the change in sign. The formulas for both are similar, but the order of signs for factoring the sum or difference of cubes can be remembered by using the acronym **SOAP**, which stands for "same, opposite, always positive." The first sign is the same as the sign in the first expression, the second is opposite, and the third is always positive. The next formula factors the difference of cubes:

$$x^3 - y^3 = (x - y)(x^2 + xy + y^2)$$

The following two examples are expansions of cubed binomials. Similarly, these polynomials always follow a pattern:

$$x^3 + 3x^2y + 3xy^2 + y^3 = (x + y)^3$$
$$x^3 - 3x^2y + 3xy^2 - y^3 = (x - y)^3$$

These rules can be used in many combinations with one another. For example, the expression $3x^3 - 24$ has a common factor of 3, which becomes:

$$3(x^3 - 8)$$

A difference of cubes still remains which can then be factored out:

$$3(x - 2)(x^2 + 2x + 4)$$

There are no other terms to be pulled out, so this expression is completely factored.

When factoring polynomials, a good strategy is to multiply the factors to check the result. Let's try another example:

$$4x^3 + 16x^2$$

Both sides of the expression can be divided by 4, and both contain x^2, because $4x^3$ can be thought of as $4x^2(x)$, so the common term can simply be factored out:

$$4x^2(x + 4)$$

It sometimes can be necessary to rewrite the polynomial in some clever way before applying the above rules. Consider the problem of factoring $x^4 - 1$. This does not immediately look like any of the previous polynomials. However, it's possible to think of this polynomial as $x^4 - 1 = (x^2)^2 - (1^2)^2$, and now it can be treated as a difference of squares to simplify this:

$$(x^2)^2 - (1^2)^2$$

$$(x^2)^2 - x^2 1^2 + x^2 1^2 - (1^2)^2$$

$$x^2(x^2 - 1^2) + 1^2(x^2 - 1^2)$$

$$(x^2 + 1^2)(x^2 - 1^2)$$

$$(x^2 + 1)(x^2 - 1)$$

Expanding Polynomials

Some polynomials may need to be expanded to identify the final solution—**polynomial expansion** means that parenthetical polynomials are multiplied out so that the parentheses no longer exist. The polynomials will be in the form $(a + b)^n$ where n is a whole number greater than 2. The expression can be simplified using the **distributive property**, which states that a number, variable, or polynomial that is multiplied by a polynomial in parentheses should be multiplied by each item in the parenthetical polynomial. Here's one example:

$$(a + b)^2 = (a + b)(a + b)$$

$$a^2 + ab + ab + b^2 = a^2 + 2ab + b^2$$

Here's another example to consider:

$$(a + b)^3 = (a + b)(a + b)(a + b)$$

$$(a^2 + ab + ab + b^2)(a + b) = (a^2 + 2ab + b^2)(a + b)$$

$$a^3 + 2a^2b + ab^2 + a^2b + 2ab^2 + b^3 = a^3 + 3a^2b + 3ab^2 + b^3$$

FOIL Method

FOIL is a technique for generating polynomials through the multiplication of binomials. A polynomial is an expression of multiple variables (for example, x, y, z) in at least three terms involving only the four basic operations and exponents. FOIL is an acronym for First, Outer, Inner, and Last. "First" represents the multiplication of the terms appearing first in the binomials. "Outer" means multiplying the outermost terms. "Inner" means multiplying the terms inside. "Last" means multiplying the last terms of each binomial.

After completing FOIL and solving the operations, like terms are combined. To identify like terms, look for terms with the same variable and the same exponent. For example, look at:

$$4x^2 - x^2 + 15x + 2x^2 - 8$$

The $4x^2, -x^2$, and $2x^2$ are all like terms because they have the variable (x) and exponent (2). Thus, after combining the like terms, the polynomial has been simplified to $5x^2 + 15x - 8$.

The purpose of FOIL is to simplify an equation involving multiple variables and operations. Although it sounds complicated, working through some examples will provide some clarity:

1) Simplify $(x + 10)(x + 4) = (x \times x) + (x \times 4) + (10 \times x) + (10 \times 4)$

$\qquad\qquad\qquad\qquad\quad$ First $\qquad$ Outer $\qquad$ Inner $\qquad$ Last

After multiplying these binomials, it's time to solve the operations and combine like terms. Thus, the expression becomes:

$$x^2 + 4x + 10x + 40 = x^2 + 14x + 40$$

2) Simplify $2x(4x^3 - 7y^2 + 3x^2 + 4)$

Here, a monomial $(2x)$ is multiplied into a polynomial $(4x^3 - 7y^2 + 3x^2 + 4)$. Using the distributive property, multiply the monomial against each term in the polynomial. This becomes:

$$2x(4x^3) - 2x(7y^2) + 2x(3x^2) + 2x(4)$$

Now, simplify each monomial. Start with the coefficients:

$$(2 \times 4)(x \times x^3) - (2 \times 7)(x \times y^2) + (2 \times 3)(x \times x^2) + (2 \times 4)(x)$$

When multiplying powers with the same base, add their exponents. Remember, a variable with no listed exponent has an exponent of 1, and exponents of distinct variables cannot be combined. This produces the answer:

$$8x^{1+3} - 14xy^2 + 6x^{1+2} + 8x = 8x^4 - 14xy^2 + 6x^3 + 8x$$

3) Simplify $(8x^{10}y^2z^4) \div (4x^2y^4z^7)$

First, divide the coefficients of the first two polynomials: $8 \div 4 = 2$. Second, divide exponents with the same variable, which requires subtracting the exponents. This results in:

$$2(x^{10-2}y^{2-4}z^{4-7}) = 2x^8y^{-2}z^{-3}$$

However, the most simplified answer should include only positive exponents. Thus, $y^{-2}z^{-3}$ need to be converted into fractions, respectively $\frac{1}{y^2}$ and $\frac{1}{z^3}$. Since the $2x^8$ has a positive exponent, it is placed in the numerator, and $\frac{1}{y^2}$ and $\frac{1}{z^3}$ are combined into the denominator, leaving $\frac{2x^8}{y^2z^3}$ as the final answer.

The Evaluation of Positive Rational Roots and Exponents

There are a few rules for working with exponents. For any numbers a, b, m, n, the following hold true:

$$a^1 = a$$

$$1^a = 1$$

$$a^0 = 1$$

$$a^m \times a^n = a^{m+n}$$

$$a^m \div a^n = a^{m-n}$$

$$(a^m)^n = a^{m \times n}$$

$$(a \times b)^m = a^m \times b^m$$

$$(a \div b)^m = a^m \div b^m$$

Any number, including a fraction, can be an exponent. The same rules apply.

Zeros of Polynomials

Finding the zeros of polynomial functions is the same process as finding the solutions of polynomial equations. These are the points at which the graph of the function crosses the x-axis. As stated previously, factors can be used to find the zeros of a polynomial function. The degree of the function shows the number of possible zeros. If the highest exponent on the independent variable is 4, then the degree is 4, and the number of possible zeros is 4. If there are complex solutions, the number of roots is less than the degree.

Given the function $y = x^2 + 7x + 6$, y can be set equal to zero, and the polynomial can be factored. The equation turns into $0 = (x + 1)(x + 6)$, where $x = -1$ and $x = -6$ are the zeros. Since this is a quadratic equation, the shape of the graph will be a parabola. Knowing that zeros represent the points where the parabola crosses the x-axis, the maximum or minimum point is the only other piece needed to sketch a rough graph of the function. By looking at the function in standard form, the coefficient of x is positive; therefore, the parabola opens *up*. Using the zeros and the minimum, the following rough sketch of the graph can be constructed:

used when the exponent on a binomial is larger than 2, and the multiplication would take a long time. The binomial theorem is given as:

$$(a+b)^n = \sum_{k=0}^{n} \binom{n}{k} a^{n-k} b^k$$

$$where \quad \binom{n}{k} = \frac{n!}{k!(n-k)!}$$

The **Remainder Theorem** can be helpful when evaluating polynomial functions $P(x)$ for a given value of x. A polynomial can be divided by $(x-a)$, if there is a remainder of 0. This also means that $P(a) = 0$ and $(x-a)$ is a factor of $P(x)$. In a similar sense, if P is evaluated at any other number b, $P(b)$ is equal to the remainder of dividing $P(x)$ by $(x-b)$.

Operations with Polynomials

Addition and subtraction operations can be performed on polynomials with like terms. **Like terms** *refers to terms* that have the same variable and exponent. The two following polynomials can be added together by collecting like terms: $(x^2 + 3x - 4) + (4x^2 - 7x + 8)$. The x^2 terms can be added as $x^2 + 4x^2 = 5x^2$. The x terms can be added as $3x + -7x = -4x$, and the constants can be added as $-4 + 8 = 4$. The following expression is the result of the addition: $5x^2 - 4x + 4$. When subtracting polynomials, the same steps are followed, only subtracting like terms together.

Multiplication of polynomials can also be performed. Given the two polynomials, $(y^3 - 4)$ and $(x^2 + 8x - 7)$, each term in the first polynomial must be multiplied by each term in the second polynomial. The steps to multiply each term in the given example are as follows:

$$(y^3 \times x^2) + (y^3 \times 8x) + (y^3 \times -7) + (-4 \times x^2) + (-4 \times 8x) + (-4 \times -7)$$

Simplifying each multiplied part, yields:

$$x^2 y^3 + 8xy^3 - 7y^3 - 4x^2 - 32x + 28$$

None of the terms can be combined because there are no like terms in the final expression. Any polynomials can be multiplied by each other by following the same set of steps, then collecting like terms at the end.

Standard Algorithms and Concepts

Order of Operations

When solving equations with multiple operations, special rules apply. These rules are known as the **Order of Operations**. The order is as follows: Parentheses, Exponents, Multiplication and Division from left to right, and Addition and Subtraction from left to right. A popular mnemonic device to help remember the order is **Please Excuse My Dear Aunt Sally (PEMDAS)**. Evaluate the following two problems to understand the Order of Operations:

1) $4 + (3 \times 2)^2 \div 4$

First, solve the operation within the parentheses: $4 + 6^2 \div 4$.
Second, solve the exponent: $4 + 36 \div 4$.
Third, solve the division operation: $4 + 9$.
Fourth, finish the operation with addition for the answer, 13.

2) $2 \times (6 + 3) \div (2 + 1)^2$

$2 \times 9 \div (3)^2$
$2 \times 9 \div 9$
$18 \div 9$
2

Positive and Negative Numbers

Signs

Aside from 0, numbers can be either positive or negative. The sign for a positive number is the plus sign or the + symbol, while the sign for a negative number is the minus sign or the − symbol. If a number has no designation, then it's assumed to be positive.

Absolute Values

Both positive and negative numbers are valued according to their distance from 0. Look at this number line for $+3$ and -3:

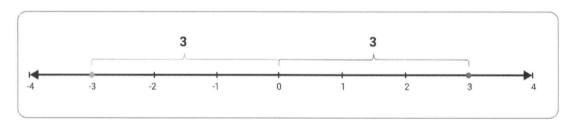

Both 3 and −3 are three spaces from 0. The distance from 0 is called its absolute value. Thus, both −3 and 3 have an absolute value of 3 since they're both three spaces away from 0.

An **absolute number** is written by placing | | around the number. So, |3| and |−3| both equal 3, as that's their common absolute value.

Implications for Addition and Subtraction

For addition, if all numbers are either positive or negative, simply add them together. For example, $4 + 4 = 8$ and $-4 + -4 = -8$. However, things get tricky when some of the numbers are negative, and some are positive.

Take $6 + (-4)$ as an example. First, take the absolute values of the numbers, which are 6 and 4. Second, subtract the smaller value from the larger. The equation becomes $6 - 4 = 2$. Third, place the sign of the original larger number on the sum. Here, 6 is the larger number, and it's positive, so the sum is 2.

Here's an example where the negative number has a larger absolute value: $(-6) + 4$. The first two steps are the same as the example above. However, on the third step, the negative sign must be placed on the sum, as the absolute value of (-6) is greater than 4. Thus, $-6 + 4 = -2$.

The absolute value of numbers implies that subtraction can be thought of as flipping the sign of the number following the subtraction sign and simply adding the two numbers. This means that subtracting a negative number will in fact be adding the positive absolute value of the negative number. Here are some examples:

$$-6 - 4 = -6 + -4 = -10$$

$$3 - -6 = 3 + 6 = 9$$

$$-3 - 2 = -3 + -2 = -5$$

Implications for Multiplication and Division

For multiplication and division, if both numbers are positive, then the product or quotient is always positive. If both numbers are negative, then the product or quotient is also positive. However, if the numbers have opposite signs, the product or quotient is always negative.

Simply put, the product in multiplication and quotient in division is always positive, unless the numbers have opposing signs, in which case it's negative. Here are some examples:

$$(-6) \times (-5) = 30$$

$$(-50) \div 10 = -5$$

$$8 \times |-7| = 56$$

$$(-48) \div (-6) = 8$$

If there are more than two numbers in a multiplication or division problem, then whether the product or quotient is positive or negative depends on the number of negative numbers in the problem. If there is an odd number of negatives, then the product or quotient is negative. If there is an even number of negative numbers, then the result is positive.

Here are some examples:

$$(-6) \times 5 \times (-2) \times (-4) = -240$$

$$(-6) \times 5 \times 2 \times (-4) = 240$$

Factorization

Factors are the numbers multiplied to achieve a product. Thus, every product in a multiplication equation has, at minimum, two factors. Of course, some products will have more than two factors. For the sake of most discussions, assume that factors are positive integers.

To find a number's factors, start with 1 and the number itself. Then divide the number by 2, 3, 4, and so on, seeing if any divisors can divide the number without a remainder, keeping a list of those that do. Stop upon reaching either the number itself or another factor.

Let's find the factors of 45. Start with 1 and 45. Then try to divide 45 by 2, which fails. Now divide 45 by 3. The answer is 15, so 3 and 15 are now factors. Dividing by 4 doesn't work, and dividing by 5 leaves 9. Lastly, dividing 45 by 6, 7, and 8 all don't work. The next integer to try is 9, but this is already known to be a factor, so the factorization is complete. The factors of 45 are 1, 3, 5, 9, 15 and 45.

Prime Factorization

Prime factorization involves an additional step after breaking a number down to its factors: breaking down the factors until they are all prime numbers. A **prime number** is any number that can only be divided by 1 and itself. The prime numbers between 1 and 20 are 2, 3, 5, 7, 11, 13, 17, and 19. As a simple test, numbers that are even or end in 5 are not prime.

Let's break 129 down into its prime factors. First, the factors are 3 and 43. Both 3 and 43 are prime numbers, so we're done. But if 43 was not a prime number, then it would also need to be factorized until all of the factors are expressed as prime numbers.

Common Factor

A **common factor** is a factor shared by two numbers. Let's take 45 and 30 and find the common factors:

The factors of 45 are: 1, 3, 5, 9, 15, and 45.
The factors of 30 are: 1, 2, 3, 5, 6, 10, 15, and 30.
The common factors are 1, 3, 5, and 15.

Greatest Common Factor

The **greatest common factor** is the largest number among the shared, common factors. From the factors of 45 and 30, the common factors are 3, 5, and 15. Thus, 15 is the greatest common factor, as it's the largest number.

Least Common Multiple

The **least common multiple** is the smallest number that's a multiple of two numbers. Let's try to find the least common multiple of 4 and 9. The multiples of 4 are 4, 8, 12, 16, 20, 24, 28, 32, 36, and so on. For 9, the multiples are 9, 18, 27, 36, 45, 54, etc. Thus, the least common multiple of 4 and 9 is 36, the lowest number where 4 and 9 share multiples.

If two numbers share no factors besides 1 in common, then their least common multiple will be simply their product. If two numbers have common factors, then their least common multiple will be their product divided by their greatest common factor. This can be visualized by the formula $LCM = \frac{x \times y}{GCF}$, where x and y are some integers, and LCM and GCF are their least common multiple and greatest common factor, respectively.

Manipulating Roots and Exponents

A **root** is a different way to write an exponent when the exponent is the reciprocal of a whole number. We use the **radical symbol** to write this in the following way: $\sqrt[n]{a} = a^{\frac{1}{n}}$. This quantity is called the *n-th root* of a. The n is called the **index of the radical**.

Note that if the n-th root of a is multiplied by itself n times, the result will just be a. If no number n is written by the radical, it is assumed that n is 2:

$$\sqrt{5} = 5^{\frac{1}{2}}$$

The special case of the 2nd root is called the **square root**, and the third root is called the **cube root**.

A **perfect square** is a whole number that is the square of another whole number. For example, 16 and 64 are perfect squares because 16 is the square of 4, and 64 is the square of 8.

The Use of Absolute Values

The **absolute value** represents the distance a number is from 0. The **absolute value symbol** is | | with a number between the bars. The $|10| = 10$ and the $|-10| = 10$.

When simplifying an algebraic expression, the value of the absolute value expression is determined first, much like parenthesis in the order of operations. See the example below:

$$|8 - 12| + 5 = |-4| + 5 = 4 + 5 = 9$$

Ordering

Exponents are shorthand for longer multiplications or divisions. The exponent is written to the upper right of a number. In the expression 2^3, the exponent is 3. The number with the exponent is called the **base**.

When the exponent is a whole number, it means to multiply the base by itself as many times as the number in the exponent. So, $2^3 = 2 \times 2 \times 2 = 8$.

If the exponent is a negative number, it means to take the reciprocal of the positive exponent:

$$2^{-3} = \frac{1}{2^3} = \frac{1}{8}$$

When the exponent is 0, the result is always 1: $2^0 = 1, 5^0 = 1$, and so on.

When the exponent is 2, the number is *squared*, and when the exponent is 3, it is *cubed*.

When working with longer expressions, parentheses are used to show the order in which the operations should be performed. Operations inside the parentheses should be completed first. Thus, $(3 - 1) \div 2$ means one should first subtract 1 from 3, and then divide that result by 2.

The **order of operations** gives an order for how a mathematical expression is to be simplified:

- Parentheses
- Exponents
- Multiplication
- Division
- Addition
- Subtraction

To help remember this, many students like to use the mnemonic PEMDAS. Some students associate this word with a phrase to help them, such as "Pirates Eat Many Donuts at Sea." Here is a quick example:

$$\text{Evaluate: } 2^2 \times (3 - 1) \div 2 + 3.$$

$$\text{Parenthesis: } 2^2 \times 2 \div 2 + 3.$$

$$\text{Exponents: } 4 \times 2 \div 2 + 3$$

$$\text{Multiply: } 8 \div 2 + 3.$$

$$\text{Divide: } 4 + 3.$$

$$\text{Addition: } 7$$

Computation with Integers and Negative Rational Numbers

Integers are the whole numbers together with their negatives. They include numbers like 5, 24, 0, -6, and 15. They do not include fractions or numbers that have digits after the decimal point.

Rational numbers are all numbers that can be written as a fraction using integers. A **fraction** is written as $\frac{x}{y}$ and represents the quotient of x being divided by y. More practically, it means dividing the whole into y equal parts, then taking x of those parts.

Examples of rational numbers include $\frac{1}{2}$ and $\frac{5}{4}$. The number on the top is called the **numerator**, and the number on the bottom is called the **denominator**. Because every integer can be written as a fraction with a denominator of 1, (e.g. $\frac{3}{1} = 3$), every integer is also a rational number.

When adding integers and negative rational numbers, there are some basic rules to determine if the solution is negative or positive:

Adding two positive numbers results in a positive number: $3.3 + 4.8 = 8.1$.

Adding two negative numbers results in a negative number: $(-8) + (-6) = -14$.

Adding one positive and one negative number requires taking the absolute values and finding the difference between them. Then, the sign of the number that has the higher absolute value for the final solution is used.

For example, $(-9) + 11$, has a difference of absolute values of 2. The final solution is 2 because 11 has the higher absolute value. Another example is $9 + (-11)$, which has a difference of absolute values of 2. The final solution is -2 because 11 has the higher absolute value.

When subtracting integers and negative rational numbers, one has to change the problem to adding the opposite and then apply the rules of addition.

Subtracting two positive numbers is the same as adding one positive and one negative number.

For example, $4.9 - 7.1$ is the same as $4.9 + (-7.1)$. The solution is -2.2 since the absolute value of -7.1 is greater. Another example is $8.5 - 6.4$ which is the same as $8.5 + (-6.4)$. The solution is 2.1 since the absolute value of 8.5 is greater.

Subtracting a positive number from a negative number results in negative value.

For example, $(-12) - 7$ is the same as $(-12) + (-7)$ with a solution of -19.

Subtracting a negative number from a positive number results in a positive value.

For example, $12 - (-7)$ is the same as $12 + 7$ with a solution of 19.

For multiplication and division of integers and rational numbers, if both numbers are positive or both numbers are negative, the result is a positive value.

For example, $(-1.7)(-4)$ has a solution of 6.8 since both numbers are negative values.

If one number is positive and another number is negative, the result is a negative value.

For example, $\frac{-15}{5}$ has a solution of -3 since there is one negative number.

Determinants

A **matrix** is a rectangular arrangement of numbers in rows and columns. The **determinant** of a matrix is a special value that can be calculated for any square matrix.

Using the *square 2 x 2 matrix* $\begin{bmatrix} a & b \\ c & d \end{bmatrix}$, the determinant is $ad - bc$.

For example, the determinant of the matrix $\begin{bmatrix} -5 & 1 \\ 3 & 4 \end{bmatrix}$ is $-5(4) - 1(3) = -20 - 3 = -23$.

Using a *3 x 3 matrix* $\begin{bmatrix} a & b & c \\ d & e & f \\ g & h & i \end{bmatrix}$, the determinant is $a(ei - fh) - b(di - fg) + c(dh - eg)$.

For example, the determinant of the matrix $\begin{bmatrix} 2 & 0 & 1 \\ -1 & 3 & 2 \\ 2 & -2 & -1 \end{bmatrix}$ is:

$$2\big(3(-1) - 2(-2)\big) - 0\big(-1(-1) - 2(2)\big) + 1\big(-1(-2) - 3(2)\big)$$

$$= 2(-3 + 4) - 0(1 - 4) + 1(2 - 6)$$

$$= 2(1) - 0(-3) + 1(-4)$$

$$= 2 - 0 - 4 = -2$$

The pattern continues for larger square matrices.

Fractions and Word Problems

Work word problems are examples of people working together in a situation that uses fractions.

Example

One painter can paint a designated room in 6 hours, and a second painter can paint the same room in 5 hours. How long will it take them to paint the room if they work together?

The first painter paints $\frac{1}{6}$ of the room in an hour, and the second painter paints $\frac{1}{5}$ of the room in an hour.

Together, they can paint $\frac{1}{x}$ of the room in an hour. The equation is the sum of the painter's rate equal to the total job or $\frac{1}{6} + \frac{1}{5} = \frac{1}{x}$.

The equation can be solved by multiplying all terms by a common denominator of $30x$ with a result of $5x + 6x = 30$.

The left side can be added together to get $11x$, and then divide by 11 for a solution of $\frac{30}{11}$ or about 2.73 hours.

Functions

A **function** is defined as a relationship between inputs and outputs where there is only one output value for a given input. As an example, the following function is in function notation:

$$f(x) = 3x - 4$$

The $f(x)$ represents the output value for an input of x. If $x = 2$, the equation becomes:

$$f(2) = 3(2) - 4 = 6 - 4 = 2$$

The input of 2 yields an output of 2, forming the ordered pair $(2, 2)$. The following set of ordered pairs corresponds to the given function: $(2, 2), (0, -4), (-2, -10)$. The set of all possible inputs of a function is its *domain*, and all possible outputs is called the *range*. By definition, each member of the domain is paired with only one member of the range.

Functions can also be defined recursively. In this form, they are not defined explicitly in terms of variables. Instead, they are defined using previously-evaluated function outputs, starting with either $f(0)$ or $f(1)$. An example of a recursively-defined function is $f(1) = 2, f(n) = 2f(n-1) + 2n, n > 1$. The domain of this function is the set of all integers.

Domain and Range

The domain and range of a function can be found visually by its plot on the coordinate plane. In the function $f(x) = x^2 - 3$, for example, the domain is all real numbers because the parabola stretches as far left and as far right as it can go, with no restrictions. This means that any input value from the real number system will yield an answer in the real number system. For the range, the inequality $y \geq -3$ would be used to describe the possible output values because the parabola has a minimum at $y = -3$. This means there will not be any real output values less than -3 because -3 is the lowest value it reaches on the y-axis.

These same answers for domain and range can be found by observing a table. The table below shows that from input values $x = -1$ to $x = 1$, the output results in a minimum of -3. On each side of $x = 0$, the numbers increase, showing that the range is all real numbers greater than or equal to -3.

x (domain/input)	y (range/output)
-2	1
-1	-2
0	-3
-1	-2
2	1

Algebraic

A function is called *algebraic* if it is built up from polynomials by adding, subtracting, multiplying, dividing, and taking radicals. This means that, for example, the variable can never appear in an exponent. Thus, polynomials and rational functions are algebraic, but exponential functions are not algebraic. It turns out that logarithms and trigonometric functions are not algebraic either.

A function of the form $f(x) = a_n x^n + a_{n-1} x^{n-1} + a_{n-2} x^{n-2} + \cdots + a_1 x + a_0$ is called a **polynomial function**. The value of n is called the **degree of the polynomial**. In the case where $n = 1$, it is called a *linear function*. In the case where $n = 2$, it is called a **quadratic function**. In the case where $n = 3$, it is called a **cubic function**.

When n is even, the polynomial is called **even**, and not all real numbers will be in its range. When n is odd, the polynomial is called **odd**, and the range includes all real numbers.

The graph of a quadratic function $f(x) = ax^2 + bx + c$ will be a **parabola**. To see whether or not the parabola opens up or down, it's necessary to check the coefficient of x^2, which is the value a.

If the coefficient is positive, then the parabola opens upward. If the coefficient is negative, then the parabola opens downward.

The quantity $D = b^2 - 4ac$ is called the **discriminant of the parabola**. If the discriminant is positive, then the parabola has two real zeros. If the discriminant is negative, then it has no real zeros.

If the discriminant is zero, then the parabola's highest or lowest point is on the x-axis, and it has a single real zero.

The highest or lowest point of the parabola is called the **vertex**. The coordinates of the vertex are given by the point $(-\frac{b}{2a}, -\frac{D}{4a})$. The roots of a quadratic function can be found with the quadratic formula, which is:

$$x = \frac{-b \pm \sqrt{b^2 - 4ac}}{2a}$$

A **rational function** is a function $f(x) = \frac{p(x)}{q(x)}$, where p and q are both polynomials. The domain of f will be all real numbers except the (real) roots of q.

At these roots, the graph of f will have a **vertical asymptote**, unless they are also roots of p. Here is an example to consider:

$$p(x) = p_n x^n + p_{n-1} x^{n-1} + p_{n-2} x^{n-2} + \cdots + p_1 x + p_0$$

$$q(x) = q_m x^m + q_{m-1} x^{m-1} + q_{m-2} x^{m-2} + \cdots + q_1 x + q_0$$

When the degree of p is less than the degree of q, there will be a **horizontal asymptote** of $y = 0$. If p and q have the same degree, there will be a horizontal asymptote of $y = \frac{p_n}{q_n}$. If the degree of p is exactly one greater than the degree of q, then f will have an oblique asymptote along the line:

$$y = \frac{p_n}{q_{n-1}} x + \frac{p_{n-1}}{q_{n-1}}$$

Exponentials

An **exponential function** is a function of the form $f(x) = b^x$, where b is a positive real number other than 1. In such a function, b is called the *base*.

The *domain* of an exponential function is all real numbers, and the *range* is all positive real numbers. There will always be a horizontal asymptote of $y = 0$ on one side. If b is greater than 1, then the graph will be increasing moving to the right. If b is less than 1, then the graph will be decreasing moving to the right. Exponential functions are one-to-one. The basic exponential function graph will go through the point $(0, 1)$.

Example
Solve $5^{x+1} = 25$.

Get the x out of the exponent by rewriting the equation $5^{x+1} = 5^2$ so that both sides have a base of 5.

Since the bases are the same, the exponents must be equal to each other.

This leaves $x + 1 = 2$ or $x = 1$.

To check the answer, the x-value of 1 can be substituted back into the original equation.

Logarithmic

A **logarithmic function** is an inverse for an exponential function. The inverse of the base b exponential function is written as $\log_b(x)$, and is called the **base b logarithm**. The domain of a logarithm is all positive real numbers. It has the properties that $\log_b(b^x) = x$. For positive real values of x,

$$b^{\log_b(x)} = x$$

When there is no chance of confusion, the parentheses are sometimes skipped for logarithmic functions: $\log_b(x)$ may be written as $\log_b x$. For the special number e, the base e logarithm is called the **natural logarithm** and is written as $\ln x$. Logarithms are one-to-one.

When working with logarithmic functions, it is important to remember the following properties. Each one can be derived from the definition of the logarithm as the inverse to an exponential function:

$$\log_b 1 = 0$$

$$\log_b b = 1$$

$$\log_b b^p = p$$

$$\log_b MN = \log_b M + \log_b N$$

$$\log_b \frac{M}{N} = \log_b M - \log_b N$$

$$\log_b M^p = p \log_b M$$

When solving equations involving exponentials and logarithms, the following fact should be used:

If f is a one-to-one function, $a = b$ is equivalent to $f(a) = f(b)$.

Using this, together with the fact that logarithms and exponentials are inverses, allows manipulations of the equations to isolate the variable.

Example
Solve $4 = \ln(x - 4)$.

Using the definition of a logarithm, the equation can be changed to $e^4 = e^{\ln(x-4)}$.

The functions on the right side cancel with a result of $e^4 = x - 4$.

This then gives $x = 4 + e^4$.

Trigonometric Functions

Trigonometric functions are built out of two basic functions, the **sine** and **cosine**, written as $\sin \theta$ and $\cos \theta$ respectively. Note that similar to logarithms, it is customary to drop the parentheses as long as the result is not confusing.

The sine and cosine are defined using the *unit circle*. If θ is the angle going counterclockwise around the origin from the x-axis, then the point on the unit circle in that direction will have the coordinates $(\cos\theta, \sin\theta)$.

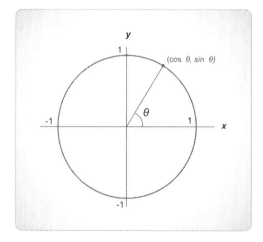

Since the angle returns to the start every 2π radians (or 360 degrees), the graph of these functions will be *periodic*, with period 2π. This means that the graph repeats itself as one moves along the x-axis because $\sin\theta = \sin(\theta + 2\pi)$. Cosine works similarly.

From the unit circle definition, the sine function starts at 0 when $\theta = 0$. It grows to 1 as θ grows to $\frac{\pi}{2}$, and then back to 0 at $\theta = \pi$. Then it decreases to -1 as θ grows to $\frac{3\pi}{2}$, and back up to 0 at $\theta = 2\pi$.

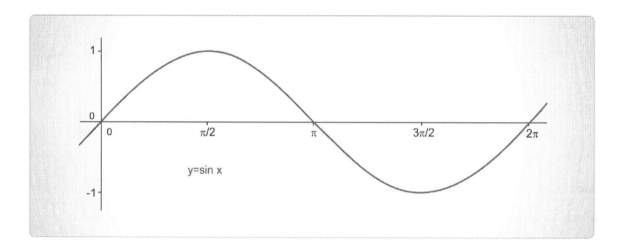

The graph of the cosine is similar. The cosine will start at 1, decreasing to 0 at $\frac{\pi}{2}$ and continuing to decrease to -1 at $\theta = \pi$. Then, it grows to 0 as θ grows to $\frac{3\pi}{2}$ and back up to 1 at $\theta = 2\pi$.

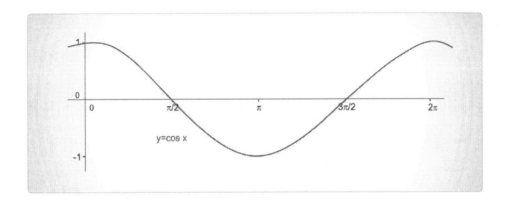

Another trigonometric function, which is frequently used, is the **tangent function**. This is defined as the following equation: $\tan \theta = \frac{\sin \theta}{\cos \theta}$.

The tangent function is a period of π rather than 2π because the sine and cosine functions have the same absolute values after a change in the angle of π, but flip their signs. Since the tangent is a ratio of the two functions, the changes in signs cancel.

The tangent function will be zero when the sine is zero, and it will have a vertical asymptote whenever cosine is zero. The following graph shows the tangent function:

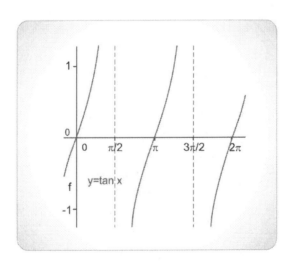

Three other trigonometric functions are sometimes useful. These are the **reciprocal trigonometric functions**, so named because they are just the reciprocals of sine, cosine, and tangent. They are the **cosecant**, defined as $\csc \theta = \frac{1}{\sin \theta}$, the **secant**, $\sec \theta = \frac{1}{\cos \theta}$, and the **cotangent**, $\cot \theta = \frac{1}{\tan \theta}$. Note that from the definition of tangent, $\cot \theta = \frac{\cos \theta}{\sin \theta}$.

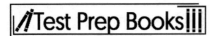

In addition, there are three identities that relate the trigonometric functions to one another:

$$\cos\theta = \sin(\frac{\pi}{2} - \theta)$$

$$\csc\theta = \sec\left(\frac{\pi}{2} - \theta\right)$$

$$\cot\theta = \tan(\frac{\pi}{2} - \theta)$$

Here is a list of commonly-needed values for trigonometric functions, given in radians, for the first quadrant:

Table for trigonometric functions

$\sin 0 = 0$	$\cos 0 = 1$	$\tan 0 = 0$
$\sin\frac{\pi}{6} = \frac{1}{2}$	$\cos\frac{\pi}{6} = \frac{\sqrt{3}}{2}$	$\tan\frac{\pi}{6} = \frac{\sqrt{3}}{3}$
$\sin\frac{\pi}{4} = \frac{\sqrt{2}}{2}$	$\cos\frac{\pi}{4} = \frac{\sqrt{2}}{2}$	$\tan\frac{\pi}{4} = 1$
$\sin\frac{\pi}{3} = \frac{\sqrt{3}}{2}$	$\cos\frac{\pi}{3} = \frac{1}{2}$	$\tan\frac{\pi}{3} = \sqrt{3}$
$\sin\frac{\pi}{2} = 1$	$\cos\frac{\pi}{2} = 0$	$\tan\frac{\pi}{2} = undefined$
$\csc 0 = undefined$	$\sec 0 = 1$	$\cot 0 = undefined$
$\csc\frac{\pi}{6} = 2$	$\sec\frac{\pi}{6} = \frac{2\sqrt{3}}{3}$	$\cot\frac{\pi}{6} = \sqrt{3}$
$\csc\frac{\pi}{4} = \sqrt{2}$	$\sec\frac{\pi}{4} = \sqrt{2}$	$\cot\frac{\pi}{4} = 1$
$\csc\frac{\pi}{3} = \frac{2\sqrt{3}}{3}$	$\sec\frac{\pi}{3} = 2$	$\cot\frac{\pi}{3} = \frac{\sqrt{3}}{3}$
$\csc\frac{\pi}{2} = 1$	$\sec\frac{\pi}{2} = undefined$	$\cot\frac{\pi}{2} = 0$

To find the trigonometric values in other quadrants, complementary angles can be used. The **complementary angle** is the smallest angle between the x-axis and the given angle.

Once the complementary angle is known, the following rule is used:

For an angle θ with complementary angle x, the absolute value of a trigonometry function evaluated at θ is the same as the absolute value when evaluated at x.

The correct sign is used based on the functions sine and cosine are given by the x and y coordinates on the unit circle.

Sine will be positive in quadrants I and II and negative in quadrants III and IV.

Cosine will be positive in quadrants I and IV, and negative in II and III.

Tangent will be positive in I and III, and negative in II and IV.

The signs of the reciprocal functions will be the same as the sign of the function of which they are a reciprocal.

Example
Find $\sin \frac{3\pi}{4}$.

First, the complementary angle must be found.

This angle is in the II quadrant, and the angle between it and the x-axis is $\frac{\pi}{4}$.

Now, $\sin \frac{\pi}{4} = \frac{\sqrt{2}}{2}$.

Since this is in the II quadrant, sine takes on positive values (the y coordinate is positive in the II quadrant).

Therefore, $\sin \frac{3\pi}{4} = \frac{\sqrt{2}}{2}$.

In addition to the six trigonometric functions defined above, there are inverses for these functions. However, since the trigonometric functions are not one-to-one, one can only construct inverses for them on a restricted domain.

Usually, the domain chosen will be $[0, \pi)$ for cosine and $(-\frac{\pi}{2}, \frac{\pi}{2}]$ for sine. The inverse for tangent can use either of these domains. The inverse functions for the trigonometric functions are also called **arc functions**. In addition to being written with a -1 in the exponent to denote that the function is an inverse, they will sometimes be written with an "a" or "arc" in front of the function name, so $\cos^{-1} \theta = a\cos \theta = \arccos \theta$.

When solving equations that involve trigonometric functions, there are often multiple solutions. For example, $2\sin \theta = \sqrt{2}$ can be simplified to $\sin \theta = \frac{\sqrt{2}}{2}$. This has solutions $\theta = \frac{\pi}{4}, \frac{3\pi}{4}$, but in addition, because of the periodicity, any integer multiple of 2π can also be added to these solutions to find another solution.

The full set of solutions is $\theta = \frac{\pi}{4} + 2\pi k, \frac{3\pi}{4} + 2\pi k$ for all integer values of k. It is very important to remember to find all possible solutions when dealing with equations that involve trigonometric functions.

The name **trigonometric** comes from the fact that these functions play an important role in the geometry of triangles, particularly right triangles.

Consider the right triangle shown in this figure:

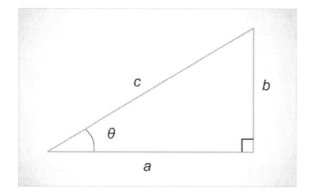

The following hold true:

- $c \sin \theta = b$

- $c \cos \theta = a$

- $\tan \theta = \dfrac{b}{a}$

- $b \csc \theta = c$

- $a \sec \theta = c$

- $\cot \theta = \dfrac{a}{b}$

Remember also the angles of a triangle must add up to π radians (180 degrees).

Coordinate Plane

The Coordinate Plane

The **coordinate plane** can be divided into four *quadrants*. The upper-right part of the plane is called the **first quadrant**, where both x and y are positive. The **second quadrant** is the upper-left, where x is negative but y is positive. The **third quadrant** is the lower left, where both x and y are negative. Finally, the **fourth quadrant** is in the lower right, where x is positive but y is negative. These quadrants are often written with Roman numerals:

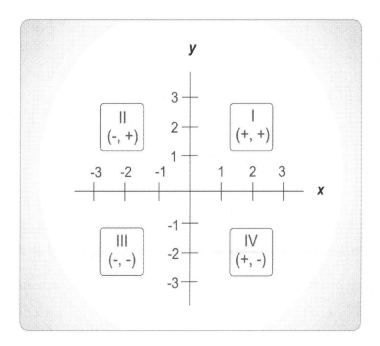

In addition to graphing individual points as shown above, the graph lines and curves in the plane can be graphed corresponding to equations. In general, if there is some equation involving x and y, then the *graph* of that equation consists of all the points (x, y) in the Cartesian coordinate plane, which satisfy this equation.

Given the equation $y = x + 2$, the point $(0, 2)$ is in the graph, since $2 = 0 + 2$ is a true equation. However, the point $(1, 4)$ will *not* be in the graph, because $4 = 1 + 2$ is false.

Plane Geometry

Algebraic equations can be used to describe geometric figures in the plane. The method for doing so is to use the **Cartesian coordinate plane**. The idea behind these Cartesian coordinates (named for mathematician and philosopher Descartes) is that from a specific point on the plane, known as the **center**, one can specify any other point by saying *how far to the right or left* and *how far up or down*.

The plane is covered with a grid. The two directions, right to left and bottom to top, are called **axes** (singular *axis*). When working with x- and y-variables, the x-variable corresponds to the right and left axis, and the y-variable corresponds to the up and down axis.

Any point on the grid is found by specifying how far to travel from the center along the x-axis and how far to travel along the y-axis. The ordered pair can be written as (x, y). A positive x value means go to the right on the x-axis, while a negative x-value means to go to the left. A positive y-value means to go up, while a negative value means to go down. Several points are shown as examples in the figure.

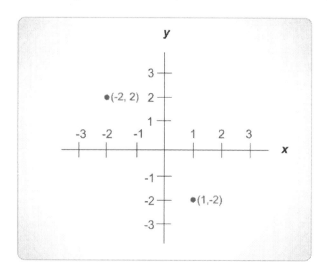

Cartesian Coordinate Plane

Straight Lines

The simplest equations to graph are the equations whose graphs are lines, called **linear equations**. Every linear equation can be rewritten algebraically so that it looks like $Ax + By = C$.

First, the ratio of the change in the y coordinate to the change in the x coordinate is constant for any two distinct points on the line. In any pair of points on a line, two points, (x_1, y_1) and (x_2, y_2) — where $x_1 \neq x_2$ — the ratio $\frac{y_2 - y_1}{x_2 - x_1}$ will always be the same, even if another pair of points is used.

This ratio, $\frac{y_2 - y_1}{x_2 - x_1}$, is called the *slope* of the line and is often denoted with the letter m. If the slope is *positive*, then the line goes upward when moving to the right. If the slope is *negative*, then it moves downward when moving to the right. If the slope is 0, then the line is *horizontal*, and the y coordinate is constant along the entire line. For lines where the x coordinate is constant along the entire line, the slope is not defined, and these lines are called *vertical* lines.

The y-coordinate of the point where the line touches the y-axis is called the *y-intercept* of the line. It is often denoted by the letter b, used in the form of the linear equation $y = mx + b$. The x coordinate of the point where the line touches the x-axis is called the *x-intercept*. It is also called the *zero* of the line.

Suppose two lines have slopes m_1 and m_2. If the slopes are equal, $m_1 = m_2$, then the lines are *parallel*. **Parallel lines** never meet one another. If $m_1 = -\frac{1}{m_2}$, then the lines are called **perpendicular or orthogonal**. Their slopes can also be called opposite reciprocals of each other.

There are several convenient ways to write down linear equations. The common forms are listed here:

Standard Form: $Ax + By = C$, where the slope is given by $\frac{-A}{B}$, and the y-intercept is given by $\frac{C}{B}$.

Slope-Intercept Form: $y = mx + b$, where the slope is m, and the y-intercept is b.

Point-Slope Form: $y - y_1 = m(x - x_1)$, where m is the slope, and (x_1, y_1) is any point on the line.

Two-Point Form: $\frac{y - y_1}{x - x_1} = \frac{y_2 - y_1}{x_2 - x_1}$, where (x_1, y_1), and (x_2, y_2) are any two distinct points on the line.

Intercept Form: $\frac{x}{x_1} + \frac{y}{y_1} = 1$, where x_1 is the x-intercept, and y_1 is the y-intercept.

Depending upon the given information, different forms of the linear equation can be easier to write down than others. When given two points, the two-point form is easy to write down. If the slope and a single point is known, the point-slope form is easiest to start with. In general, which form to start with depends upon the given information.

Conics

The graph of an equation of the form $y = ax^2 + bx + c$ or $x = ay^2 + by + c$ is called a **parabola**.

The graph of an equation of the form $\frac{x^2}{a^2} - \frac{y^2}{b^2} = 1$ or $-\frac{x^2}{a^2} + \frac{y^2}{b^2} = 1$ is called a **hyperbola**.

The graph of an equation of the form $\frac{(x-x_0)^2}{a^2} + \frac{(y-y_0)^2}{b^2} = 1$ is called an **ellipse**. If $a = b$ then this is a **circle with radius** $r = \frac{1}{a}$.

Sets of Points in the Plane

The **midpoint** between two points, (x_1, y_1) and (x_2, y_2), is given by taking the average of the x coordinates and the average of the y coordinates:

$$\left(\frac{x_1 + x_2}{2}, \frac{y_1 + y_2}{2} \right)$$

The *distance* between two points, (x_1, y_1) and (x_2, y_2), is given by the **Pythagorean formula**:

$$\sqrt{(x_2 - x_1)^2 + (y_2 - y_1)^2}$$

To find the perpendicular distance between a line $Ax + By = C$ and a point (x_1, y_1) not on the line, we need to use this formula:

$$\frac{|Ax_1 + By_1 + C|}{\sqrt{A^2 + B^2}}$$

57

Solving Problems in the Coordinate Plane

The location of a point on a coordinate grid is identified by writing it as an ordered pair. An **ordered pair** is a set of numbers indicating the x-and y-coordinates of the point. Ordered pairs are written in the form (x, y) where x and y are values which indicate their respective coordinates. For example, the point $(3, -2)$ has an x-coordinate of 3 and a y-coordinate of -2.

Plotting a point on the coordinate plane with a given coordinate means starting from the origin $(0, 0)$. To determine the value of the x-coordinate, move right (positive number) or left (negative number) along the x-axis. Next, move up (positive number) or down (negative number) to the value of the y-coordinate. Finally, plot and label the point. For example, plotting the point $(1, -2)$ requires starting from the origin and moving right along the x-axis to positive one, then moving down until straight across from negative 2 on the y-axis. The point is plotted and labeled. This point, along with three other points, are plotted and labeled on the graph below.

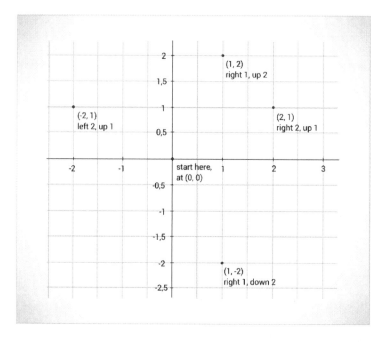

To write the coordinates of a point on the coordinate grid, a line should be traced directly above or below the point until reaching the x-axis (noting the value on the x-axis). Then, returning to the point, a line should be traced directly to the right or left of the point until reaching the y-axis (noting the value on the y-axis). The ordered pair (x, y) should be written with the values determined for the x- and y-coordinates.

Polygons can be drawn in the coordinate plane given the coordinates of their vertices. These coordinates can be used to determine the perimeter and area of the figure. Suppose triangle RQP has vertices located at the points: $R(-2, 0)$, $Q(2, 2)$, and $P(2, 0)$. By plotting the points for the three vertices, the triangle can be constructed as follows:

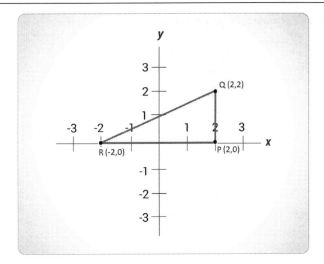

Because points R and P have the same y-coordinates (they are directly across from each other), the distance between them is determined by subtracting their x-coordinates (or simply counting units from one point to the other):

$$2 - (-2) = 4$$

Therefore, the length of side RP is 4 units. Because points Q and P have the same x-coordinate (they are directly above and below each other), the distance between them is determined by subtracting their y-coordinates (or counting units between them): $2 - 0 = 2$. Therefore, the length of side PQ is 2 units. Knowing the length of side RP, which is the base of the triangle, and the length of side PQ, which is the height of the triangle, the area of the figure can be determined by using the formula $A = \frac{1}{2}bh$.

To determine the perimeter of the triangle, the lengths of all three sides are needed. Points R and Q are neither directly across nor directly above and below each other. Therefore, the distance formula must be used to find the length of side RQ. The distance formula is as follows:

$$d = \sqrt{(x_2 - x_1)^2 + (y_2 - y_1)^2}$$

$$d = \sqrt{\left(2 - (-2)\right)^2 + (2 - 0)^2}$$

$$d = \sqrt{(4)^2 + (2)^2}$$

$$d = \sqrt{16 + 4} \rightarrow d = \sqrt{20}$$

The perimeter is determined by adding the lengths of the three sides of the triangle.

Circles on the Coordinate Plane

If a circle is placed on the coordinate plane with the center of the circle at the origin $(0, 0)$, then point (x, y) is a point on the circle. Furthermore, the line extending from the center to point (x, y) is the radius, or r. By applying the Pythagorean Theorem ($a^2 + b^2 = c^2$), it can be stated that $x^2 + y^2 = r^2$. However, the center of the circle does not always need to be on the origin of the coordinate plane.

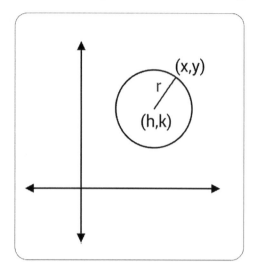

In the diagram above, the center of the circle is noted by (h, k). By applying the distance formula, the equation becomes:

$$\sqrt{(x - h)^2 + (y - k)^2}$$

When squaring both sides of the equation, the result is the standard form of a circle with the center (h, k) and radius r. Namely, $r^2 = (x - h)^2 + (y - k)^2$, where $r = radius$ and $center = (h, k)$. The following examples may be solved by using this information:

Example: Graph the equation $-x^2 + y^2 = 25$.

To graph this equation, first note that the center of the circle is $(0, 0)$. The radius is the positive square root of 25 or 5.

Example: Find the equation for the circle below.

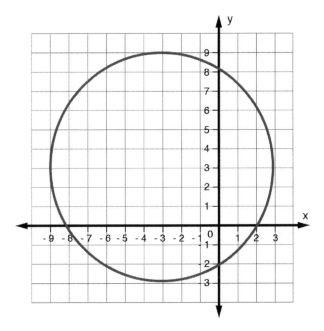

To find the equation for the circle, note that its center is not zero. Therefore, to find the circle's center, draw vertical and horizontal diameters to examine where they intersect. The center is located at point: $(-3, 3)$. Next, count the number of spaces from the center to the outside of the circle. This number is 6. Therefore, 6 is the radius. Finally, plug in the numbers that are known into the standard equation for a circle:

$$36 = \left(x - (-3)\right)^2 + (y - 3)^2$$

or

$$36 = (x + 3)^2 + (y - 3)^2$$

It is possible to determine whether a point lies on a circle or not within the coordinate plane. For example, a circle has a center of $(2, -5)$, and a radius of 6 centimeters. The first step is to apply the equation of a circle, which is $r^2 = (x - h)^2 + (y - k)^2$, where $r = radius$ and the $center = (h, k)$. Next, substitute the numbers for the center point and the number for the radius. This action simplifies the equation to $36 = (x - 2)^2 + (y + 5)^2$. Note that the radius of 6 was squared to get 36.

To prove that the point $(2, -1)$ lies on the circle, apply the equation of the circle that was just used and input the values of $(2, -1)$ for x and y in the equation.

$$36 = (x - 2)^2 + (y + 5)^2$$

$$36 = (2 - 2)^2 + (1 + 5)^2$$

$$36 = (0)^2 + (6)^2$$

$$36 = 36$$

Because the left side of the equation equals the right side of the equation, point $(2, 1)$ lies on the given circle.

Simultaneous Equations

Systems of Equations

A **system of equations** is a group of equations that have the same variables or unknowns. These equations can be linear, but they are not always so. Finding a solution to a system of equations means finding the values of the variables that satisfy each equation. For a linear system of two equations and two variables, there could be a single solution, no solution, or infinitely many solutions.

A single solution occurs when there is one value for x and y that satisfies the system. This would be shown on the graph where the lines cross at exactly one point. When there is no solution, the lines are parallel and do not ever cross. With infinitely many solutions, the equations may look different, but they are the same line. One equation will be a multiple of the other, and on the graph, they lie on top of each other.

The process of elimination can be used to solve a system of equations. For example, the following equations make up a system: $x + 3y = 10$ and $2x - 5y = 9$. Immediately adding these equations does not eliminate a variable, but it is possible to change the first equation by multiplying the whole equation by -2. This changes the first equation to:

$$-2x - 6y = -20$$

The equations can be then added to obtain $-11y = -11$. Solving for y yields $y = 1$. To find the rest of the solution, 1 can be substituted in for y in either original equation to find the value of $x = 7$. The solution to the system is $(7, 1)$ because it makes both equations true, and it is the point in which the lines intersect. If the system is *dependent*—having infinitely many solutions—then both variables will cancel out when the elimination method is used, resulting in an equation that is true for many values of x and y. Since the system is dependent, both equations can be simplified to the same equation or line.

A system can also be solved using **substitution**. This involves solving one equation for a variable and then plugging that solved equation into the other equation in the system. For example, $x - y = -2$ and $3x + 2y = 9$ can be solved using substitution. The first equation can be solved for x, where $x = -2 + y$. Then it can be plugged into the other equation:

$$3(-2 + y) + 2y = 9$$

Solving for y yields $-6 + 3y + 2y = 9$, where $y = 3$. If $y = 3$, then $x = 1$. This solution can be checked by plugging in these values for the variables in each equation to see if it makes a true statement.

Finally, a solution to a system of equations can be found graphically. The solution to a linear system is the point or points where the lines cross. The values of x and y represent the coordinates (x, y) where the lines intersect. Using the same system of equations as above, they can be solved for y to put them in slope-intercept form, $y = mx + b$. These equations become $y = x + 2$ and $y = -\frac{3}{2}x + 4.5$. The slope

62

This material is provided for exam preparation purposes only and does not indicate an endorsement of any specific scientific, political, or religious point of view. © TPB Publishing. You have been licensed one copy of this document for personal use only. Any other reproduction or redistribution is strictly prohibited. All rights reserved.

is the coefficient of x, and the y-intercept is the constant value. This system with the solution is shown below:

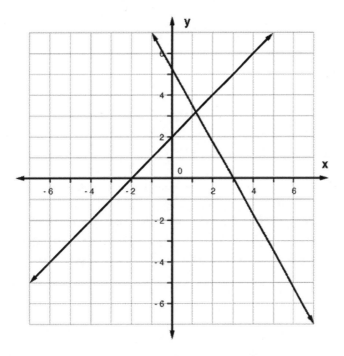

A system of equations may also be made up of a linear and a quadratic equation. These systems may have one solution, two solutions, or no solutions. The graph of these systems involves one straight line and one parabola. Algebraically, these systems can be solved by solving the linear equation for one variable and plugging that answer into the quadratic equation. If possible, the equation can then be solved to find part of the answer. The graphing method is commonly used for these types of systems. On a graph, these two lines can be found to intersect at one point, at two points across the parabola, or at no points.

Matrices can also be used to solve systems of linear equations. Specifically, for systems, the coefficients of the linear equations in standard form are the entries in the matrix. Using the same system of linear equations as above, $x - y = -2$ and $3x + 2y = 9$, the matrix to represent the system is:

$$\begin{bmatrix} 1 & -1 \\ 3 & 2 \end{bmatrix} \begin{bmatrix} x \\ y \end{bmatrix} = \begin{bmatrix} -2 \\ 9 \end{bmatrix}$$

To solve this system using matrices, the inverse matrix must be found. For a general 2x2 matrix, $\begin{bmatrix} a & b \\ c & d \end{bmatrix}$, the inverse matrix is found by the expression:

$$\frac{1}{ad - bc} \begin{bmatrix} d & -b \\ -c & a \end{bmatrix}$$

The inverse matrix for the system given above is:

$$\frac{1}{2 - -3} \begin{bmatrix} 2 & 1 \\ -3 & 1 \end{bmatrix} = \frac{1}{5} \begin{bmatrix} 2 & 1 \\ -3 & 1 \end{bmatrix}$$

63

The next step in solving is to multiply this identity matrix by the system matrix above. This is given by the following equation: $\frac{1}{5}\begin{bmatrix} 2 & 1 \\ -3 & 1 \end{bmatrix}\begin{bmatrix} 1 & -1 \\ 3 & 2 \end{bmatrix}\begin{bmatrix} x \\ y \end{bmatrix} = \begin{bmatrix} 2 & 1 \\ -3 & 1 \end{bmatrix}\begin{bmatrix} -2 \\ 9 \end{bmatrix}\frac{1}{5}$, which simplifies to:

$$\frac{1}{5}\begin{bmatrix} 5 & 0 \\ 0 & 5 \end{bmatrix}\begin{bmatrix} x \\ y \end{bmatrix} = \frac{1}{5}\begin{bmatrix} 5 \\ 15 \end{bmatrix}$$

Solving for the solution matrix, the answer is:

$$\begin{bmatrix} 1 & 0 \\ 0 & 1 \end{bmatrix}\begin{bmatrix} x \\ y \end{bmatrix} = \begin{bmatrix} 1 \\ 3 \end{bmatrix}$$

Since the first matrix is the identity matrix, the solution is $x = 1$ and $y = 3$.

Finding solutions to systems of equations is essentially finding what values of the variables make both equations true. It is finding the input value that yields the same output value in both equations. For functions $g(x)$ and $f(x)$, the equation $g(x) = f(x)$ means the output values are being set equal to each other. Solving for the value of x means finding the x-coordinate that gives the same output in both functions. For example, $f(x) = x + 2$ and $g(x) = -3x + 10$ is a system of equations. Setting $f(x) = g(x)$ yields the equation:

$$x + 2 = -3x + 10$$

Solving for x, gives the x-coordinate $x = 2$ where the two lines cross. This value can also be found by using a table or a graph. On a table, both equations can be given the same inputs, and the outputs can be recorded to find the point(s) where the lines cross. Any method of solving finds the same solution, but some methods are more appropriate for some systems of equations than others.

Tips for Equation Systems

There are a few basic rules to keep in mind when solving systems of equations.

A single equation can be changed by doing the same operation to both sides, just as with one equation.

If one of the equations gives an expression for one of the variables in terms of other variables and constants, the expression can be substituted into the other equation, in place of the variable. This means the other equations will have one less variable in them.

If two equations are in the form of $a = b$ and $c = d$, then a new equation can be formed by adding the equations together, $a + c = b + d$, or subtracting the equations, $a - c = b - d$. This can eliminate one of the variables from an equation.

The general approach is to find a way to change one of the equations so that one variable is isolated, and then substitute that value (or expression) for the variable into the other equations.

The simplest case is a **linear system of two equations**, which has the form $ax + by = c$ and $dx + ey = f$.

To solve linear systems of equations, use the same process to solve one equation in order to isolate one of the variables. Here's an example, using the linear system of equations:

$$2x - 3y = 2, 4x + 4y = 3$$

The first equation is multiplied on both sides by -2, which gives $-4x + 6y = -4$.

Adding this equation to the second equation will allow cancellation of the x term:

$$4x + 4y - 4x + 6y = 3 - 4$$

The result can be simplified to get $10y = -1$, which simplifies to $y = -\frac{1}{10}$.

The solution can be substituted into either of the original equations to find a value for x. Using the first equation:

$$2x - 3\left(-\frac{1}{10}\right) = 2$$

This simplifies to $2x + \frac{3}{10} = 2$, then to $2x = \frac{17}{10}$, and finally $x = \frac{17}{20}$.

The final solution is $x = \frac{17}{20}, y = -\frac{1}{10}$.

To check the validity of the answer, both solutions can be substituted into either original equation, which should result in a true statement.

An alternative way to solve this system would be to solve the first equation to get an expression for y in terms of x.

Subtracting $2x$ from both sides results in $-3y = 2 - 2x$.

Dividing both sides by -3 would be $y = \frac{2}{3}x - \frac{2}{3}$.

Then, this expression can be substituted into the second equation, getting:

$$4x + 4\left(\frac{2}{3}x - \frac{2}{3}\right) = 3$$

This only involves the variable x, which can now be solved. Once the value for x is obtained, it can be substituted into either equation to solve for y.

There is one important issue to note here. If one of the equations in the system can be made to look identical to another equation, then it is **redundant**. The set of solutions will then be all pairs that satisfy the other equation.

For instance, in the system of equations $2x - y = 1$ and $-4x + 2y = -2$, the second equation can be made into the first equation by dividing both sides by -2. Thus, the solution set will be all pairs satisfying $2x - y = 1$, which simplifies to $y = 2x - 1$.

For a pair of linear equations, the simplest way to see if one equation is redundant is to rewrite each equation to the form $ax + by = c$. If one equation can be obtained from the other in this form by multiplying both sides by some constant, then the equations are redundant, and the answer to the system would be all real numbers.

It is also possible for the two equations to be **inconsistent**, which occurs when the two equations can be made into the form $ax + by = c, ax + by = d$, with c and d being different numbers. The two equations are inconsistent if, while trying to solve them, it is determined that an equation is false, such as $3 = 2$. This result shows that there are no solutions to that system of equations.

For linear systems of two equations with two variables, there will always be a single solution unless one of the two equations is redundant or the equations are inconsistent, in which case there are no solutions.

Solving a System of One Linear Equation and One Quadratic Equation

As mentioned, a system of equations consists of two variables in two equations. A solution to the system is an ordered pair (x, y) that makes both equations true. When displayed graphically, a solution to a system is a point of intersection between the graphs of the equations. When a system consists of one linear equation and one quadratic equation, there may be one, two, or no solutions. If the line and parabola intersect at two points, there are two solutions to the system; if they intersect at one point, there is one solution; if they do not intersect, there is no solution.

Systems with One Linear Equation and One Quadratic Equation

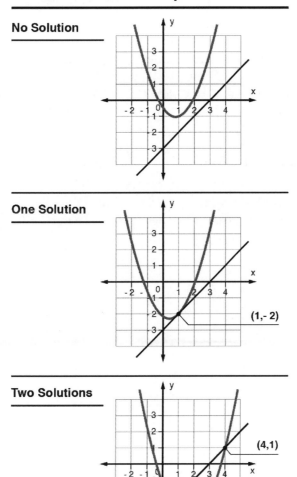

No Solution

One Solution

(1,- 2)

Two Solutions

(4,1)

$(\frac{1}{2}, \frac{-5}{2})$

One method for solving a system of one linear equation and one quadratic equation is to graph both functions and identify point(s) of intersection. This, however, is not always practical. Graph paper may not be available, or the intersection points may not be easily identified. Solving the system algebraically involves using the substitution method. Consider the following system: $y = x^2 + 9x + 11$; $y = 2x - 1$. The equivalent value of y should be substituted from the linear equation ($2x - 1$) into the quadratic equation. The resulting equation is:

$$2x - 1 = x^2 + 9x + 11$$

Next, this quadratic equation should be solved using the appropriate method: factoring, taking square roots, or using the quadratic formula (see section *Solving a Quadratic Equation*). Solving this quadratic

67

equation by factoring results in $x = -4$ or $x = -3$. Next, the corresponding y-values should be found by substituting the x-values into the original linear equation: $y = 2(-4) - 1$; $y = 2(-3) - 1$. The solutions should be written as ordered pairs: $(-4, -9)$ and $(-3, -7)$. Finally, the possible solutions should be checked by substituting each into both of the original equations. In this case, both solutions "check out."

Systems of Linear Inequalities

Systems of linear inequalities are like systems of equations, but the solutions are different. Since inequalities have infinitely many solutions, their systems also have infinitely many solutions. Finding the solutions of inequalities involves graphs. A system of two equations and two inequalities is linear; thus, the lines can be graphed using slope-intercept form. If the inequality has an equals sign, the line is solid. If the inequality only has a greater than or less than symbol, the line on the graph is dotted. Dashed lines indicate that points lying on the line are not included in the solution. After the lines are graphed, a region is shaded on one side of the line. This side is found by determining if a point—known as a **test point**—lying on one side of the line produces a true inequality. If it does, that side of the graph is shaded. If the point produces a false inequality, the line is shaded on the opposite side from the point. The graph of a system of inequalities involves shading the intersection of the two shaded regions.

Practice Quiz

1. What is the answer to $(2 + 2i)(2 - 2i)$?
   a. 8
   b. $8i$
   c. 4
   d. $4i$

2. At the store, Jan spends $90 on apples and oranges. Apples cost $1 each and oranges cost $2 each. If Jan buys the same number of apples as oranges, how many oranges did she buy?
   a. 20
   b. 25
   c. 30
   d. 35

3. What is the equation of a circle whose center is $(1, 5)$ and whole radius is 4?
   a. $(x - 1)^2 + (y - 25)^2 = 4$
   b. $(x - 1)^2 + (y - 25)^2 = 16$
   c. $(x + 1)^2 + (y + 5)^2 = 16$
   d. $(x - 1)^2 + (y - 5)^2 = 16$

4. Where does the point $(-3, -4)$ lie on the circle with the equation $(x)^2 + (y)^2 = 25$?
   a. Inside of the circle
   b. Outside of the circle
   c. On the circle
   d. There is not enough information to tell

5. Shawna buys $2\frac{1}{2}$ gallons of paint. If she uses $\frac{1}{3}$ of it on the first day, how much does she have left?
   a. $1\frac{5}{6}$ gallons

   b. $1\frac{1}{2}$ gallons

   c. $1\frac{2}{3}$ gallons

   d. 2 gallons

See answers on next page.

Answer Explanations

1. A: This answer is correct because $(2 + 2i)(2 - 2i)$, using the FOIL method and rules for imaginary numbers, is:

$$4 - 4i + 4i - 4i^2 = 8$$

Choice *B* is not the answer because there is no *i* in the final answer, since the *i*'s cancel out in the FOIL. Choice *C*, 4, is not the final answer because we add $4 + 4$ in the end to equal 8. Choice *D*, $4i$, is not the final answer because there is neither a 4 nor an *i* in the final answer.

2. C: One apple/orange pair costs \$3 total. Therefore, Jan bought $90 \div 3 = 30$ total pairs, and hence, she bought 30 oranges.

3. D: The standard form for the equation of a circle is $(x - h)^2 + (y - k)^2 = r^2$, where (h, k) is the center and *r* is the radius. Subtract the center from the *x* and *y* values of the equation and square the radius on the right side of the equation. Choice *A* is not the correct answer because you need to square the radius of the equation. Choice *B* is not the correct answer because you do not square the centers of the equation. Choice *C* is not the correct answer because you need to subtract (not add) the centers of the equation.

4. C: Plug in the values for *x* and *y* to discover that the solution works, which is:

$$(-3)^2 + (-4)^2 = 25$$

Choices *A* and *B* are not the correct answers since the solution works. Choice *D* is not the correct answer because there is enough information to tell where the given point lies on the circle.

5. C: If she has used $\frac{1}{3}$ of the paint, she has $\frac{2}{3}$ remaining. The mixed fraction can be converted because $2\frac{1}{2}$ gallons is the same as $\frac{5}{2}$ gallons. The calculation is:

$$\frac{2}{3} \times \frac{5}{2} = \frac{5}{3} = 1\frac{2}{3} \text{ gal}$$

Reading

Summarizing the Most Important Ideas, Events, or Information

Topic Versus the Main Idea

It is very important to know the difference between the topic and the main idea of the text. Even though these two are similar because they both present the central point of a text, they have distinctive differences. A **topic** is the subject of the text; it can usually be described in a one- to two-word phrase and appears in the simplest form. On the other hand, the **main idea** is more detailed and provides the author's central point of the text. It can be expressed through a complete sentence and is often found in the beginning, middle, or end of a paragraph. In most nonfiction books, the first sentence of the passage usually (but not always) states the main idea. Review the passage below to explore the topic versus the main idea.

Cheetahs

Cheetahs are one of the fastest mammals on the land, reaching up to 70 miles an hour over short distances. Even though cheetahs can run as fast as 70 miles an hour, they usually only have to run half that speed to catch up with their choice of prey. Cheetahs cannot maintain a fast pace over long periods of time because their bodies will overheat. After a chase, cheetahs need to rest for approximately 30 minutes prior to eating or returning to any other activity.

In the example above, the topic of the passage is "Cheetahs" simply because that is the subject of the text. The main idea of the text is "Cheetahs are one of the fastest mammals on the land but can only maintain a fast pace for shorter distances." While it covers the topic, it is more detailed and refers to the text in its entirety. The text continues to provide additional details called **supporting details**, which will be discussed in the next section.

Supporting Details

Supporting details help readers better develop and understand the main idea. Supporting details answer questions like *who, what, where, when, why,* and *how.* Different types of supporting details include examples, facts and statistics, anecdotes, and sensory details.

Persuasive and informative texts often use supporting details. In persuasive texts, authors attempt to make readers agree with their points of view, and supporting details are often used as "selling points." If authors make a statement, they need to support the statement with evidence in order to adequately persuade readers. Informative texts use supporting details such as examples and facts to inform readers. Review the previous "Cheetahs" passage to find examples of supporting details.

Cheetahs

Cheetahs are one of the fastest mammals on the land, reaching up to 70 miles an hour over short distances. Even though cheetahs can run as fast as 70 miles an hour, they

71

usually only have to run half that speed to catch up with their choice of prey. Cheetahs cannot maintain a fast pace over long periods of time because their bodies will overheat. After a chase, cheetahs need to rest for approximately 30 minutes prior to eating or returning to any other activity.

In the example, supporting details include:

1. Cheetahs reach up to 70 miles per hour over short distances.
2. They usually only have to run half that speed to catch up with their prey.
3. Cheetahs will overheat if they exert a high speed over longer distances.
4. Cheetahs need to rest for 30 minutes after a chase.

Look at the diagram below (applying the cheetah example) to help determine the hierarchy of topic, main idea, and supporting details.

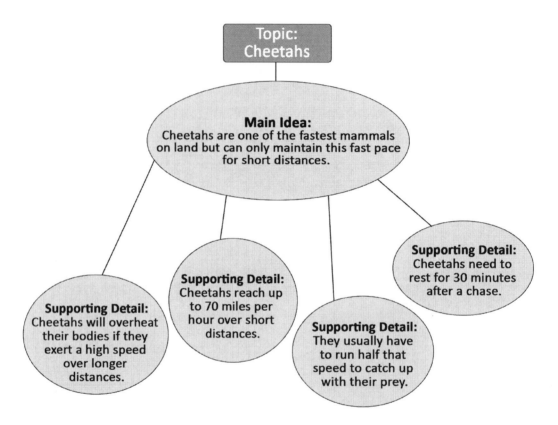

Summarizing and Paraphrasing a Passage

As an aid to drawing conclusions, outlining the information contained in the passage should be a familiar skill to readers. An effective outline will reveal the structure of the passage and will lead to solid conclusions. An effective outline will have a title that refers to the basic subject of the text though the title needs not recapitulate the main idea. In most outlines, the main idea will be the first major section. Each major idea of the passage will be established as the head of a category. For instance, the most common outline format calls for the main ideas of the passage to be indicated with Roman numerals. In an effective outline of this kind, each of the main ideas will be represented by a Roman numeral and none of the Roman numerals will designate minor details or secondary ideas. Moreover, all supporting ideas and details should be placed in the appropriate place on the outline. An outline does not need to include every detail listed in the text, but the outline should feature all of those that are central to the argument or message. Each of these details should be listed under the appropriate main idea.

Ideas from a text can also be organized using graphic organizers. A graphic organizer is a way to simplify information and take key points from the text. A graphic organizer such as a timeline may have an event listed for a corresponding date on the timeline while an outline may have an event listed under a key point that occurs in the text. Each reader needs to create the type of graphic organizer that works the best for him or her in terms of being able to recall information from a story. Examples include a **spider-map**, which takes a main idea from the story and places it in a bubble with supporting points branching off the main idea. An *outline* is useful for diagramming the main and supporting points of the entire story, and a **Venn diagram** classifies information as separate or overlapping.

A helpful tool is the ability to summarize the information that you have read in a paragraph or passage format. This process is similar to creating an effective outline. First, a summary should accurately define the main idea of the passage though the summary does not need to explain this main idea in exhaustive detail. The summary should continue by laying out the most important supporting details or arguments from the passage. All of the significant supporting details should be included, and none of the details included should be irrelevant or insignificant. Also, the summary should accurately report all of these details. Too often, the desire for brevity in a summary leads to the sacrifice of clarity or accuracy. Summaries are often difficult to read because they omit all of the graceful language, digressions, and asides that distinguish great writing. However, an effective summary should contain much the same message as the original text.

Paraphrasing is another method that the reader can use to aid in comprehension. When paraphrasing, one puts what they have read into their words by rephrasing what the author has written, or one "translates" all of what the author shared into their words by including as many details as they can.

Outlining

As mentioned, an *outline* is a system used to organize writing. When reading texts, outlining is important because it helps readers organize important information in a logical pattern using Roman numerals. Usually, outlines start out with the main idea(s) and then branch out into subgroups or subsidiary thoughts or subjects. Not only do outlines provide a visual tool for readers to reflect on how events, characters, settings, or other key parts of the text or passage relate to one another, but they can also lead readers to a stronger conclusion.

The sample below demonstrates what a general outline looks like.

I. Main Topic 1
    a. Subtopic 1
    b. Subtopic 2
        1. Detail 1
        2. Detail 2
II. Main Topic 2
    a. Subtopic 1
    b. Subtopic 2
        1. Detail 1
        2. Detail 2

Summarizing

At the end of a text or passage, it is important to summarize what the readers read. **Summarizing** is a strategy in which readers determine what is important throughout the text or passage, shorten those ideas, and rewrite or retell it in their own words. A summary should identify the main idea of the text or passage. Important details or supportive evidence should also be accurately reported in the summary. If writers provide irrelevant details in the summary, it may cloud the greater meaning of the text or passage. When summarizing, writers should not include their opinions, quotes, or what they thought the author should have said. A clear summary provides clarity of the text or passage to the readers. The following checklist lists items that writers should include in a summary:

Summary Checklist

1. Title of the story
2. Someone: Who is or are the main character(s)?
3. Wanted: What did the character(s) want?
4. But: What was the problem?
5. So: How did the character(s) solve the problem?
6. Then: How did the story end? What was the resolution?

Paraphrasing

Another strategy readers can use to help them fully comprehend a text or passage is *paraphrasing.* **Paraphrasing** is when readers take the author's words and put them into their own words. When readers and writers paraphrase, they need to avoid copying the text—that is **plagiarism**. It is also important to include as many details as possible when restating the facts. Not only will this help readers

74

and writers recall information, but by putting the information into their own words, they demonstrate if they fully comprehend the text or passage. The example below shows an original text and how to paraphrase it.

> *Original Text*: Fenway Park is home to the beloved Boston Red Sox. The stadium opened on April 20, 1912. The stadium currently seats over 37,000 fans, many of whom travel from all over the country to experience the iconic team and nostalgia of Fenway Park.

> *Paraphrased*: On April 20, 1912, Fenway Park opened. Home to the Boston Red Sox, the stadium now seats over 37,000 fans. Many spectators travel to watch the Red Sox and experience the spirit of Fenway Park.

Paraphrasing, summarizing, and quoting can often cross paths with one another. The chart below shows the similarities and differences between the three strategies:

PARAPHRASING	SUMMARIZING	QUOTING
Uses own words	Puts main ideas into own words	Uses words that are identical to text
References original source	References original source	Requires quotation marks
Uses own sentences	Shows important ideas of source	Uses author's words and ideas

Drawing Conclusions

When drawing conclusions about texts or passages, readers should do two main things: 1) Use the information that they already know and 2) Use the information they have learned from the text or passage. Authors write with an intended purpose, and it is the readers' responsibility to understand and form logical conclusions of authors' ideas. It is important to remember that the readers' conclusions should be supported by information directly from the text. Readers cannot simply form conclusions based off of only information they already know.

Determining conclusions requires being an active reader, as a reader must make a prediction and analyze facts to identify a conclusion. A reader should identify key words in a passage to determine the logical conclusion or outcome that flows from the information presented. Consider the passage below:

> Lindsay, covered in flour, moved around the kitchen frantically. Her mom yelled from another room, "Lindsay, we're going to be late!"

You can conclude that Lindsay's next steps are to finish baking, clean herself up, and head off somewhere with her baked goods. Notice that the conclusion cannot be verified factually. Many conclusions are not spelled out specifically in the text; thus, they have to be identified and drawn out by the reader.

Supporting or Challenging Assertions about a Text

There are several ways readers can understand assertions made in a text and decide whether they support or challenge these ideas. Critical readers can consider text evidence, text credibility, and directly stated information versus implications.

Text Evidence

Text evidence is the information readers find in a text or passage that supports the main idea or point(s) in a story. In turn, text evidence can help readers draw conclusions about the text or passage. The information should be taken directly from the text or passage and placed in quotation marks. Text evidence provides readers with information to support ideas about the text or passage so that they simply do not just rely on their own thoughts. Details should be precise, descriptive, and factual. Statistics are a great piece of text evidence because it provides readers with exact numbers and not just a generalization. For example, instead of saying "Asia has a larger population than Europe," authors could provide detailed information such as "In Asia there are over 7 billion people, whereas in Europe there are a little over 750 million." More definitive information provides better evidence to readers to help support their conclusions about texts or passages.

Text Credibility

Credible sources are important when drawing conclusions because readers need to be able to trust what they are reading. Authors should always use credible sources to help gain the trust of their readers. A text is **credible** when it is believable and the author is objective and unbiased. If readers do not trust authors' words, they may simply dismiss the text completely. For example, if an author writes a persuasive essay, he or she is outwardly trying to sway readers' opinions to align with their own, providing readers with the liberty to do what they please with the text. Readers may agree or disagree with the author, which may, in turn, lead them to believe that the author is credible or not credible. Also, readers should keep in mind the source of the text. If readers review a journal about astronomy, would a more reliable source be a NASA employee or a plumber? Overall, text credibility is important when drawing conclusions because readers want reliable sources that support the decisions they have made about the author's ideas.

Directly Stated Information Versus Implications

Engaged readers should constantly self-question while reviewing texts to help them form conclusions. Self-questioning is when readers review a paragraph, page, passage, or chapter and ask themselves, "Did I understand what I read?," "What was the main event in this section?," "Where is this taking place?," and so on. Authors can provide clues or pieces of evidence throughout a text or passage to guide readers toward a conclusion. This is why active and engaged readers should read the text or passage in its entirety before forming a definitive conclusion. If readers do not gather all the necessary pieces of evidence, then they may jump to an illogical conclusion.

At times, authors directly state conclusions while others simply imply them. Of course, it is easier if authors outwardly provide conclusions to readers because this does not leave any information open to interpretation. However, implications are things that authors do not directly state but can be assumed based off of information they provided. If authors only imply what may have happened, readers can form a menagerie of ideas for conclusions. For example, in the statement: *Once we heard the sirens, we hunkered down in the storm shelter*, the author does not directly state that there was a tornado, but clues such as "sirens" and "storm shelter" provide insight to the readers to help form that conclusion.

76

Meaning of Words and Phrases in Context

In order to successfully complete the Reading section of the PERT, the test taker should be able to identify words in context. This involves a set of skills that requires the test taker to answer questions about unfamiliar words within a particular text passage. Additionally, the test taker may be asked to answer critical thinking questions based on unfamiliar word meanings. Identifying the meaning of different words in context is very much like solving a puzzle. By using a variety of techniques, a test taker should be able to correctly identify the meaning of unfamiliar words and concepts with ease.

Using Context Clues

A **context clue** is a hint that an author provides to the reader in order to help define difficult or unique words. When reading a passage, a test taker should take note of any unfamiliar words, and then examine the sentence around them to look for clues to the word meanings. Let's look at an example:

> He faced a *conundrum* in making this decision. He felt as if he had come to a crossroads. This was truly a puzzle, and what he did next would determine the course of his future.

The word *conundrum* may be unfamiliar to the reader. By looking at context clues, the reader should be able to determine its meaning. In this passage, context clues include the idea of making a decision and of being unsure. Furthermore, the author restates the definition of conundrum in using the word *puzzle* as a synonym. Therefore, the reader should be able to determine that the definition of the word *conundrum* is a difficult puzzle.

Similarly, a reader can determine difficult vocabulary by identifying antonyms. Let's look at an example:

> Her *gregarious* nature was completely opposite of her twin's, who was shy, retiring, and socially nervous.

The word *gregarious* may be unfamiliar. However, by looking at the surrounding context clues, the reader can determine that *gregarious* does not mean shy. The twins' personalities are being contrasted. Therefore, *gregarious* must mean sociable, or something similar to it.

At times, an author will provide contextual clues through a cause and effect relationship. Look at the next sentence as an example:

> The athletes were excited with *elation* when they won the tournament; unfortunately, their off-court antics caused them to forfeit the win.

The word elated may be unfamiliar to the reader. However, the author defines the word by presenting a cause and effect relationship. The athletes were so elated at the win that their behavior went overboard, and they had to forfeit. In this instance, *elated* must mean something akin to overjoyed, happy, and overexcited.

Cause and effect is one technique authors use to demonstrate relationships. A **cause** is why something happens. The **effect** is what happens as a result. For example, a reader may encounter text such as *Because he was unable to sleep, he was often restless and irritable during the day.* The cause is insomnia due to lack of sleep. The effect is being restless and irritable. When reading for a cause and effect relationship, look for words such as "if", "then", "such", and "because." By using cause and effect, an author can describe direct relationships, and convey an overall theme, particularly when taking a stance on their topic.

An author can also provide contextual clues through comparison and contrast. Let's look at an example:

Her torpid state caused her parents, and her physician, to worry about her seemingly sluggish well-being.

The word *torpid* is probably unfamiliar to the reader. However, the author has compared *torpid* to a state of being and, moreover, one that's worrisome. Therefore, the reader should be able to determine that *torpid* is not a positive, healthy state of being. In fact, through the use of comparison, it means sluggish. Similarly, an author may contrast an unfamiliar word with an idea. In the sentence *Her torpid state was completely opposite of her usual, bubbly self,* the meaning of *torpid*, or sluggish, is contrasted with the words *bubbly self*.

A test taker should be able to critically assess and determine unfamiliar word meanings through the use of an author's context clues in order to fully comprehend difficult text passages.

Relating Unfamiliar Words to Familiar Words

The PERT will test a reader's ability to use context clues, and then relate unfamiliar words to more familiar ones. Using the word *torpid* as an example, the test may ask the test taker to relate the meaning of the word to a list of vocabulary options and choose the more familiar word as closest in meaning. In this case, the test may say something like the following:

Which of the following words means the same as the word *torpid* in the above passage?

Then they will provide the test taker with a list of familiar options such as happy, disgruntled, sluggish, and animated. By using context clues, the reader has already determined the meaning of *torpid* as slow or sluggish, so the reader should be able to correctly identify the word *sluggish* as the correct answer.

One effective way to relate unfamiliar word meanings to more familiar ones is to substitute the provided word in each answer option for the unfamiliar word in question. Although this will not always lead to a correct answer every time, this strategy will help the test taker narrow answer options. Be careful when utilizing this strategy. Pay close attention to the meaning of sentences and answer choices because it's easy to mistake answer choices as correct when they are easily substituted, especially when they are the same part of speech. Does the sentence mean the same thing with the substituted word option in place or does it change entirely? Does the substituted word make sense? Does it possibly mean the same as the unfamiliar word in question?

Meaning, Word Choices, Tone, and Organizational Structure of a Text

How an Author's Word Choice Shapes Meaning, Style, and Tone

Authors choose their words carefully in order to artfully depict meaning, style, and tone, which is most commonly inferred through the use of adjectives and verbs. The tone is the predominant emotion present in the text and represents the attitude or feelings that an author has towards a character or event..

To review, an **adjective** is a word used to describe something, and usually precedes the noun, a person, place, or object. A **verb** is a word describing an action. For example, the sentence "The scary woodpecker ate the spider" includes the adjective "scary," the noun "woodpecker," and the verb "ate." Reading this sentence may rouse some negative feelings, as the word "scary" carries a negative charge. The **charge** is the emotional connotation that can be derived from the adjectives and verbs and is either positive or negative. Recognizing the charge of a particular sentence or passage is an effective way to understand the meaning and tone the author is trying to convey.

Many authors have conflicting charges within the same text, but a definitive tone can be inferred by understanding the meaning of the charges relative to each other. It's important to recognize key conjunctions, or words that link sentences or clauses together. There are several types and subtypes of conjunctions. Three are most important for reading comprehension:

- *Cumulative conjunctions* add one statement to another.
- Examples: and, both, also, as well as, not only
- e.g. The juice is sweet *and* sour.
- *Adversative conjunctions* are used to contrast two clauses.
- Examples: but, while, still, yet, nevertheless
- e.g. She was tired, *but* she was happy.
- *Alternative conjunctions* express two alternatives.
- Examples: or, either, neither, nor, else, otherwise
- e.g. He must eat, *or* he will die.

Identifying the meaning and tone of a text can be accomplished with the following steps:

- Identify the adjectives and verbs.
- Recognize any important conjunctions.
- Label the adjectives and verbs as positive or negative.
- Understand what the charge means about the text.

To demonstrate these steps, examine the following passage from the classic children's poem, "The Sheep":

> Lazy sheep, pray tell me why
>
> In the pleasant fields you lie,
>
> Eating grass, and daisies white,

79

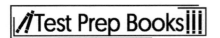

From the morning till the night?

Everything can something do,

But what kind of use are you?

–Taylor, Jane and Ann. "The Sheep."

This selection is a good example of conflicting charges that work together to express an overall tone. Following the first two steps, identify the adjectives, verbs, and conjunctions within the passage. For this example, the adjectives are <u>underlined</u>, the verbs are in **bold**, and the conjunctions *italicized*:

<u>Lazy</u> sheep, pray **tell** me why

In the <u>pleasant</u> fields you **lie**,

Eating grass, and daisies <u>white,</u>

From the morning till the night?

Everything can something do,

But what kind of use are you?

For step three, read the passage and judge whether feelings of positivity or negativity arose. Then assign a charge to each of the words that were outlined. This can be done in a table format, or simply by writing a + or − next to the word.

The word <u>lazy</u> carries a negative connotation; it usually denotes somebody unwilling to work. To **tell** someone something has an exclusively neutral connotation, as it depends on what's being told, which has not yet been revealed at this point, so a charge can be assigned later. The word <u>pleasant</u> is an inherently positive word. To **lie** could be positive or negative depending on the context, but as the subject (the sheep) is lying in a pleasant field, then this is a positive experience. **Eating** is also generally positive.

After labeling the charges for each word, it might be inferred that the tone of this poem is happy and maybe even admiring or innocuously envious. However, notice the adversative conjunction, "but" and what follows. The author has listed all the pleasant things this sheep gets to do all day, but the tone changes when the author asks, "What kind of use are you?" Asking someone to prove their value is a rather hurtful thing to do, as it implies that the person asking the question doesn't believe the subject has any value, so this could be listed under negative charges. Referring back to the verb **tell**, after

80

reading the whole passage, it can be deduced that the author is asking the sheep to tell what use the sheep is, so this has a negative charge.

+	−
• Pleasant • Lie in fields • From morning to night	• Lazy • Tell me • What kind of use are you

Upon examining the charges, it might seem like there's an even amount of positive and negative emotion in this selection, and that's where the conjunction "but" becomes crucial to identifying the tone. The conjunction "but" indicates there's a contrasting view to the pleasantness of the sheep's daily life, and this view is that the sheep is lazy and useless, which is also indicated by the first line, "lazy sheep, pray tell me why."

It might be helpful to look at questions pertaining to tone. For this selection, consider the following question:

The author of the poem regards the sheep with a feeling of what?
    a. Respect
    b. Disgust
    c. Apprehension
    d. Intrigue

Considering the author views the sheep as lazy with nothing to offer, Choice *A* appears to reflect the opposite of what the author is feeling.

Choice *B* seems to mirror the author's feelings towards the sheep, as laziness is considered a disreputable trait, and people (or personified animals, in this case) with unfavorable traits might be viewed with disgust.

Choice *C* doesn't make sense within context, as laziness isn't usually feared.

Choice *D* is tricky, as it may be tempting to argue that the author is intrigued with the sheep because they ask, "pray tell me why." This is another out-of-scope answer choice as it doesn't *quite* describe the feelings the author experiences and there's also a much better fit in Choice *B*.

Style, Tone, and Mood
Style, tone, and mood are often thought to be the same thing. Though they're closely related, there are important differences to keep in mind. The easiest way to do this is to remember that style "creates and affects" tone and mood. More specifically, style is how the writer uses words to create the desired tone and mood for their writing.

81

Style

Style can include any number of technical writing choices. A few examples of style choices include:

- Sentence Construction: When presenting facts, does the writer use shorter sentences to create a quicker sense of the supporting evidence, or do they use longer sentences to elaborate and explain the information?

- Technical Language: Does the writer use jargon to demonstrate their expertise in the subject, or do they use ordinary language to help the reader understand things in simple terms?

- Formal Language: Does the writer refrain from using contractions such as *won't* or *can't* to create a more formal tone, or do they use a colloquial, conversational style to connect to the reader?

- Formatting: Does the writer use a series of shorter paragraphs to help the reader follow a line of argument, or do they use longer paragraphs to examine an issue in great detail and demonstrate their knowledge of the topic?

On the test, examine the writer's style and how their writing choices affect the way the text comes across.

Tone

Tone refers to the writer's attitude toward the subject matter. Tone is usually explained in terms of a work of fiction. For example, the tone conveys how the writer feels about their characters and the situations in which they're involved. Nonfiction writing is sometimes thought to have no tone at all; however, this is incorrect.

A lot of nonfiction writing has a neutral tone, which is an important tone for the writer to take. A neutral tone demonstrates that the writer is presenting a topic impartially and letting the information speak for itself. On the other hand, nonfiction writing can be just as effective and appropriate if the tone isn't neutral. For instance, take this example involving seat belts:

> Seat belts save more lives than any other automobile safety feature. Many studies show that airbags save lives as well; however, not all cars have airbags. For instance, some older cars don't. Furthermore, air bags aren't entirely reliable. For example, studies show that in 15% of accidents airbags don't deploy as designed, but, on the other hand, seat belt malfunctions are extremely rare. The number of highway fatalities has plummeted since laws requiring seat belt usage were enacted.

In this passage, the writer mostly chooses to retain a neutral tone when presenting information. If the writer would instead include their own personal experience of losing a friend or family member in a car accident, the tone would change dramatically. The tone would no longer be neutral and would show that the writer has a personal stake in the content, allowing them to interpret the information in a different way. When analyzing tone, consider what the writer is trying to achieve in the text and how they *create* the tone using style.

Mood

Mood refers to the feelings and atmosphere that the writer's words create for the reader. Like tone, many nonfiction texts can have a neutral mood. To return to the previous example, if the writer would choose to include information about a person they know being killed in a car accident, the text would suddenly carry an emotional component that is absent in the previous example. Depending on how they present the information, the writer can create a sad, angry, or even hopeful mood. When analyzing the mood, consider what the writer wants to accomplish and whether the best choice was made to achieve that end.

Point of View

As mentioned, point of view is an important writing device to consider. In fiction writing, **point of view** refers to who tells the story or from whose perspective readers are observing the story. In non-fiction writing, the **point of view** refers to whether the author refers to himself/herself, their readers, or chooses not to mention either. Whether fiction or nonfiction, the author will carefully consider the impact the perspective will have on the purpose and main point of the writing.

- **First-person point of view**: The story is told from the writer's perspective. In fiction, this would mean that the main character is also the narrator. First-person point of view is easily recognized by the use of personal pronouns such as *I, me, we, us, our, my,* and *myself*.

- **Third-person point of view**: In a more formal essay, this would be an appropriate perspective because the focus should be on the subject matter, not the writer or the reader. Third-person point of view is recognized by the use of the pronouns *he, she, they,* and *it*. In fiction writing, third-person point of view has a few variations.

    o *Third-person limited* point of view refers to a story told by a narrator who has access to the thoughts and feelings of just one character.

    o In *third-person omniscient* point of view, the narrator has access to the thoughts and feelings of all the characters.

    o In *third-person objective* point of view, the narrator is like a fly on the wall and can see and hear what the characters do and say but does not have access to their thoughts and feelings.

- **Second-person point of view**: This point of view isn't commonly used in fiction or nonfiction writing because it directly addresses the reader using the pronouns *you, your,* and *yourself*.

Second-person perspective is more appropriate in direct communication, such as business letters or emails.

Point of View	Pronouns Used
First person	I, me, we, us, our, my, myself
Second person	You, your, yourself
Third person	He, she, it, they

Figurative Language

Literary texts also employ rhetorical devices. Figurative language like simile and metaphor is a type of rhetorical device commonly found in literature. In addition to rhetorical devices that play on the *meanings* of words, there are also rhetorical devices that use the *sounds* of words. These devices are most often found in poetry but may also be found in other types of literature and in non-fiction writing like speech texts.

Alliteration and *assonance* are both varieties of sound repetition. Other types of sound repetition include: anaphora, repetition that occurs at the beginning of the sentences; epiphora, repetition occurring at the end of phrases; antimetabole, repetition of words in reverse order; and antiphrasis, a form of denial of an assertion in a text.

Alliteration refers to the repetition of the first sound of each word. Recall Robert Burns' opening line:

> My love is like a red, red rose

This line includes two instances of alliteration: "love" and "like" (repeated *L* sound), as well as "red" and "rose" (repeated *R* sound). Next, **assonance** refers to the repetition of vowel sounds, and can occur anywhere within a word (not just the opening sound). Here is the opening of a poem by John Keats:

> When I have fears that I may cease to be

> Before my pen has glean'd my teeming brain

Assonance can be found in the words "fears," "cease," "be," "glean'd," and "teeming," all of which stress the long *E* sound. Both alliteration and assonance create a harmony that unifies the writer's language.

Another sound device is **onomatopoeia**, or words whose spelling mimics the sound they describe. Words such as "crash," "bang," and "sizzle" are all examples of onomatopoeia. Use of onomatopoetic language adds auditory imagery to the text.

Readers are probably most familiar with the technique of *pun*. A **pun** is a play on words, taking advantage of two words that have the same or similar pronunciation. Puns can be found throughout Shakespeare's plays, for instance:

> Now is the winter of our discontent
> Made glorious summer by this son of York

These lines from *Richard III* contain a play on words. Richard III refers to his brother, the newly crowned King Edward IV, as the "son of York," referencing their family heritage from the house of York. However, while drawing a comparison between the political climate and the weather (times of political trouble were the "winter," but now the new king brings "glorious summer"), Richard's use of the word "son" also implies another word with the same pronunciation, "sun"—so Edward IV is also like the sun, bringing light, warmth, and hope to England. Puns are a clever way for writers to suggest two meanings at once.

Some examples of figurative language are included in the following graphic.

	Definition	Example
Simile	Compares two things using "like" or "as"	Her hair was like gold.
Metaphor	Compares two things as if they are the same	He was a giant teddy bear.
Idiom	Using words with predictable meanings to create a phrase with a different meaning	The world is your oyster.
Alliteration	Repeating the same beginning sound or letter in a phrase for emphasis	The busy baby babbled.
Personification	Attributing human characteristics to an object or an animal	The house glowered menacingly with a dark smile.
Foreshadowing	Giving an indication that something is going to happen later in the story	I wasn't aware at the time, but I would come to regret those words.
Symbolism	Using symbols to represent ideas and provide a different meaning	The ring represented the bond between us.
Onomatopoeia	Using words that imitate sound	The tire went off with a bang and a crunch.
Imagery	Appealing to the senses by using descriptive language	The sky was painted with red and pink and streaked with orange.
Hyperbole	Using exaggeration not meant to be taken literally	The girl weighed less than a feather.

Figurative language can be used to give additional insight into the theme or message of a text by moving beyond the usual and literal meaning of words and phrases. It can also be used to appeal to the senses of readers and create a more in-depth story.

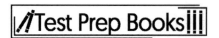

Identifying Modes of Writing

<u>Distinguishing Between Common Modes of Writing</u>
To distinguish between the common modes of writing, it is important to identify the primary purpose of the work. This can be determined by considering what the author is trying to say to the reader. Although there are countless different styles of writing, all written works tend to fall under four primary categories: argumentative/persuasive, informative expository, descriptive, and narrative.

The table below highlights the purpose, distinct characteristics, and examples of each rhetorical mode.

Writing Mode	Purpose	Distinct Characteristics	Examples
Argumentative	To persuade	Opinions, loaded or subjective language, evidence, suggestions of what the reader should do, calls to action	Critical reviews Political journals Letters of recommendation Cover letters Advertising
Informative	To teach or inform	Objective language, definitions, instructions, factual information	Business and scientific reports Textbooks Instruction manuals News articles Personal letters Wills Informative essays Travel guides Study guides
Descriptive	To deliver sensory details to the reader	Heavy use of adjectives and imagery, language that appeals to any of the five senses	Poetry Journal entries Often used in narrative mode
Narrative	To tell a story, share an experience, entertain	Series of events, plot, characters, dialogue, conflict	Novels Short stories Novellas Anecdotes Biographies Epic poems Autobiographies

<u>Identifying Common Types of Writing</u>
The following steps help to identify examples of common types within the modes of writing:

1. Identifying the audience—to whom or for whom the author is writing
2. Determining the author's purpose—why the author is writing the piece
3. Analyzing the word choices and how they are used

86

To demonstrate, the following passage has been marked to illustrate *the addressee*, the author's purpose, and <u>word choices</u>:

> *To Whom It May Concern*:
>
> I am <u>extraordinarily excited</u> to be applying to the Master of Environmental Science program at Australian National University. I believe the richness in biological and cultural diversity, as well as Australia's close proximity to the Great Barrier Reef, would provide a <u>deeply fulfilling</u> educational experience. *I am writing to express why I believe I would be an <u>excellent</u> addition to the program.*
>
> While in college, I participated in a three-month public health internship in Ecuador, where I spent time both learning about medicine in a third world country and also about the Ecuadorian environment, including the Amazon Jungle and the Galápagos Islands. <u>My favorite experience</u> through the internship, besides swimming with sea lions in San Cristóbal, was helping to neutralize parasitic potable water and collect samples for analysis in Puyo.
>
> Though my undergraduate studies related primarily to the human body, I took several courses in natural science, including a year of chemistry, biology, and physics as well as a course in a calculus. <u>I am confident</u> that my fundamental knowledge in these fields will prepare me for the science courses integral to the Masters of Environmental Science.

Having identified the *addressee*, it is evident that this selection is a letter of some kind. Further inspection into the author's purpose, seen in *bold*, shows that the author is trying to explain why he or she should be accepted into the environmental science program, which automatically places it into the argumentative mode as the writer is trying to persuade the reader to agree and to incite the reader into action by encouraging the program to accept the writer as a candidate. In addition to revealing the purpose, the use of emotional language—extraordinarily, excellent, deeply fulfilling, favorite experience, confident—illustrates that this is a persuasive piece. It also provides evidence for why this person would be an excellent addition to the program—their experience in Ecuador and with scientific curriculum.

The following passage presents an opportunity to solidify this method of analysis and practice the steps above to determine the mode of writing:

> The biological effects of laughter have long been an interest of medicine and psychology. Laughing is often speculated to reduce blood pressure because it induces feelings of relaxation and elation. Participating students watched a series of videos that elicited laughter, and their blood pressure was taken before and after the viewings. An average decrease in blood pressure was observed, though resulting p-values attest that the results were not significant.

This selection contains factual and scientific information, is devoid of any adjectives or flowery descriptions, and is not trying to convince the reader of any particular stance. Though the audience is not directly addressed, the purpose of the passage is to present the results of an experiment to those who would be interested in the biological effects of laughter—most likely a scientific community. Thus, this passage is an example of informative writing.

Below is another passage to help identify examples of the common writing modes, taken from *The Endeavor Journal of Sir Joseph Banks*:

10th May 1769 – THE ENGLISH CREW GET TAHITIAN NAMES

> We have now got the Indian name of the Island, Otahite, so therefore for the future I shall call it. As for our own names the Indians find so much dificulty in pronouncing them that we are forcd to indulge them in calling us what they please, or rather what they say when they attempt to pronounce them. I give here the List: Captn Cooke *Toote*, Dr Solander *Torano*, Mr Hicks *Hete*, Mr Gore *Toárro*, Mr Molineux *Boba* from his Christian name Robert, Mr Monkhouse *Mato*, and myself *Tapáne*. In this manner they have names for almost every man in the ship.

This extract contains no elements of an informative or persuasive intent and does not seem to follow any particular line of narrative. The passage gives a list of the different names that the Indians have given the crew members, as well as the name of an island. Although there is no context for the selection, through the descriptions, it is clear that the author and his comrades are on an island trying to communicate with the native inhabitants. Hence, this passage is a journal that reflects the descriptive mode.

These are only a few of the many examples that can be found in the four primary modes of writing.

Determining the Appropriate Mode of Writing

The author's **primary purpose** is defined as the reason an author chooses to write a selection, and it is often dependent on their *audience*. A biologist writing a textbook, for example, does so to communicate scientific knowledge to an audience of people who want to study biology. An audience can be as broad as the entire global population or as specific as women fighting for equal rights in the bicycle repair industry. Whatever the audience, it is important that the author considers its demographics—age, gender, culture, language, education level, etc.

If the author's purpose is to persuade or inform, he or she will consider how much the intended audience knows about the subject. For example, if an author is writing on the importance of recycling to anyone who will listen, he or she will use the informative mode—including background information on recycling—and the argumentative mode—evidence for why it works, while also using simple diction so that it is easy for everyone to understand. If, on the other hand, the writer is proposing new methods for recycling using solar energy, the audience is probably already familiar with standard recycling processes and will require less background information, as well as more technical language inherent to the scientific community.

If the author's purpose is to entertain through a story or a poem, he or she will need to consider whom he/she is trying to entertain. If an author is writing a script for a children's cartoon, the plot, language, conflict, characters, and humor would align with the interests of the age demographic of that audience. On the other hand, if an author is trying to entertain adults, he or she may write content not suitable for children. The author's purpose and audience are generally interdependent.

Text Structure

Depending on what the author is attempting to accomplish, certain formats or text structures work better than others. For example, a sequence structure might work for narration but not for identifying similarities and differences between concepts. Similarly, a comparison-contrast structure is not useful for narration. It's the author's job to put the right information in the correct format.

Readers should be familiar with the five main literary structures:

1. **Sequence structure** (sometimes referred to as the order structure) is when the order of events proceed in a predictable order. In many cases, this means the text goes through the plot elements: exposition, rising action, climax, falling action, and resolution. Readers are introduced to characters, setting, and conflict in the exposition. In the rising action, there's an increase in tension and suspense. The climax is the height of tension and the point of no return. Tension decreases during the falling action. In the resolution, any conflicts presented in the exposition are solved, and the story concludes. An informative text that is structured sequentially will often go in order from one step to the next.

2. In the **problem-solution structure**, authors identify a potential problem and suggest a solution. This form of writing is usually divided into two paragraphs and can be found in informational texts. For example, cell phone, cable, and satellite providers use this structure in manuals to help customers troubleshoot or identify problems with services or products.

3. When authors want to discuss similarities and differences between separate concepts, they arrange thoughts in a **comparison-contrast paragraph structure**. Venn diagrams are an effective graphic organizer for comparison-contrast structures because they feature two overlapping circles that can be used to organize similarities and differences. A comparison-contrast essay organizes one paragraph based on similarities and another based on differences. A comparison-contrast essay can also be arranged with the similarities and differences of individual traits addressed within individual paragraphs. Words such as *however*, *but*, and *nevertheless* help signal a contrast in ideas.

4. **Descriptive writing** structure is designed to appeal to your senses. Much like an artist who constructs a painting, good descriptive writing builds an image in the reader's mind by appealing to the five senses: sight, hearing, taste, touch, and smell. However, overly descriptive writing can become tedious; whereas sparse descriptions can make settings and characters seem flat. Good authors strike a balance by applying descriptions only to passages, characters, and settings that are integral to the plot.

5. Passages that use the *cause-and-effect* structure are simply asking *why* by demonstrating some type of connection between ideas. Words such as *if, since, because, then, or consequently* indicate a cause-and-effect relationship. By switching the order of a complex sentence, the writer can rearrange the emphasis on different clauses. Saying *"If Sheryl is late, we'll miss the dance"* is different from saying *"We'll miss the dance if Sheryl is late."* One emphasizes Sheryl's tardiness while the other emphasizes missing the dance. Paragraphs can also be arranged in a cause-and-effect format. Since the format—before and after—is sequential, it is useful when authors wish to discuss the impact of choices. Researchers often apply this paragraph structure to the scientific method.

Relationships Within and Between Sentences

Transitional Words and Phrases

There are approximately 200 transitional words and phrases that are commonly used in the English language. Below are lists of common transition words and phrases used throughout transitions.

Time
- After
- Before
- During
- In the middle

Example About to be Given
- For example
- In fact
- For instance

Compare
- Likewise
- Also

Contrast
- However
- Yet
- But

Addition
- And
- Also
- Furthermore
- Moreover

Logical Relationships
- If
- Then
- Therefore
- As a result
- Since

Steps in a Process
- First
- Second
- Last

Transitional words and phrases are important writing devices because they connect sentences and paragraphs. Transitional words and phrases present logical order to writing and provide more coherent meaning to readers.

Transition words can be categorized based on the relationships they create between ideas:

- **General order**: signaling elaboration of an idea to emphasize a point—e.g., *for example, for instance, to demonstrate, including, such as, in other words, that is, in fact, also, furthermore, likewise, and, truly, so, surely, certainly, obviously, doubtless*

- **Chronological order**: referencing the time frame in which main event or idea occurs—e.g., *before, after, first, while, soon, shortly thereafter, meanwhile*

- **Numerical order/order of importance**: indicating that related ideas, supporting details, or events will be described in a sequence, possibly in order of importance—e.g., *first, second, also, finally, another, in addition, equally important, less importantly, most significantly, the main reason, last but not least*

- **Spatial order**: referring to the space and location of something or where things are located in relation to each other—e.g., *inside, outside, above, below, within, close, under, over, far, next to, adjacent to*

- **Cause and effect order**: signaling a causal relationship between events or ideas—e.g., *thus, therefore, since, resulted in, for this reason, as a result, consequently, hence, for, so*

- **Compare and contrast order**: identifying the similarities and differences between two or more objects, ideas, or lines of thought—e.g., *like, as, similarly, equally, just as, unlike, however, but, although, conversely, on the other hand, on the contrary*

- **Summary order**: indicating that a particular idea is coming to a close—e.g., *in conclusion, to sum up, in other words, ultimately, above all*

Sentence Structures

- **Simple sentence**: composed of one independent clause

   Many people watch hummingbirds.

Note that it has one subject and one verb; however, a simple sentence can have a compound subject and/or a compound verb.

   Adults and children often enjoy watching and photographing hummingbirds.

- **Compound sentence**: composed of two independent clauses

   The wind knocked down lots of trees, but no trees in my yard were affected.

- **Complex sentence**: composed of one independent clause and one dependent clause

   Although the wind knocked down lots of trees, no trees in my yard were affected.

Forming Paragraphs

A good *paragraph* should have the following characteristics:

- Be logical with organized sentences
- Have a *unified* purpose within itself
- Use sentences as *building blocks*
- Be a *distinct section* of a piece of writing
- Present a *single theme* introduced by a *topic sentence*
- Maintain a *consistent flow* through subsequent, relevant, well-placed sentences
- *Tell a story* of its own or have its own purpose, yet connect with what is written before and after
- Enlighten, entertain, and/or inform

Though certainly not set in stone, the length should be a consideration for the reader's sake, not merely for the sake of the topic. When paragraphs are especially short, the reader might experience an irregular, uneven effect; when they're much longer than 250 words, the reader's attention span, and probably their retention, is challenged. While a paragraph can technically be a sentence long, a good rule of thumb is for paragraphs to be at least three sentences long and no more than ten sentence long. An optimal word length is 100 to 250 words.

Coherent Paragraphs

Coherence is simply defined as the quality of being logical and consistent. In order to have coherent paragraphs, therefore, authors must be logical and consistent in their writing, whatever the document might be. Two words are helpful to understanding coherence: flow and relationship. Earlier, transitions were referred to as being the "glue" to put organized thoughts together. Now, let's look at the topic sentence from which flow and relationship originate.

The **topic sentence**, usually the first in a paragraph, holds the essential features that will be brought forth in the paragraph. It is also here that authors either grab or lose readers. It may be the only writing that a reader encounters from that writer, so it is a good idea to summarize and represent ideas accurately.

The coherent paragraph has a logical order. It utilizes transitional words and phrases, parallel sentence structure, clear pronoun references, and reasonable repetition of key words and phrases. Use common sense for repetition. Consider synonyms for variety. Be consistent in verb tense whenever possible.

When writers have accomplished their paragraph's purpose, they prepare it to receive the next paragraph. While writing, read the paragraph over, edit, examine, evaluate, and make changes accordingly. Possibly, a paragraph has gone on too long. If that occurs, it needs to be broken up into other paragraphs, or the length should be reduced. If a paragraph didn't fully accomplish its purpose, consider revising it.

Main Point of a Paragraph

What is the **main point of a paragraph**? It is *the* point all of the other important and lesser important points should lead up to, and it should be summed up in the topic sentence.

Sometimes there is a fine line between a paragraph's topic sentence and its main point. In fact, they actually might be one and the same. Often, though, they are two separate, but closely related, aspects of the same paragraph.

Depending upon the writer's purpose, the topic sentence or the paragraph's main point might not be fully revealed until the paragraph's conclusion.

Sometimes, while developing paragraphs, authors deviate from the main point, which means they have to delete and rework their materials to stay on point.

Examining Paragraphs

Throughout this text, composing and combining sentences, using basic grammar skills, employing rules and guidelines, identifying differing points of view, using appropriate context, constructing accurate word usage, and discerning correct punctuation have all been discussed. Whew! The types of sentences, patterns, transitions, and overall structure have been covered as well.

While authors write, thoughts coalesce to form words on "paper" (aka a computer screen). Authors strategically place those thoughts in sentences to give them "voice" in an orderly manner, and then they manipulate them into cohesive sentences for cohesion to express ideas. Like a hunk of modeling clay (thanks to computers, people are no longer bound to erasers and whiteout), sentences can be worked and reworked until they cooperate and say what was originally intended.

Before calling a paragraph complete, identify its main point, making sure that related sentences stay on point. Pose questions such as, "Did I sufficiently develop the main point? Did I say it succinctly enough? Did I give it time to develop? *Is* it developed?"

Let's examine the following two paragraphs, each an example of a movie review. Read them and form a critique.

Example 1: *Eddie the Eagle* is a movie about a struggling athlete. Eddie was crippled at birth. He had a lot of therapy and he had a dream. Eddie trained himself for the Olympics. He went far away to learn how to ski jump. It was hard for him, but he persevered. He got a coach and kept trying. He qualified for the Olympics. He was the only one from Britain who could jump. When he succeeded, they named him, "Eddie the Eagle."

Example 2: The last movie I saw in the theater was *Eddie the Eagle,* a story of extraordinary perseverance inspired by real life events. Eddie was born in England with a birth defect that he slowly but surely overcame, but not without trial and error (not the least of which was his father's perpetual *dis*couragement). In fact, the old man did everything to get him to give up, but Eddie was dogged beyond anyone in the neighborhood; in fact, maybe beyond anyone in the whole town or even the whole world! Eddie, simply, did not know to quit. As he grew up, so did his dream; a strange one, indeed, for someone so unaccomplished: to compete in the Winter Olympics as a ski jumper (which he knew absolutely nothing about). Eddie didn't just keep on dreaming about it. He actually went to Germany and *worked* at it, facing unbelievable odds, defeats, and put-downs by Dad and the other Men in Charge, aka the Olympic decision-makers. Did that stop him? No way! Eddie got a coach and persevered. Then, when he failed, he persevered some more, again and again. You should be able to open up a dictionary, look at the

93

word "persevere," and see a picture of Eddie the Eagle because, when everybody told him he couldn't, he did. The result? He is forever dubbed, "Eddie the Eagle."

Both reviews tell something about the movie *Eddie the Eagle*. Does one motivate the reader to want to see the movie more than the other? Does one just provide a few facts while the other paints a virtual picture of the movie? Does one give a carrot and the other a rib eye steak, mashed potatoes, and chocolate silk pie?

Paragraphs sometimes only give facts. Sometimes that's appropriate and all that is needed. Sometimes, though, writers want to use the blank documents on their computer screens to paint a picture. Writers must "see" the painting come to life. To do so, pick a familiar topic, write a simple sentence, and add to it. Pretend, for instance, there's a lovely view. What does one see? Is it a lake? Try again – picture it as though it were the sea! Visualize a big ship sailing out there. Is it sailing away or approaching ? Who is on it? Is it dangerous? Is it night and are there crazy pirates on board? Uh-oh! Did one just jump ship and start swimming toward shore?

The Author's Purpose and the Relation of Events in a Text

Author's Intent

No matter the genre or format, all authors are writing to persuade, inform, entertain, or express feelings. Often, these purposes are blended, with one dominating the rest. It's useful to learn to recognize the author's intent.

Persuasive writing is used to persuade or convince readers of something. It often contains two elements: the argument and the counterargument. The **argument** takes a stance on an issue, while the **counterargument** pokes holes in the opposition's stance. Authors rely on logic, emotion, and writer credibility to persuade readers to agree with them. If readers are opposed to the stance before reading, they are unlikely to adopt that stance. However, those who are undecided or committed to the same stance are more likely to agree with the author.

Informative writing tries to teach or inform. Workplace manuals, instructor lessons, statistical reports, and cookbooks are examples of informative texts. Informative writing is usually based on facts and is often void of emotion and persuasion. Informative texts generally contain statistics, charts, and graphs. Though most informative texts lack a persuasive agenda, readers still must examine the text carefully to determine whether one exists within a given passage.

Stories or **narratives** are designed to entertain. When you go to the movies, you often want to escape for a few hours, not necessarily to think critically. Entertaining writing is designed to delight and engage the reader. However, sometimes this type of writing can be woven into more serious materials, such as persuasive or informative writing to hook the reader before transitioning into a more scholarly discussion.

Emotional writing works to evoke the reader's feelings, such as anger, euphoria, or sadness. The connection between reader and author is an attempt to cause the reader to share the author's intended emotion or tone. Sometimes in order to make a piece more poignant, the author simply wants readers to feel the same emotions that the author has felt. Other times, the author attempts to persuade or manipulate the reader into adopting his stance. While it's okay to sympathize with the author, be aware of the individual's underlying intent.

Understanding the Task, Purpose, and Audience

Identifying the Task, Purpose, and Intended Audience

An author's **writing style**—the way in which words, grammar, punctuation, and sentence fluidity are used—is the most influential element in a piece of writing, and it is dependent on the purpose and the audience for whom it is intended. Together, a writing style and mode of writing form the foundation of a written work, and a good writer will choose the most effective mode and style to convey a message to readers.

Writers should first determine what they are trying to say and then choose the most effective mode of writing to communicate that message. Different writing modes and *word choices* will affect the tone of a piece—that is, its underlying attitude, emotion, or character. The argumentative mode may utilize words that are earnest, angry, passionate, or excited whereas an informative piece may have a sterile, germane, or enthusiastic tone. The tones found in narratives vary greatly, depending on the purpose of the writing. *Tone* will also be affected by the audience—teaching science to children or those who may be uninterested would be most effective with enthusiastic language and exclamation points whereas teaching science to college students may take on a more serious and professional tone, with fewer charged words and punctuation choices that are inherent to academia.

Sentence fluidity—whether sentences are long and rhythmic or short and succinct—also affects a piece of writing as it determines the way in which a piece is read. Children or audiences unfamiliar with a subject do better with short, succinct sentence structures as these break difficult concepts up into shorter points. A period, question mark, or exclamation point is literally a signal for the reader to stop and takes more time to process. Thus, longer, more complex sentences are more appropriate for adults or educated audiences as they can fit more information in between processing time.

The amount of *supporting detail* provided is also tailored to the audience. A text that introduces a new subject to its readers will focus more on broad ideas without going into greater detail whereas a text that focuses on a more specific subject is likely to provide greater detail about the ideas discussed.

Writing styles, like modes, are most effective when tailored to their audiences. Having awareness of an audience's demographic is one of the most crucial aspects of properly communicating an argument, a story, or a set of information.

Choosing the Most Appropriate Type of Writing

Before beginning any writing, it is imperative that a writer have a firm grasp on the message he or she wishes to convey and how he or she wants readers to be affected by the writing. For example, does the author want readers to be more informed about the subject? Does the writer want readers to agree with their opinion? Does the writer want readers to get caught up in an exciting narrative? The following steps are a guide to determining the appropriate type of writing for a task, purpose, and audience:

1. Identifying the purpose for writing the piece
2. Determining the audience
3. Adapting the writing mode, word choices, tone, and style to fit the audience and the purpose

It is important to distinguish between a work's purpose and its main idea. The essential difference between the two is that the **main idea** is what the author wants to communicate about the topic at hand whereas the **primary purpose** is why the author is writing in the first place. The primary purpose is what will determine the type of writing an author will choose to utilize, not the main idea, though the two are related. For example, if an author writes an article on the mistreatment of animals in factory farms and, at the end, suggests that people should convert to vegetarianism, the main idea is that vegetarianism would reduce the poor treatment of animals. The primary purpose is to convince the reader to stop eating animals. Since the primary purpose is to galvanize an audience into action, the author would choose the argumentative writing mode.

The next step is to consider to whom the author is appealing as this will determine the type of details to be included, the diction to be used, the tone to be employed, and the sentence structure to be used. An audience can be identified by considering the following questions:

- What is the purpose for writing the piece?

- To whom is it being written?

- What is their age range?

- Are they familiar with the material being presented, or are they just being newly introduced to it?

- Where are they from?

- Is the task at hand in a professional or casual setting?

- Is the task at hand for monetary gain?

These are just a few of the numerous considerations to keep in mind, but the main idea is to become as familiar with the audience as possible. Once the audience has been understood, the author can then adapt the writing style to align with the readers' education and interests. The audience is what determines the **rhetorical appeal** the author will use—ethos, pathos, or logos. **Ethos** is a rhetorical appeal to an audience's ethics and/or morals. Ethos is most often used in argumentative and informative writing modes. **Pathos** is an appeal to the audience's emotions and sympathies, and it is found in argumentative, descriptive, and narrative writing modes. **Logos** is an appeal to the audience's logic and reason and is used primarily in informative texts as well as in supporting details for argumentative pieces. Rhetorical appeals are discussed in depth in the informational texts and rhetoric section of the test.

If the author is trying to encourage global conversion to vegetarianism, he or she may choose to use all three rhetorical appeals to reach varying personality types. Those who are less interested in the welfare of animals but are interested in facts and science would relate more to logos. Animal lovers would relate better to an emotional appeal. In general, the most effective works utilize all three appeals.

Finally, after determining the writing mode and rhetorical appeal, the author will consider word choice, sentence structure, and tone, depending on the purpose and audience. The author may choose words that convey sadness or anger when speaking about animal welfare if writing to persuade, or he or she will stick to dispassionate and matter-of-fact tones, if informing the public on the treatment of animals in factory farms. If the author is writing to a younger or less-educated audience, he or she may choose to shorten and simplify sentence structures and word choice. If appealing to an audience with more expert knowledge on a particular subject, writers will more likely employ a style of longer sentences and more complex vocabulary.

Depending on the task, the author may choose to use a first person, second person, or third person point of view. First person and second person perspectives are inherently more casual in tone, including the author and the reader in the rhetoric, while third person perspectives are often seen in more professional settings.

Evaluating the Effectiveness of a Piece of Writing

An effective and engaging piece of writing will cause the reader to forget about the author entirely. Readers will become so engrossed in the subject, argument, or story at hand that they will almost identify with it, readily adopting beliefs proposed by the author or accepting all elements of the story as believable. On the contrary, poorly written works will cause the reader to be hyperaware of the author, doubting the writer's knowledge of a subject or questioning the validity of a narrative. Persuasive or expository works that are poorly researched will have this effect, as well as poorly planned stories with significant plot holes. An author must consider the task, purpose, and audience to sculpt a piece of writing effectively.

When evaluating the effectiveness of a piece, the most important thing to consider is how well the purpose is conveyed to the audience through the mode, use of rhetoric, and writing style.

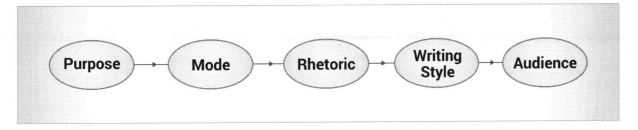

The purpose must pass through these three aspects for effective delivery to the audience. If any elements are not properly considered, the reader will be overly aware of the author, and the message will be lost. The following is a checklist for evaluating the effectiveness of a piece:

- Does the writer choose the appropriate writing mode—argumentative, narrative, descriptive, informative—for their purpose?

- Does the writing mode employed contain characteristics inherent to that mode?

- Does the writer consider the personalities/interests/demographics of the intended audience when choosing rhetorical appeals?

- Does the writer use appropriate vocabulary, sentence structure, voice, and tone for the audience demographic?

- Does the author properly establish himself/herself as having authority on the subject, if applicable?

- Does the piece make sense?

Another thing to consider is the medium in which the piece was written. If the medium is a blog, diary, or personal letter, the author may adopt a more casual stance towards the audience. If the piece of writing is a story in a book, a business letter or report, or a published article in a journal or if the task is to gain money or support or to get published, the author may adopt a more formal stance. Ultimately, the writer will want to be very careful in how he or she addresses the reader.

Finally, the effectiveness of a piece can be evaluated by asking how well the purpose was achieved. For example, if students are assigned to read a persuasive essay, instructors can ask whether the author influences students' opinions. Students may be assigned two differing persuasive texts with opposing perspectives and be asked which writer was more convincing. Students can then evaluate what factors contributed to this—for example, whether one author uses more credible supporting facts, appeals more effectively to readers' emotions, presents more believable personal anecdotes, or offers stronger counterargument refutation. Students can then use these evaluations to strengthen their own writing skills.

Inferences in a Text

Readers should be able to make *inferences*. Making an inference requires the reader to read between the lines and look for what is implied rather than what is explicitly stated. That is, using information that is known from the text, the reader is able to make a logical assumption about information that is not explicitly stated but is probably true. Read the following passage:

"Hey, do you wanna meet my new puppy?" Jonathan asked.

"Oh, I'm sorry but please don't—" Jacinta began to protest, but before she could finish, Jonathan had already opened the passenger side door of his car and a perfect white ball of fur came bouncing towards Jacinta.

"Isn't he the cutest?" beamed Jonathan.

"Yes—achoo!—he's pretty—aaaachooo!!—adora—aaa—aaaachoo!" Jacinta managed to say in between sneezes. "But if you don't mind, I—I—achoo!—need to go inside."

Which of the following can be inferred from Jacinta's reaction to the puppy?
    a. she hates animals
    b. she is allergic to dogs
    c. she prefers cats to dogs
    d. she is angry at Jonathan

An **inference** requires the reader to consider the information presented and then form their own idea about what is probably true. Based on the details in the passage, what is the best answer to the question? Important details to pay attention to include the tone of Jacinta's dialogue, which is overall polite and apologetic, as well as her reaction itself, which is a long string of sneezes. Answer choices (a) and (d) both express strong emotions ("hates" and "angry") that are not evident in Jacinta's speech or actions. Answer choice (c) mentions cats, but there is nothing in the passage to indicate Jacinta's feelings about cats. Answer choice (b), "she is allergic to dogs," is the most logical choice—based on the fact that she began sneezing as soon as a fluffy dog approached her, it makes sense to guess that Jacinta

98

might be allergic to dogs. So even though Jacinta never directly states, "Sorry, I'm allergic to dogs!" using the clues in the passage, it is still reasonable to guess that this is true.

Making inferences is crucial for readers of literature because literary texts often avoid presenting complete and direct information to readers about characters' thoughts or feelings, or they present this information in an unclear way, leaving it up to the reader to interpret clues given in the text. In order to make inferences while reading, readers should ask themselves:

- What details are being presented in the text?
- Is there any important information that seems to be missing?
- Based on the information that the author *does* include, what else is probably true?
- Is this inference reasonable based on what is already known?

Apply Information

A natural extension of being able to make an inference from a given set of information is also being able to apply that information to a new context. This is especially useful in non-fiction or informative writing. Considering the facts and details presented in the text, readers should consider how the same information might be relevant in a different situation. The following is an example of applying an inferential conclusion to a different context:

> Often, individuals behave differently in large groups than they do as individuals. One example of this is the psychological phenomenon known as the bystander effect. According to the bystander effect, the more people who witness an accident or crime occur, the less likely each individual bystander is to respond or offer assistance to the victim. A classic example of this is the murder of Kitty Genovese in New York City in the 1960s. Although there were over thirty witnesses to her killing by a stabber, none of them intervened to help Kitty or contact the police.

Considering the phenomenon of the bystander effect, what would probably happen if somebody tripped on the stairs in a crowded subway station?
a. Everybody would stop to help the person who tripped
b. Bystanders would point and laugh at the person who tripped
c. Someone would call the police after walking away from the station
d. Few if any bystanders would offer assistance to the person who tripped

This question asks readers to apply the information they learned from the passage, which is an informative paragraph about the bystander effect. According to the passage, this is a concept in psychology that describes the way people in groups respond to an accident—the more people are present, the less likely any one person is to intervene. While the passage illustrates this effect with the example of a woman's murder, the question asks readers to apply it to a different context—in this case, someone falling down the stairs in front of many subway passengers. Although this specific situation is not discussed in the passage, readers should be able to apply the general concepts described in the paragraph. The definition of the bystander effect includes any instance of an accident or crime in front of a large group of people. The question asks about a situation that falls within the same definition, so the general concept should still hold true: in the midst of a large crowd, few individuals are likely to actually respond to an accident. In this case, answer choice (d) is the best response.

Identifying the Position and Purpose

Readers should always identify the author's position or stance in a text. No matter how objective a piece may seem, assume the author has preconceived beliefs. Reduce the likelihood of accepting an invalid argument by looking for multiple articles on the topic, including those with varying opinions. If several opinions point in the same direction, and are backed by reputable peer-reviewed sources, it's more likely the author has a valid argument. Positions that run contrary to widely held beliefs and existing data should invite scrutiny. There are exceptions to the rule, so be a careful consumer of information.

Though themes, symbols, and motifs are buried deep within the text and can sometimes be difficult to infer, an author's purpose is usually obvious from the beginning. There are four purposes of writing: to inform, to persuade, to describe, and to entertain. Informative writings present facts in an accessible way. Persuasive writing appeals to emotions and logic to inspire the reader to adopt a specific stance. Be wary of this type of writing, as it often lacks objectivity. Descriptive writing is designed to paint a picture in the reader's mind, while texts that entertain are often narratives designed to engage and delight the reader.

The various writing styles are usually blended, with one purpose dominating the rest. For example, a persuasive piece might begin with a humorous tale to make readers more receptive to the persuasive message, or a recipe in a cookbook designed to inform might be preceded by an entertaining anecdote that makes the recipe more appealing.

Understanding the Effect of Word Choice

An author's choice of words—also referred to as **diction**—helps to convey their meaning in a particular way. Through diction, an author can convey a particular tone—e.g., a humorous tone, a serious tone—in order to support the thesis in a meaningful way to the reader.

Connotation and Denotation

Connotation is when an author chooses words or phrases that invoke ideas or feelings other than their literal meaning. An example of the use of connotation is the word *cheap*, which suggests something is poor in value or negatively describes a person as reluctant to spend money. When something or someone is described this way, the reader is more inclined to have a particular image or feeling about it or him/her. Thus, connotation can be a very effective language tool in creating emotion and swaying opinion. However, connotations are sometimes hard to pin down because varying emotions can be associated with a word. Generally, though, connotative meanings tend to be fairly consistent within a specific cultural group.

Denotation refers to words or phrases that mean exactly what they say. It is helpful when a writer wants to present hard facts or vocabulary terms with which readers may be unfamiliar. Some examples of denotation are the words *inexpensive* and *frugal*. *Inexpensive* refers to the cost of something, not its value, and *frugal* indicates that a person is conscientiously watching their spending. These terms do not elicit the same emotions that *cheap* does.

Authors sometimes choose to use both, but what they choose and when they use it is what critical readers need to differentiate. One method isn't inherently better than the other; however, one may create a better effect, depending upon an author's intent. If, for example, an author's purpose is to inform, to instruct, and to familiarize readers with a difficult subject, their use of connotation may be

100

helpful. However, it may also undermine credibility and confuse readers. An author who wants to create a credible, scholarly effect in their text would most likely use denotation, which emphasizes literal, factual meaning and examples.

Technical Language

Test takers and critical readers alike should be very aware of technical language used within informational text. **Technical language** refers to terminology that is specific to a particular industry and is best understood by those specializing in that industry. This language is fairly easy to differentiate, since it will most likely be unfamiliar to readers. It's critical to be able to define technical language either by the author's written definition, through the use of an included glossary—if offered—or through context clues that help readers clarify word meaning.

Identifying Rhetorical Strategies

Rhetoric refers to an author's use of particular strategies, appeals, and devices to persuade an intended audience. The more effective the use of rhetoric, the more likely the audience will be persuaded.

Determining an Author's Point of View

A **rhetorical strategy**—also referred to as a **rhetorical mode**—is the structural way an author chooses to present their argument. Though the terms noted below are similar to the organizational structures noted earlier, these strategies do not imply that the entire text follows the approach. For example, a cause and effect organizational structure is solely that, nothing more. A persuasive text may use cause and effect as a strategy to convey a singular point. Thus, an argument may include several of the strategies as the author strives to convince their audience to take action or accept a different point of view. It's important that readers are able to identify an author's thesis and position on the topic in order to be able to identify the careful construction through which the author speaks to the reader.

The following are some of the more common rhetorical strategies:

- Cause and effect—establishing a logical correlation or causation between two ideas

- Classification/division—the grouping of similar items together or division of something into parts

- Comparison/contrast—the distinguishing of similarities/differences to expand on an idea

- Definition—used to clarify abstract ideas, unfamiliar concepts, or to distinguish one idea from another

- Description—use of vivid imagery, active verbs, and clear adjectives to explain ideas

- Exemplification—the use of examples to explain an idea

- Narration—anecdotes or personal experience to present or expand on a concept

- Problem/Solution—presentation of a problem or problems, followed by proposed solution(s)

Rhetorical Strategies and Devices

A **rhetorical device** is the phrasing and presentation of an idea that reinforces and emphasizes a point in an argument. A rhetorical device is often quite memorable. One of the more famous uses of a rhetorical device is in John F. Kennedy's 1961 inaugural address: "Ask not what your country can do for you, ask what you can do for your country." The contrast of ideas presented in the phrasing is an example of the rhetorical device of antimetabole. Some other common examples are provided below, but test takers should be aware that this is not a complete list.

Device	Definition	Example
Allusion	A reference to a famous person, event, or significant literary text as a form of significant comparison	"We are apt to shut our eyes against a painful truth, and listen to the song of that siren till she transforms us into beasts." Patrick Henry
Anaphora	The repetition of the same words at the beginning of successive words, phrases, or clauses, designed to emphasize an idea	"We shall not flag or fail. We shall go on to the end. We shall fight in France, we shall fight on the seas and oceans, we shall fight with growing confidence … we shall fight in the fields and in the streets, we shall fight in the hills. We shall never surrender." Winston Churchill
Understatement	A statement meant to portray a situation as less important than it actually is to create an ironic effect	"The war in the Pacific has not necessarily developed in Japan's favor." Emperor Hirohito, surrendering Japan in World War II
Parallelism	A syntactical similarity in a structure or series of structures used for impact of an idea, making it memorable	"A penny saved is a penny earned." Ben Franklin
Rhetorical question	A question posed that is not answered by the writer though there is a desired response, most often designed to emphasize a point	"Can anyone look at our reduced standing in the world today and say, 'Let's have four more years of this?'" Ronald Reagan

102

The Traits, Motivations, and Thoughts of Characters

Characters are the story's figures that assume primary, secondary, or minor roles. *Central* or *major* characters are those integral to the story—the plot cannot be resolved without them. A central character can be a **protagonist** or hero. There may be more than one protagonist, and he/she doesn't always have to possess good characteristics. A character can also be an **antagonist**—the force against a protagonist.

Character development is when the author takes the time to create dynamic characters that add uniqueness and depth to the story. **Dynamic characters** are characters that change over the course of the plot time. **Stock characters** are those that appear across genres and embrace stereotypes—e.g., the cowboy of the Wild West or the blonde bombshell in a detective novel. A **flat character** is one that does not present a lot of complexity or depth, while a **rounded character** does. Sometimes, the **narrator** of a story or the *speaker* in a poem can be a character—e.g., Nick Carraway in F. Scott Fitzgerald's *The Great Gatsby* or the speaker in Robert Browning's "My Last Duchess." The narrator might also function as a character in prose, though not be part of the story—e.g., Charles Dickens' narrator of *A Christmas Carol*.

The point of view from which a story is told also affects the understanding of the story's characters. Most stories are told in first or third person. As mentioned, in first person narration, the story is told from the writer's perspective. In fiction, this would mean that the main character is also the narrator. First-person point of view is easily recognized by the use of personal pronouns such as *I, me, we, us, our, my*, and *myself*. Third-person point of view is recognized by the use of the pronouns *he, she, they*, and *it*. In fiction writing, third-person point of view has a few variations.

1. *Third-person limited* point of view refers to a story told by a narrator who has access to the thoughts and feelings of just one character.
2. In *third-person omniscient* point of view, the narrator has access to the thoughts and feelings of all the characters.
3. In *third-person objective* point of view, the narrator is like a fly on the wall and can see and hear what the characters do and say, but does not have access to their thoughts and feelings.

Comparing Topics or Themes in Different Texts

Comparison and Contrast

One writing device authors use is *comparison and contrast*. When authors take two objects and show how they are alike or similar, a comparison is being made. When authors take the same two objects and show how they differ, they are contrasting them. Comparison and contrast essays are most commonly written in nonfiction form. The Venn diagram below presents some common words or phrases used when comparing or contrasting objects.

Compare and Contrast Venn Diagram

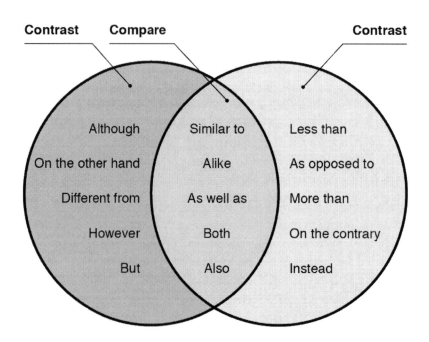

In order to understand the relationship between ideas, readers need to be able to *compare* and *contrast*. **Comparing** two things means identifying their similarities, while **contrasting** two things means finding their differences. Consider the following excerpt from "The Lamb" by William Blake:

> Little lamb, who made thee?
> Dost thou know who made thee,
> Gave thee life, and bid thee feed
> By the stream and o'er the mead;
> Gave thee clothing of delight,
> Softest clothing, woolly, bright;
> Gave thee such a tender voice,
> Making all the vales rejoice?
> Little lamb, who made thee?
> Dost thou know who made thee?

Consider that poem alongside an excerpt from another work by Blake called "The Tyger."

> Tyger! Tyger! burning bright
> In the forests of the night,
> What immortal hand or eye
> Could frame thy fearful symmetry?
> [...]

104

What the hammer? what the chain?
In what furnace was thy brain?
What the anvil? what dread grasp
Dare its deadly terrors clasp?
When the stars threw down their spears,
And watered heaven with their tears,
Did he smile his work to see?
Did he who made the Lamb make thee?

These poems have quite a few things in common. Each poem's subject is an animal—a lamb and a tiger, respectively—and each poem addresses the same question to the animal: "Who created you?" In fact, both poems are formed primarily of questions.

However, the poems also exhibit many differences. It's easy, for instance, to contrast the tone and word choice in each poem. Whereas "The Lamb" uses words with positive and gentle connotations to create a tone of innocence and serenity, "The Tyger" gives a completely different impression. Some strongly connotative words that stand out include "night," "fearful," and "deadly terrors," all of which contribute to a tone that's tense and full of danger.

When taken together, then, the two poems address the same question—who created the world and all of its creatures?—from two different perspectives. "The Lamb" considers all of the sweet and delightful things that exist, leaving "The Tyger" to ponder the problem of why evil exists. In fact, Blake relies on the contrast between the two poems to fully communicate his dilemma over the paradox of creation—"Did he who make the Lamb make thee?" Although the poems present a strong contrast to one another, it's also possible to find similarities in their subject matter.

Authors often intentionally use contrast in order to ask readers to delve deeper into the qualities of the two things being compared. When an author deliberately places two things (characters, settings, etc.) side-by-side for readers to compare, it's known as **juxtaposition**. An example of juxtaposition can be found in Emily Bronte's *Wuthering Heights*, a novel in which the protagonist Cathy is caught in a love triangle between two romantic interests, Heathcliff and Edgar Linton, who are complete opposites. Cathy compares her feelings for each man in her memorable speech:

> *My love for Linton is like the foliage in the woods: time will change it, I'm well aware, as winter changes the trees. My love for Heathcliff resembles the eternal rocks beneath: a source of little visible delight, but necessary. Nelly, I **am** Heathcliff! He's always, always in my mind: not as a pleasure, any more than I am always a pleasure to myself, but as my own being.*

When these two characters are placed next to each other, it's easier for readers to grasp their notable characteristics. Edgar is gentle and sophisticated in comparison to Heathcliff, who is rough and wild. Here, Cathy also juxtaposes her feelings about each character. Her love for Edgar is fresh and harmless, like the new spring leaves on trees; but come winter, it will fade away. Her love for Heathcliff might be less conventionally appealing, like the rocks that form the earth; but, just like those rocks, that love forms the foundation of Cathy's being and is essential to her life. By juxtaposing these two men, Cathy is better able to express her thoughts about them.

105

Understanding the Development of Themes

Identifying Theme or Central Message

The **theme** is the central message of a fictional work, whether that work is structured as prose, drama, or poetry. It is the heart of what an author is trying to say to readers through the writing, and theme is largely conveyed through literary elements and techniques.

In literature, a theme can often be determined by considering the over-arching narrative conflict within the work. Though there are several types of conflicts and several potential themes within them, the following are the most common:

- Individual against the self—relevant to themes of self-awareness, internal struggles, pride, coming of age, facing reality, fate, free will, vanity, loss of innocence, loneliness, isolation, fulfillment, failure, and disillusionment

- Individual against nature— relevant to themes of knowledge vs. ignorance, nature as beauty, quest for discovery, self-preservation, chaos and order, circle of life, death, and destruction of beauty

- Individual against society— relevant to themes of power, beauty, good, evil, war, class struggle, totalitarianism, role of men/women, wealth, corruption, change vs. tradition, capitalism, destruction, heroism, injustice, and racism

- Individual against another individual— relevant to themes of hope, loss of love or hope, sacrifice, power, revenge, betrayal, and honor

For example, in Hawthorne's *The Scarlet Letter*, one possible narrative conflict could be the individual against the self, with a relevant theme of internal struggles. This theme is alluded to through characterization—Dimmesdale's moral struggle with his love for Hester and Hester's internal struggles with the truth and her daughter, Pearl. It's also alluded to through plot—Dimmesdale's suicide and Hester helping the very townspeople who initially condemned her.

Sometimes, a text can convey a **message** or **universal lesson**—a truth or insight that the reader infers from the text, based on analysis of the literary and/or poetic elements. This message is often presented as a statement. For example, a potential message in Shakespeare's *Hamlet* could be "Revenge is what ultimately drives the human soul." This message can be immediately determined through plot and characterization in numerous ways, but it can also be determined through the setting of Norway, which is bordering on war.

How Authors Develop Theme

Authors employ a variety of techniques to present a theme. They may compare or contrast characters, events, places, ideas, or historical or invented settings to speak thematically. They may use analogies, metaphors, similes, allusions, or other literary devices to convey the theme. An author's use of diction, syntax, and tone can also help convey the theme. Authors will often develop themes through the development of characters, use of the setting, repetition of ideas, use of symbols, and through contrasting value systems. Authors of both fiction and nonfiction genres will use a variety of these techniques to develop one or more themes.

106

Regardless of the literary genre, there are commonalities in how authors, playwrights, and poets develop themes or central ideas.

Authors often do research, the results of which contributes to theme. In prose fiction and drama, this research may include real historical information about the setting the author has chosen or include elements that make fictional characters, settings, and plots seem realistic to the reader. In nonfiction, research is critical since the information contained within this literature must be accurate and, moreover, accurately represented.

In fiction, authors present a narrative conflict that will contribute to the overall theme. In fiction, this conflict may involve the storyline itself and some trouble within characters that needs resolution. In nonfiction, this conflict may be an explanation or commentary on factual people and events.

Authors will sometimes use character motivation to convey theme, such as in the example from *Hamlet* regarding revenge. In fiction, the characters an author creates will think, speak, and act in ways that effectively convey the theme to readers. In nonfiction, the characters are factual, as in a biography, but authors pay particular attention to presenting those motivations to make them clear to readers.

Authors also use literary devices as a means of conveying theme. For example, the use of moon symbolism in Mary Shelley's *Frankenstein* is significant as its phases can be compared to the phases that the Creature undergoes as he struggles with his identity.

The selected point of view can also contribute to a work's theme. The use of first-person point of view in a fiction or non-fiction work engages the reader's response differently than third person point of view. The central idea or theme from a first-person narrative may differ from a third-person limited text.

In literary nonfiction, authors usually identify the purpose of their writing, which differs from fiction, where the general purpose is to entertain. The purpose of nonfiction is usually to inform, persuade, or entertain the audience. The stated purpose of a non-fiction text will drive how the central message or theme, if applicable, is presented.

Authors identify an audience for their writing, which is critical in shaping the theme of the work. For example, the audience for J.K. Rowling's *Harry Potter* series would be different than the audience for a biography of George Washington. The audience an author chooses to address is closely tied to the purpose of the work. The choice of an audience also drives the choice of language and level of diction an author uses. Ultimately, the intended audience determines the level to which that subject matter is presented and the complexity of the theme.

Synthesize Information Across Multiple Sources

In any academic endeavor, it's essential to look to *many* sources of information to get a comprehensive and well-rounded view of the subject matter. Getting information from multiple texts, though, requires readers to synthesize their content—that is, to combine ideas from various sources and express it in an organized way.

In order to synthesize information, readers first need to understand the relationship between the different sources. One way to do so is comparing and contrasting, as described above. Comparison and contrast is also useful in evaluating non-literary sources. For example, if readers want to learn more about a controversial issue, they might decide to read articles from both sides of the argument, compare differences in the arguments on each side, and identify any areas of overlap or agreement. This will allow readers to arrive at a more balanced conclusion.

In addition to synthesizing information from persuasive sources with different opinions, readers can also combine information from different types of texts—for example, from entertaining and informative texts. Readers who are interested in medieval religious life in Europe, for instance, might read a text on medieval history by modern academics; a sociological research article about the role of religion in society; and a piece of literature from the Middle Ages such as Chaucer's *The Canterbury Tales*. By reading fiction written in that time period, readers can look at one writer's perspective on religious activities in their world; and by reading non-fiction texts by modern researchers, readers can further enhance their background knowledge of the subject.

Point of View

The **point of view** is the position the narrator takes when telling the story in prose. If a narrator is incorporated in a drama, the point of view may vary; in poetry, point of view refers to the position the speaker in a poem takes.

First Person
The **first person point of view** is when the writer uses the word "I" in the text. Poetry often uses first person, e.g., William Wordsworth's "I Wandered Lonely as a Cloud." Two examples of prose written in first person are Suzanne Collins' *The Hunger Games* and Anthony Burgess's *A Clockwork Orange*.

Second Person
The **second person point of view** is when the writer uses the pronoun "you." It is not widely used in prose fiction, but as a technique, it has been used by writers such as William Faulkner in *Absalom, Absalom!* and Albert Camus in *The Fall*. It is more common in poetry—e.g., Pablo Neruda's "If You Forget Me."

Third Person
Third person point of view is when the writer utilizes pronouns such as him, her, or them. It may be the most utilized point of view in prose as it provides flexibility to an author and is the one with which readers are most familiar. There are two main types of third person used in fiction. **Third person omniscient** uses a narrator that is all-knowing, relating the story by conveying and interpreting thoughts/feelings of all characters. In **third person limited**, the narrator relates the story through the perspective of one character's thoughts/feelings, usually the main character.

Facts Versus Opinions

As mentioned previously, authors write with a purpose. They adjust their writing for an intended audience. It is the readers' responsibility to comprehend the writing style or purpose of the author. When readers understand a writer's purpose, they can then form their own thoughts about the text(s) regardless of whether their thoughts are the same as or different from the author's. The following section will examine different writing tactics that authors use, such as facts versus opinions, bias and stereotypes, appealing to the readers' emotions, and fallacies (including false analogies, circular reasoning, false dichotomy, and overgeneralization).

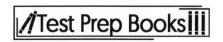

Facts Versus Opinions

Readers need to be aware of the writer's purpose to help discern facts and opinions within texts. A **fact** is a piece of information that is true. It can either prove or disprove claims or arguments presented in texts. Facts cannot be changed or altered. For example, the statement: *Abraham Lincoln was assassinated on April 15, 1865*, is a fact. The date and related events cannot be altered.

Authors not only present facts in their writing to support or disprove their claim(s), but they may also express their opinions. Authors may use facts to support their own opinions, especially in a persuasive text; however, that does not make their opinions facts. An **opinion** is a belief or view formed about something that is not necessarily based on the truth. Opinions often express authors' personal feelings about a subject and use words like *believe, think,* or *feel.* For example, the statement: *Abraham Lincoln was the best president who has ever lived*, expresses the writer's opinion. Not all writers or readers agree or disagree with the statement. Therefore, the statement can be altered or adjusted to express opposing or supporting beliefs, such as "Abraham Lincoln was the worst president who has ever lived" or "I also think Abraham Lincoln was a great president."

When authors include facts and opinions in their writing, readers may be less influenced by the text(s). Readers need to be conscious of the distinction between facts and opinions while going through texts. Not only should the intended audience be vigilant in following authors' thoughts versus valid information, readers need to check the source of the facts presented. Facts should have reliable sources derived from credible outlets like almanacs, encyclopedias, medical journals, and so on.

Bias and Stereotypes

Not only can authors state facts or opinions in their writing, they sometimes intentionally or unintentionally show bias or portray a stereotype. A **bias** is when someone demonstrates a prejudice in favor of or against something or someone in an unfair manner. When an author is biased in their writing, readers should be skeptical despite the fact that the author's bias may be correct. For example, two athletes competed for the same position. One athlete is related to the coach and is a mediocre athlete, while the other player excels and deserves the position. The coach chose the less talented player who is related to him for the position. This is a biased decision because it favors someone in an unfair way.

Similar to a bias, a **stereotype** shows favoritism or opposition but toward a specific group or place. Stereotypes create an oversimplified or overgeneralized idea about a certain group, person, or place. For example,

     Women are horrible drivers.

This statement basically labels *all* women as horrible drivers. While there may be some terrible female drivers, the stereotype implies that *all* women are bad drivers when, in fact, not *all* women are. While many readers are aware of several vile ethnic, religious, and cultural stereotypes, audiences should be cautious of authors' flawed assumptions because they can be less obvious than the despicable examples that are unfortunately pervasive in society.

Evaluating an Argument's Reasoning

Authors write to captivate the attention of their readers. Oftentimes, authors will appeal to their readers' emotions to convince or persuade their audience, especially in when trying to win weak arguments that lack factual evidence. Authors may tell sob stories or use bandwagon approaches in their writing to tap into the readers Strategies and Algorithms to Perform Operations on Rational Numbers' emotions. For example, "Everyone is voting yes" or "He only has two months to live" are statements that can tug at the heartstrings of readers. Authors may use other tactics, such as name-calling or advertising, to lead their readers into believing something is true or false. These emotional pleas are clear signs that the authors do not have a favorable point and that they are trying to distract the readers from the fact that their argument is factually weak.

Understanding Methods Used to Appeal to a Specific Audience

Rhetorical Appeals

In an argument or persuasive text, an author will strive to sway readers to an opinion or conclusion. To be effective, an author must consider their intended audience. Although an author may write text for a general audience, he or she will use methods of appeal or persuasion to convince that audience. Aristotle asserted that there were three methods or modes by which a person could be persuaded. These are referred to as **rhetorical appeals**.

The three main types of rhetorical appeals are shown in the following graphic.

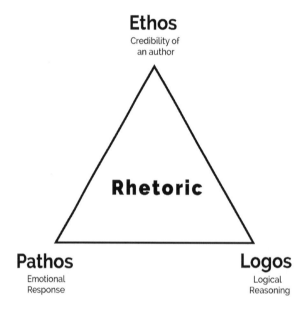

Ethos, also referred to as an **ethical appeal**, is an appeal to the audience's perception of the writer as credible (or not), based on their examination of their ethics and who the writer is, their experience or incorporation of relevant information, or their argument. For example, authors may present testimonials to bolster their arguments. The reader who critically examines the veracity of the testimonials and the credibility of those giving the testimony will be able to determine if the author's use of testimony is valid to their argument. In turn, this will help the reader determine if the author's thesis is valid. An author's careful and appropriate use of technical language can create an overall knowledgeable effect and, in turn, act as a convincing vehicle when it comes to credibility. Overuse of technical language, however, may create confusion in readers and obscure an author's overall intent.

Pathos, also referred to as a **pathetic or emotional appeal**, is an appeal to the audience's sense of identity, self-interest, or emotions. A critical reader will notice when the author is appealing to pathos

110

through anecdotes and descriptions that elicit an emotion such as anger or pity. Readers should also beware of factual information that uses generalization to appeal to the emotions. While it's tempting to believe an author is the source of truth in their text, an author who presents factual information as universally true, consistent throughout time, and common to all groups is using *generalization*. Authors who exclusively use generalizations without specific facts and credible sourcing are attempting to sway readers solely through emotion.

Logos, also referred to as a *logical appeal*, is an appeal to the audience's ability to see and understand the logic in a claim offered by the writer. A critical reader has to be able to evaluate an author's arguments for validity of reasoning and for sufficiency when it comes to argument.

Fallacies

A **fallacy** is a mistaken belief or faulty reasoning, otherwise known as a **logical fallacy**. It is important for readers to recognize logical fallacies because they discredit the author's message. Readers should continuously self-question as they go through a text to identify logical fallacies. Readers cannot simply complacently take information at face value.

There are six common types of logical *fallacies:*

1. False analogy
2. Circular reasoning
3. False dichotomy
4. Overgeneralization
5. Slippery slope
6. Hasty generalization

Each of the six logical fallacies are reviewed individually.

False Analogy
A **false analogy** is when the author assumes two objects or events are alike in all aspects despite the fact that they may be vastly different. Authors intend on making unfamiliar objects relatable to convince readers of something. For example, the letters *A* and *E* are both vowels; therefore, *A* equals *E*. Readers cannot assume that because *A* and *E* are both vowels that they perform the same function in words or independently. If authors tell readers, *A* equals *E*, then that is a false analogy. While this is a simple example, other false analogies may be less obvious.

Circular reasoning
Circular reasoning is when the reasoning is decided based upon the outcome or conclusion and then vice versa. Basically, those who use circular reasoning start out with the argument and then use false logic to try to prove it, and then, in turn, the reasoning supports the conclusion in one big circular pattern. For example, consider the two thoughts, "I don't have time to get organized" and "My disorganization is costing me time." Which is the argument? What is the conclusion? If there is not time to get organized, will more time be spent later trying to find whatever is needed? In turn, if so much time is spent looking for things, there is not time to get organized. The cycle keeps going in an endless series. One problem affects the other; therefore, there is a circular pattern of reasoning.

False dichotomy

A **false dichotomy**, also known as a false dilemma, is when the author tries to make readers believe that there are only two options to choose from when, in fact, there are more. The author creates a false sense of the situation because he or she wants the readers to believe that their claim is the most logical choice. If the author does not present the readers with options, then the author is purposefully limiting what readers may believe. In turn, the author hopes that readers will believe that their point of view is the most sensible choice. For example, in the statement: *you either love running, or you are lazy*, the fallacy lies in the options of loving to run or being lazy. Even though both statements do not necessarily have to be true, the author tries to make one option seem more appealing than the other.

Overgeneralization

An **overgeneralization** is a logical fallacy that occurs when authors write something so extreme that it cannot be proved or disproved. Words like *all, never, most,* and *few* are commonly used when an overgeneralization is being made. For example,

> All kids are crazy when they eat sugar; therefore, my son will not have a cupcake at the birthday party.

Not *all* kids are crazy when they eat sugar, but the extreme statement can influence the readers' points of view on the subject. Readers need to be wary of overgeneralizations in texts because authors may try to sneak them in to sway the readers' opinions.

Slippery slope

A **slippery slope** is when an author implies that something will inevitably happen as a result of another action. A slippery slope may or may not be true, even though the order of events or gradations may seem logical. For example, in the children's book *If You Give a Mouse a Cookie*, the author goes off on tangents such as "If you give a mouse a cookie, he will ask for some milk. When you give him the milk, he'll probably ask you for a straw." The mouse in the story follows a series of logical events as a result of a previous action. The slippery slope continues on and on throughout the story. Even though the mouse made logical decisions, it very well could have made a different choice, changing the direction of the story.

Hasty generalization

A **hasty generalization** is when the reader comes to a conclusion without reviewing or analyzing all the evidence. It is never a good idea to make a decision without all the information, which is why hasty generalizations are considered fallacies. For example, if two friends go to a hairdresser and give the hairdresser a positive recommendation, that does not necessarily mean that a new client will have the same experience. Two referrals is not quite enough information to form an educated and well-formed conclusion.

Overall, readers should carefully review and analyze authors' arguments to identify logical fallacies and come to sensible conclusions.

Counterarguments and Evaluating Arguments

If an author presents a differing opinion or a counterargument in order to refute it, the reader should consider how and why the information is being presented. It is meant to strengthen the original argument and shouldn't be confused with the author's intended conclusion, but it should also be considered in the reader's final evaluation.

Authors can also use bias if they ignore the opposing viewpoint or present their side in an unbalanced way. A strong argument considers the opposition and finds a way to refute it. Critical readers should look for an unfair or one-sided presentation of the argument and be skeptical, as a bias may be present. Even if this bias is unintentional, if it exists in the writing, the reader should be wary of the validity of the argument. Readers should also look for the use of stereotypes, which refer to specific groups. Stereotypes are often negative connotations about a person or place, and should always be avoided. When a critical reader finds stereotypes in a piece of writing, they should be critical of the argument, and consider the validity of anything the author presents. Stereotypes reveal a flaw in the writer's thinking and may suggest a lack of knowledge or understanding about the subject.

In general, readers should always heed attention to whether an author's ideas or stated facts are relevant to the argument or counterargument posed in the reading. Those that are irrelevant can cloud the argument or weaken it. In much the same way, critical readers are able to identify whether statements in a reading strengthen or weaken the author's argument.

Authors want you to accept their assertions and arguments as true but critical readers evaluate the strength of the argument instead of simply taking it at face value and accepting it as the truth or only point of view. All arguments need two parts: the claim and the supporting evidence or rationale. The claim *is* the argument. It asserts an opinion, idea, point of view, or conclusion. The supporting evidence is the rationale, assumptions, beliefs, as well as the factual evidence in support of the stated claim. The supporting evidence is what gives readers the information necessary to accept or reject the stated claim. Critical readers should assess the argument in its entirety by evaluating the claims and conclusions themselves, the process of reasoning, and the accuracy of the evidence. For example, arguments are weaker and should be skeptically considered when the supporting evidence is highly opinionated, biased, or derived from sources that are not credible. Authors should cite where statistics and other stated facts were found. Lastly, the support for a claim should be pertinent to it and consistent with the other statements and evidence.

Practice Quiz

Questions 1–5 are based upon the following passage:

My Good Friends,—When I first imparted to the committee of the projected Institute my particular wish that on one of the evenings of my readings here the main body of my audience should be composed of working men and their families, I was animated by two desires; first, by the wish to have the great pleasure of meeting you face to face at this Christmas time, and accompany you myself through one of my little Christmas books; and second, by the wish to have an opportunity of stating publicly in your presence, and in the presence of the committee, my earnest hope that the Institute will, from the beginning, recognise one great principle—strong in reason and justice—which I believe to be essential to the very life of such an Institution. It is, that the working man shall, from the first unto the last, have a share in the management of an Institution which is designed for his benefit, and which calls itself by his name.

I have no fear here of being misunderstood—of being supposed to mean too much in this. If there ever was a time when any one class could of itself do much for its own good, and for the welfare of society—which I greatly doubt—that time is unquestionably past. It is in the fusion of different classes, without confusion; in the bringing together of employers and employed; in the creating of a better common understanding among those whose interests are identical, who depend upon each other, who are vitally essential to each other, and who never can be in unnatural antagonism without deplorable results, that one of the chief principles of a Mechanics' Institution should consist. In this world a great deal of the bitterness among us arises from an imperfect understanding of one another. Erect in Birmingham a great Educational Institution, properly educational; educational of the feelings as well as of the reason; to which all orders of Birmingham men contribute; in which all orders of Birmingham men meet; wherein all orders of Birmingham men are faithfully represented—and you will erect a Temple of Concord here which will be a model edifice to the whole of England.

Contemplating as I do the existence of the Artisans' Committee, which not long ago considered the establishment of the Institute so sensibly, and supported it so heartily, I earnestly entreat the gentlemen—earnest I know in the good work, and who are now among us,—by all means to avoid the great shortcoming of similar institutions; and in asking the working man for his confidence, to set him the great example and give him theirs in return. You will judge for yourselves if I promise too much for the working man, when I say that he will stand by such an enterprise with the utmost of his patience, his perseverance, sense, and support; that I am sure he will need no charitable aid or condescending patronage; but will readily and cheerfully pay for the advantages which it confers; that he will prepare himself in individual cases where he feels that the adverse circumstances around him have rendered it necessary; in a word, that he will feel his responsibility like an honest man, and will most honestly and manfully discharge it. I now proceed to the pleasant task to which I assure you I have looked forward for a long time.

This excerpt is adapted from Charles Dickens' speech in Birmingham in England on December 30, 1853 on behalf of the Birmingham and Midland Institute.

1. Based upon the contextual evidence provided in the passage above, what is the meaning of the term *enterprise* in the third paragraph?
   a. Company
   b. Courage
   c. Game
   d. Cause

2. The speaker addresses his audience as *My Good Friends*—what kind of credibility does this salutation give to the speaker?
   a. The speaker is an employer addressing his employees, so the salutation is a way for the boss to bridge the gap between himself and his employees.
   b. The speaker's salutation is one from an entertainer to his audience and uses the friendly language to connect to his audience before a serious speech.
   c. The salutation gives the serious speech that follows a somber tone, as it is used ironically.
   d. The speech is one from a politician to the public, so the salutation is used to grab the audience's attention.

3. According to the aforementioned passage, what is the speaker's second desire for his time in front of the audience?
   a. To read a Christmas story
   b. For the working man to have a say in his institution which is designed for his benefit
   c. To have an opportunity to stand in their presence
   d. For the life of the institution to be essential to the audience as a whole

4. The speaker's tone in the passage can be described as:
   a. Happy and gullible
   b. Lazy and entitled
   c. Confident and informed
   d. Angry and frustrated

5. Which of the following is one of the main purposes of the last paragraph?
   a. To persuade the audience to support the Institute no matter what, since it provided so much support to the working class
   b. To market the speaker's new book, while at the same time, supporting the activities of the Institute
   c. To inform the audience that the Institute is corrupt and will not help them out when the time comes to give them compensation
   d. To provide credibility to the working man and share confidence in their ability to take on responsibilities if they are compensated appropriately

See answers on next page.

Answer Explanations

1. D: *Enterprise* most closely means *cause*. Choices *A, B,* and *C* are all related to the term *enterprise*. However, Dickens speaks of a *cause* here, not a company, courage, or a game. *He will stand by such an enterprise* is a call to stand by a cause to enable the working man to have a certain autonomy over his own economic standing. The very first paragraph ends with the statement that the working man *shall . . . have a share in the management of an institution which is designed for his benefit.*

2. B: The speaker's salutation is one from an entertainer to his audience and uses the friendly language to connect to his audience before a serious speech. Recall in the first paragraph that the speaker is there to "accompany [the audience] . . . through one of my little Christmas books," making him an author there to entertain the crowd with his own writing. The speech preceding the reading is the passage itself, and, as the tone indicates, a serious speech addressing the "working man." Although the passage speaks of employers and employees, the speaker himself is not an employer of the audience, so Choice *A* is incorrect. Choice *C* is also incorrect, as the salutation is not used ironically, but sincerely, as the speech addresses the wellbeing of the crowd. Choice *D* is incorrect because the speech is not given by a politician, but by a writer.

3. B: Choice *A* is incorrect because that is the speaker's first desire, not his second. Choices *C* and *D* are tricky because the language of both of these is mentioned after the word *second*. However, the speaker doesn't get to the second wish until the next sentence. Choices *C* and *D* are merely preliminary remarks before the statement of the main clause, Choice *B*.

4. C: The speaker's tone can best be described as *confident and informed.* The speaker addresses the audience as "My good friends," and says, "I have no fear of being misunderstood," which implies confidence. Additionally, the speaker's knowledge of the proposal and topic can be seen in the text as well, especially in the second paragraph.

5. D: To provide credibility to the working man and share confidence in their ability to take on responsibilities if they are compensated appropriately. The speaker provides credibility by saying "he will stand by such an enterprise with the utmost of his patience," and displays their responsibilities by saying "he will feel his responsibility like an honest man."

116

Writing

Sustaining Focus on a Specific Topic or Argument

Focus

Good writing stays *focused* and on topic. During the test, determine the main idea for each passage and then look for times when the writer strays from the point they're trying to make. Consider an argumentative essay about the importance of seat belts in preventing automobile accident-related deaths. If the writer suddenly begins talking about how well airbags, crumple zones, or other safety features work to save lives, they might be losing focus from the topic of "safety belts."

Focus can also refer to individual sentences. Sometimes the writer does address the main topic, but in a confusing way. For example:

> Thanks to seat belt usage, survival in serious car accidents has shown a consistently steady increase since the development of the retractable seat belt in the 1950s.

This statement is definitely on topic, but it's not easy to follow. A simpler, more focused version of this sentence might look like this:

> Seat belts have consistently prevented car fatalities since the 1950s.

Providing *adequate information* is another aspect of focused writing. Statements like "seat belts are important" and "many people drive cars" are true, but they're so general that they don't contribute much to the writer's case. When reading a passage, watch for these kinds of unfocused statements.

Establishing a Topic or Thesis

Proposition

The **proposition** (also called the *claim* since it can be true or false) is a clear statement of the point or idea the writer is trying to make. The length or format of a proposition can vary, but it often takes the form of a *topic sentence*. A good topic sentence is:

- Clear: does not weave a complicated web of words for the reader to decode or unwrap
- Concise: presents only the information needed to make the claim and doesn't clutter up the statement with unnecessary details
- Precise: clarifies the exact point the writer wants to make and doesn't use broad, overreaching statements

Look at the following example:

> The civil rights movement, from its genesis in the Emancipation Proclamation to its current struggles with de facto discrimination, has changed the face of the United States more than any other factor in its history.

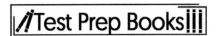

Is the statement clear? Yes, the statement is fairly clear, although other words can be substituted for "genesis" and "de facto" to make it easier to understand.

Is the statement concise? No, the statement is not concise. Details about the Emancipation Proclamation and the current state of the movement are unnecessary for a topic sentence. Those details should be saved for the body of the text.

Is the statement precise? No, the statement is not precise. What exactly does the writer mean by "changed the face of the United States"? The writer should be more specific about the effects of the movement. Also, suggesting that something has a greater impact than anything else in U.S. history is far too ambitious a statement to make.

A better version might look like this:

> The civil rights movement has greatly increased the career opportunities available for Black Americans.

The unnecessary language and details are removed, and the claim can now be measured and supported.

The Conventions of Standard English

Understanding the Conventions of Standard English

Parts of Speech

The English language has eight parts of speech, each serving a different grammatical function.

Verb

Verbs describe an action—e.g., *run*, *play*, *eat*—or a state of being—e.g., *is*, *are*, *was*. It is impossible to make a grammatically-complete sentence without a verb.

> He *runs* to the store.

> She *is* eight years old.

Noun

Nouns can be a person, place, or thing. They can refer to concrete objects—e.g., chair, apple, house—or abstract things—love, knowledge, friendliness.

> Look at the *dog*!

> Where are my *keys*?

Some nouns are **countable**, meaning they can be counted as separate entities—one chair, two chairs, three chairs. They can be either singular or plural. Other nouns, usually substances or concepts, are **uncountable**—e.g., air, information, wealth—and some nouns can be both countable and uncountable depending on how they are used.

> I bought three *dresses*.

> *Respect* is important to me.

> I ate way too much *food* last night.

> At the international festival, you can sample *foods* from around the world.

Proper nouns are the specific names of people, places, or things and are almost always capitalized.

> *Marie Curie studied at the Flying University in Warsaw, Poland.*

Pronoun

Pronouns function as substitutes for nouns or noun phrases. Pronouns are often used to avoid constant repetition of a noun or to simplify sentences. **Personal pronouns** are used for people. Some pronouns are **subject pronouns**; they are used to replace the subject in a sentence—I, we, he, she, they.

> Is *he* your friend?

> *We* work together.

Object pronouns can function as the object of a sentence—me, us, him, her, them.

> Give the documents to *her*.

> Did you call *him* back yet?

Some pronouns can function as either the subject or the object—e.g., you, it. The subject of a sentence is the noun of the sentence that is doing or being something.

> *You* should try it.

> *It* tastes great.

Possessive pronouns indicate ownership. They can be used alone—mine, yours, his, hers, theirs, ours—or with a noun—my, your, his, her, their, ours. In the latter case, they function as a determiner, which is described in detail in the below section on adjectives.

> This table is *ours*.

> I can't find *my* phone!

Reflexive pronouns refer back to the person being spoken or written about. These pronouns end in -*self/-selves*.

> I've heard that New York City is gorgeous in the autumn, but I've never seen it for *myself*.

> After moving away from home, young people have to take care of *themselves*.

Indefinite pronouns are used for things that are unknown or unspecified. Some examples are *anybody*, *something*, and *everything*.

> I'm looking for *someone* who knows how to fix computers.

> I wanted to buy some shoes today, but I couldn't find *any* that I liked.

Adjective

An **adjective** modifies a noun, making it more precise or giving more information about it. Adjectives answer these questions: What kind? Which one?

> I just bought a *red* car.

> I don't like *cold* weather.

One special type of word that modifies a noun is a **determiner.** In fact, some grammarians classify determiners as a separate part of speech because whereas adjectives simply describe additional qualities of a noun, a determiner is often a necessary part of a noun phrase, without which the phrase is grammatically incomplete. A determiner indicates whether a noun is definite or indefinite and can identify which noun is being discussed. It also introduces context to the noun in terms of quantity and possession. The most commonly-used determiners are articles—a, an, the.

> I ordered *a* pizza.

> She lives in *the* city.

120

Possessive pronouns discussed above, such as *my*, *your*, and *our*, are also determiners, along with **demonstratives**—this, that—and **quantifiers**—much, many, some. These determiners can take the place of an article.

> Are you using *this* chair?

> I need *some* coffee!

Adverb

Adverbs modify verbs, adjectives, and other adverbs. Words that end in –ly are usually adverbs. Adverbs answer these questions: When? Where? In what manner? To what degree?

> She talks *quickly*.

> The mountains are *incredibly* beautiful!

> The students arrived *early*.

> Please take your phone call *outside*.

Preposition

Prepositions show the relationship between different elements in a phrase or sentence and connect nouns or pronouns to other words in the sentence. Some examples of prepositions are words such as *after*, *at*, *behind*, *by*, *during*, *from*, *in*, *on*, *to*, and *with*.

> Let's go *to* class.

> Starry Night was painted *by* Vincent van Gogh *in* 1889.

Conjunction

Conjunctions join words, phrases, clauses, or sentences together, indicating the type of connection between these elements.

> I like pizza, *and* I enjoy spaghetti.

> I like to play baseball, *but* I'm allergic to mitts.

Some conjunctions are *coordinating*, meaning they give equal emphasis to two main clauses. **Coordinating conjunctions** are short, simple words that can be remembered using the mnemonic FANBOYS: for, and, nor, but, or, yet, so. Other conjunctions are *subordinating*. **Subordinating conjunctions** introduce dependent clauses and include words such as *because*, *since*, *before*, *after*, *if*, and *while*.

Interjection

An **interjection** is a short word that shows greeting or emotion. Examples of interjections include *wow*, *ouch*, *hey*, *oops*, *alas*, and *hey*.

> *Wow*! Look at that sunset!

> Was It your birthday yesterday? *Oops*! I forgot.

Errors in Standard English Grammar, Usage, Syntax, and Mechanics

Sentence Fragments

A **complete sentence** requires a verb and a subject, and it must express a complete thought. Sometimes, the subject is omitted in the case of the implied *you*, used in sentences that are the command or imperative form—e.g., "Look!" or "Give me that." It is understood that the subject of the command is *you*, the listener or reader, so it is possible to have a structure without an explicit subject. Without these elements, though, the sentence is incomplete—it is a **sentence fragment**. While sentence fragments often occur in conversational English or creative writing, they are generally not appropriate in academic writing. Sentence fragments often occur when dependent clauses are not joined to an independent clause:

Sentence fragment: Because the airline overbooked the flight.

The sentence above is a dependent clause that does not express a complete thought. What happened as a result of this cause? With the addition of an independent clause, this now becomes a complete sentence:

Complete sentence: Because the airline overbooked the flight, several passengers were unable to board.

Sentences fragments may also occur through improper use of conjunctions:

I'm going to the Bahamas for spring break. And to New York City for New Year's Eve.

While the first sentence above is a complete sentence, the second one is not because it is a prepositional phrase that lacks a subject [I] and a verb [am going]. Joining the two together with the coordinating conjunction forms one grammatically-correct sentence:

I'm going to the Bahamas for spring break and to New York City for New Year's Eve.

Run-ons

A **run-on** is a sentence with too many independent clauses that are improperly connected to each other:

This winter has been very cold some farmers have suffered damage to their crops.

The sentence above has two subject-verb combinations. The first is "this winter has been"; the second is "some farmers have suffered." However, they are simply stuck next to each other without any punctuation or conjunction. Therefore, the sentence is a run-on.

Another type of run-on occurs when writers use inappropriate punctuation:

This winter has been very cold, some farmers have suffered damage to their crops.

Though a comma has been added, this sentence is still not correct. When a comma alone is used to join two independent clauses, it is known as a ***comma splice***. Without an appropriate conjunction, a comma cannot join two independent clauses by itself.

Run-on sentences can be corrected by either dividing the independent clauses into two or more separate sentences or inserting appropriate conjunctions and/or punctuation. The run-on sentence can be amended by separating each subject-verb pair into its own sentence:

> This winter has been very cold. Some farmers have suffered damage to their crops.

The run-on can also be fixed by adding a comma and conjunction to join the two independent clauses with each other:

> This winter has been very cold, so some farmers have suffered damage to their crops.

Parallelism

Parallel structure occurs when phrases or clauses within a sentence contain the same structure. Parallelism increases readability and comprehensibility because it is easy to tell which sentence elements are paired with each other in meaning.

> Jennifer enjoys cooking, knitting, and to spend time with her cat.

This sentence is not parallel because the items in the list appear in two different forms. Some are *gerunds*, which is the verb + ing: *cooking, knitting*. The other item uses the *infinitive* form, which is to + verb: *to spend*. To create parallelism, all items in the list may reflect the same form:

> Jennifer enjoys cooking, knitting, and spending time with her cat.

All of the items in the list are now in gerund forms, so this sentence exhibits parallel structure. Here's another example:

> The company is looking for employees who are responsible and with a lot of experience.

Again, the items that are listed in this sentence are not parallel. "Responsible" is an adjective, yet "with a lot of experience" is a prepositional phrase. The sentence elements do not utilize parallel parts of speech.

> The company is looking for employees who are responsible and experienced.

"Responsible" and "experienced" are both adjectives, so this sentence now has parallel structure.

Dangling and Misplaced Modifiers

Modifiers enhance meaning by clarifying or giving greater detail about another part of a sentence. However, incorrectly-placed modifiers have the opposite effect and can cause confusion. A *misplaced modifier* is a modifier that is not located appropriately in relation to the word or phrase that it modifies:

> Because he was one of the greatest thinkers of Renaissance Italy, John idolized Leonardo da Vinci.

In this sentence, the modifier is "because he was one of the greatest thinkers of Renaissance Italy," and the noun it is intended to modify is "Leonardo da Vinci." However, due to the placement of the modifier next to the subject, John, it seems as if the sentence is stating that John was a Renaissance genius, not Da Vinci.

123

John idolized Leonard da Vinci because he was one of the greatest thinkers of Renaissance Italy.

The modifier is now adjacent to the appropriate noun, clarifying which of the two men in this sentence is the greatest thinker.

Dangling modifiers modify a word or phrase that is not readily apparent in the sentence. That is, they "dangle" because they are not clearly attached to anything:

After getting accepted to college, Amir's parents were proud.

The modifier here, "after getting accepted to college," should modify who got accepted. The noun immediately following the modifier is "Amir's parents"—but they are probably not the ones who are going to college.

After getting accepted to college, Amir made his parents proud.

The subject of the sentence has been changed to Amir himself, and now the subject and its modifier are appropriately matched.

Inconsistent Verb Tense

Verb tense reflects when an action occurred or a state existed. For example, the tense known as **simple present** expresses something that is happening right now or that happens regularly:

She *works* in a hospital.

Present continuous tense expresses something in progress. It is formed by to be + verb + -ing.

Sorry, I can't go out right now. I *am doing* my homework.

Past tense is used to describe events that previously occurred. However, in conversational English, speakers often use present tense or a mix of past and present tense when relating past events because it gives the narrative a sense of immediacy. In formal written English, though, consistency in verb tense is necessary to avoid reader confusion.

I traveled to Europe last summer. As soon as I stepped off the plane, I feel like I'm in a movie! I'm surrounded by quaint cafes and impressive architecture.

The passage above abruptly switches from past tense—*traveled, stepped*—to present tense—*feel, am surrounded*.

I *traveled* to Europe last summer. As soon as I *stepped* off the plane, I *felt* like I was in a movie! I *was surrounded* by quaint cafes and impressive architecture.

All verbs are in past tense, so this passage now has consistent verb tense.

Split Infinitives

The **infinitive form** of a verb consists of "to + base verb"—e.g., to walk, to sleep, to approve. A **split infinitive** occurs when another word, usually an adverb, is placed between *to* and the verb:

I decided *to simply walk* to work to get more exercise every day.

124

The infinitive *to walk* is split by the adverb *simply*.

It was a mistake *to hastily approve* the project before conducting further preliminary research.

The infinitive *to approve* is split by *hastily*.

Although some grammarians still advise against split infinitives, this syntactic structure is common in both spoken and written English and is widely accepted in standard usage.

Subject-Verb Agreement

In English, verbs must agree with the subject. The form of a verb may change depending on whether the subject is singular or plural, or whether it is first, second, or third person. For example, the verb *to be* has various forms:

I am a student.

You are a student.

She is a student.

We are students.

They are students.

Errors occur when a verb does not agree with its subject. Sometimes, the error is readily apparent:

We is hungry.

Is is not the appropriate form of *to be* when used with the third person plural *we*.

We are hungry.

This sentence now has correct subject-verb agreement.

However, some cases are trickier, particularly when the subject consists of a lengthy noun phrase with many modifiers:

Students who are hoping to accompany the anthropology department on its annual summer trip to Ecuador needs to sign up by March 31st.

The verb in this sentence is *needs*. However, its subject is not the noun adjacent to it—Ecuador. The subject is the noun at the beginning of the sentence—students. Because *students* is plural, *needs* is the incorrect verb form.

Students who are hoping to accompany the anthropology department on its annual summer trip to Ecuador *need* to sign up by March 31st.

This sentence now uses correct agreement between *students* and *need*.

Another case to be aware of is a *collective noun*. A collective noun refers to a group of many things or people but can be singular in itself—e.g., family, committee, army, pair team, council, jury. Whether or

125

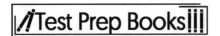
not a collective noun uses a singular or plural verb depends on how the noun is being used. If the noun refers to the group performing a collective action as one unit, it should use a singular verb conjugation:

>   The family is moving to a new neighborhood.

The whole family is moving together in unison, so the singular verb form *is* is appropriate here.

>   The committee has made its decision.

The verb *has* and the possessive pronoun *its* both reflect the word *committee* as a singular noun in the sentence above; however, when a collective noun refers to the group as individuals, it can take a plural verb:

>   The newlywed pair spend every moment together.

This sentence emphasizes the love between two people in a pair, so it can use the plural verb *spend*.

>   The council are all newly elected members.

The sentence refers to the council in terms of its individual members and uses the plural verb *are*.

Overall, though, American English is more likely to pair a collective noun with a singular verb, while British English is more likely to pair a collective noun with a plural verb.

Grammar, Usage, Syntax, and Mechanics Choices

Colons and Semicolons

In a sentence, **colons** are used before a list, a summary or elaboration, or an explanation related to the preceding information in the sentence:

>   There are two ways to reserve tickets for the performance: by phone or in person.

>   One thing is clear: students are spending more on tuition than ever before.

As these examples show, a colon must be preceded by an independent clause. However, the information after the colon may be in the form of an independent clause or in the form of a list.

Semicolons can be used in two different ways—to join ideas or to separate them. In some cases, semicolons can be used to connect what would otherwise be stand-alone sentences. Each part of the sentence joined by a semicolon must be an independent clause. The use of a semicolon indicates that these two independent clauses are closely related to each other:

>   The rising cost of childcare is one major stressor for parents; healthcare expenses are another source of anxiety.

>   Classes have been canceled due to the snowstorm; check the school website for updates.

Semicolons can also be used to divide elements of a sentence in a more distinct way than simply using a comma. This usage is particularly useful when the items in a list are especially long and complex and contain other internal punctuation.

Retirees have many modes of income: some survive solely off their retirement checks; others supplement their income through part time jobs, like working in a supermarket or substitute teaching; and others are financially dependent on the support of family members, friends, and spouses.

Its and It's

These pronouns are some of the most confused in the English language as most possessives contain the suffix –'s. However, for *it*, it is the opposite. *Its* is a possessive pronoun:

The government is reassessing *its* spending plan.

It's is a contraction of the words *it is*:

It's snowing outside.

Saw and Seen

Saw and *seen* are both conjugations of the verb *to see*, but they express different verb tenses. *Saw* is used in the simple past tense. *Seen* is the past participle form of *to see* and can be used in all perfect tenses.

I seen her yesterday.

This sentence is incorrect. Because it expresses a completed event from a specified point in time in the past, it should use simple past tense:

I *saw* her yesterday.

This sentence uses the correct verb tense. Here's how the past participle is used correctly:

I *have seen* her before.

The meaning in this sentence is slightly changed to indicate an event from an unspecific time in the past. In this case, present perfect is the appropriate verb tense to indicate an unspecified past experience. Present perfect conjugation is created by combining *to have* + past participle.

Then and Than

Then is generally used as an adverb indicating something that happened next in a sequence or as the result of a conditional situation:

We parked the car and *then* walked to the restaurant.

If enough people register for the event, *then* we can begin planning.

Than is a conjunction indicating comparison:

This watch is more expensive *than* that one.

The bus departed later *than* I expected.

They're, Their, and There

They're is a contraction of the words *they are*:

127

They're moving to Ohio next week.

Their is a possessive pronoun:

The baseball players are training for *their* upcoming season.

There can function as multiple parts of speech, but it is most commonly used as an adverb indicating a location:

Let's go to the concert! Some great bands are playing *there*.

Insure and Ensure

These terms are both verbs. *Insure* means to guarantee something against loss, harm, or damage, usually through an insurance policy that offers monetary compensation:

The robbers made off with her prized diamond necklace, but luckily it was *insured* for one million dollars.

Ensure means to make sure, to confirm, or to be certain:

Ensure that you have your passport before entering the security checkpoint.

Accept and Except

Accept is a verb meaning to take or agree to something:

I would like to *accept* your offer of employment.

Except is a preposition that indicates exclusion:

I've been to every state in America *except* Hawaii.

Affect and Effect

Affect is a verb meaning to influence or to have an impact on something:

The amount of rainfall during the growing season *affects* the flavor of wine produced from these grapes.

Effect can be used as either a noun or a verb. As a noun, *effect* is synonymous with a result:

If we implement the changes, what will the *effect* be on our profits?

As a verb, *effect* means to bring about or to make happen:

In just a few short months, the healthy committee has *effected* real change in school nutrition.

Components of Sentences

Clauses

Clauses contain a subject and a verb. An **independent clause** can function as a complete sentence on its own, but it might also be one component of a longer sentence. **Dependent clauses** cannot stand alone

128

as complete sentences. They rely on independent clauses to complete their meaning. Dependent clauses usually begin with a subordinating conjunction. Independent and dependent clauses are sometimes also referred to as **main clauses** and **subordinate clauses**, respectively. The following structure highlights the differences:

Apiculturists raise honeybees because they love insects.

Apiculturists raise honeybees is an independent or main clause. The subject is *apiculturists*, and the verb is *raise*. It expresses a complete thought and could be a standalone sentence.

Because they love insects is a dependent or subordinate clause. If it were not attached to the independent clause, it would be a sentence fragment. While it contains a subject and verb—*they love*—this clause is dependent because it begins with the subordinate conjunction *because*. Thus, it does not express a complete thought on its own.

Another type of clause is a **relative clause**, and it is sometimes referred to as an **adjective clause** because it gives further description about the noun. A relative clause begins with a *relative pronoun*: *that, which, who, whom, whichever, whomever,* or *whoever*. It may also begin with a *relative adverb*: *where, why,* or *when.* Here's an example of a relative clause, functioning as an adjective:

The strawberries that I bought yesterday are already beginning to spoil.

Here, the relative clause is *that I bought yesterday*; the relative pronoun is *that*. The subject is *I*, and the verb is *bought*. The clause modifies the subject *strawberries* by answering the question, "Which strawberries?" Here's an example of a relative clause with an adverb:

The tutoring center is a place where students can get help with homework.

The relative clause is *where students can get help with homework*, and it gives more information about a place by describing what kind of place it is. It begins with the relative adverb *where* and contains the noun *students* along with its verb phrase *can get*.

Relative clauses may be further divided into two types: essential or nonessential. **Essential clauses** contain identifying information without which the sentence would lose significant meaning or not make sense. These are also sometimes referred to as *restrictive clauses*. The sentence above contains an example of an essential relative clause. Here is what happens when the clause is removed:

The tutoring center is a place where students can get help with homework.

The tutoring center is a place.

Without the relative clause, the sentence loses the majority of its meaning; thus, the clause is essential or restrictive.

Nonessential clauses—also referred to as **non-restrictive clauses**—offer additional information about a noun in the sentence, but they do not significantly control the overall meaning of the sentence. The following example indicates a nonessential clause:

New York City, which is located in the northeastern part of the country, is the most populated city in America.

129

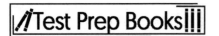

New York City is the most populated city in America.

Even without the relative clause, the sentence is still understandable and continues to communicate its central message about New York City. Thus, it is a nonessential clause.

Punctuation differs between essential and nonessential relative clauses, too. Nonessential clauses are set apart from the sentence using commas whereas essential clauses are not separated with commas. Also, the relative pronoun *that* is generally used for essential clauses, while *which* is used for nonessential clauses. The following examples clarify this distinction:

Romeo and Juliet is my favorite play *that Shakespeare wrote.*

The relative clause *that Shakespeare wrote* contains essential, controlling information about the noun *play*, limiting it to those plays by Shakespeare. Without it, it would seem that *Romeo and Juliet* is the speaker's favorite play out of every play ever written, not simply from Shakespeare's repertoire.

Romeo and Juliet, which Shakespeare wrote, is my favorite play.

Here, the nonessential relative clause—"which Shakespeare wrote"—modifies *Romeo and Juliet.* It doesn't provide controlling information about the play, but simply offers further background details. Thus, commas are needed.

Phrases
Phrases are groups of words that do not contain the subject-verb combination required for clauses. Phrases are classified by the part of speech that begins or controls the phrase.

A **noun phrase** consists of a noun and all its modifiers—adjectives, adverbs, and determiners. Noun phrases can serve many functions in a sentence, acting as subjects, objects, and object complements:

The shallow yellow bowl sits on the top shelf.

Nina just bought *some incredibly fresh organic produce.*

Prepositional phrases are made up of a preposition and its object. The object of a preposition might be a noun, noun phrase, pronoun, or gerund. Prepositional phrases may function as either an adjective or an adverb:

Jack picked up the book *in front of him.*

The prepositional phrase *in front of him* acts as an adjective indicating which book Jack picked up.

The dog ran into the back yard.

The phrase *into the backyard* describes where the dog ran, so it acts as an adverb.

Verb phrases include all of the words in a verb group, even if they are not directly adjacent to each other:

I *should have woken up* earlier this morning.

The company **is** now *offering* membership discounts for new enrollers.

130

This sentence's verb phrase is *is offering*. Even though they are separated by the word *now*, they function together as a single verb phrase.

Structures of Sentences

All sentences contain the same basic elements: a subject and a verb. The **subject** is who or what the sentence is about; the **verb** describes the subject's action or condition. However, these elements, subjects and verbs, can be combined in different ways. The following graphic describes the different types of sentence structures.

Sentence Structure	Independent Clauses	Dependent Clauses
Simple	1	0
Compound	2 or more	0
Complex	1	1 or more
Compound-Complex	2 or more	1 or more

A **simple sentence** expresses a complete thought and consists of one subject and verb combination:

> The children ate pizza.

The subject is *children*. The verb is *ate*.

Either the subject or the verb may be *compound*—that is, it could have more than one element:

> *The children and their parents* ate pizza.

> The children *ate pizza and watched a movie.*

All of these are still simple sentences. Despite having either compound subjects or compound verbs, each sentence still has only one subject and verb combination.

Compound sentences combine two or more simple sentences to form one sentence that has multiple subject-verb combinations:

> *The children ate pizza,* and *their parents watched a movie.*

This structure is comprised of two independent clauses: (1) *the children ate pizza* and (2) *their parents watched a movie.* Compound sentences join different subject-verb combinations using a comma and a coordinating conjunction.

> I called my mom**,** *but* she didn't answer the phone.

> The weather was stormy**,** *so* we canceled our trip to the beach.

A **complex sentence** consists of an independent clause and one or more dependent clauses. Dependent clauses join a sentence using **subordinating conjunctions**. Some examples of subordinating conjunctions are *although, unless, as soon as, since, while, when, because, if,* and *before.*

> I missed class yesterday *because* my mother was ill.

> *Before* traveling to a new country, you need to exchange your money to the local currency.

The order of clauses determines their punctuation. If the dependent clause comes first, it should be separated from the independent clause with a comma. However, if the complex sentence consists of an independent clause followed by a dependent clause, then a comma is not always necessary.

A **compound-complex sentence** can be created by joining two or more independent clauses with at least one dependent clause:

> After the earthquake struck, thousands of homes were destroyed, and many families were left without a place to live.

The first independent clause in the compound structure includes a dependent clause—*after the earthquake struck*. Thus, the structure is both complex and compound.

Understanding the Use of Affixes, Context, and Syntax

Affixes

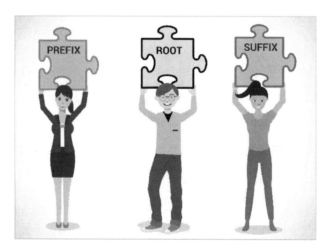

Individual words are constructed from building blocks of meaning. An **affix** is an element that is added to a root or stem word that can change the word's meaning.

For example, the stem word *fix* is a verb meaning *to repair*. When the ending *–able* is added, it becomes the adjective *fixable*, meaning "capable of being repaired." Adding *un–* to the beginning changes the word to *unfixable*, meaning "incapable of being repaired." In this way, affixes attach to the word stem to create a new word and a new meaning. Knowledge of affixes can assist in deciphering the meaning of unfamiliar words.

Affixes are also related to inflection. **Inflection** is the modification of a base word to express a different grammatical or syntactical function. For example, countable nouns such as *car* and *airport* become plural with the addition of *–s* at the end: *cars* and *airports*.

Verb tense is also expressed through inflection. **Regular verbs**—those that follow a standard inflection pattern—can be changed to past tense using the affixes *–ed*, *–d*, or *–ied*, as in *cooked* and *studied*. Verbs can also be modified for continuous tenses by using *–ing*, as in *working* or *exploring*. Thus, affixes are used not only to express meaning but also to reflect a word's grammatical purpose.

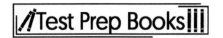

A **prefix** is an affix attached to the beginning of a word. The meanings of English prefixes mainly come from Greek and Latin origins. The chart below contains a few of the most commonly used English prefixes.

Prefix	Meaning	Example
a-	not	amoral, asymptomatic
anti-	against	antidote, antifreeze
auto-	self	automobile, automatic
circum-	around	circumference, circumspect
co-, com-, con-	together	coworker, companion
contra-	against	contradict, contrary
de-	negation or reversal	deflate, deodorant
extra-	outside, beyond	extraterrestrial, extracurricular
in-, im-, il-, ir-	not	impossible, irregular
inter-	between	international, intervene
intra-	within	intramural, intranet
mis-	wrongly	mistake, misunderstand
mono-	one	monolith, monopoly
non-	not	nonpartisan, nonsense
pre-	before	preview, prediction
re-	again	review, renew
semi-	half	semicircle, semicolon
sub-	under	subway, submarine
super-	above	superhuman, superintendent
trans-	across, beyond, through	trans-Siberian, transform
un-	not	unwelcome, unfriendly

133

While the addition of a prefix alters the meaning of the base word, the addition of a **suffix** may also affect a word's part of speech. For example, adding a suffix can change the noun *material* into the verb *materialize* and back to a noun again in *materialization*.

Suffix	Part of Speech	Meaning	Example
-able, -ible	adjective	having the ability to	honorable, flexible
-acy, -cy	noun	state or quality	intimacy, dependency
-al, -ical	adjective	having the quality of	historical, tribal
-en	verb	to cause to become	strengthen, embolden
-er, -ier	adjective	comparative	happier, longer
-est, -iest	adjective	superlative	sunniest, hottest
-ess	noun	female	waitress, actress
-ful	adjective	full of, characterized by	beautiful, thankful
-fy, -ify	verb	to cause, to come to be	liquefy, intensify
-ism	noun	doctrine, belief, action	Communism, Buddhism
-ive, -ative, -itive	adjective	having the quality of	creative, innovative
-ize	verb	to convert into, to subject to	Americanize, dramatize
-less	adjective	without, missing	emotionless, hopeless
-ly	adverb	in the manner of	quickly, energetically
-ness	noun	quality or state	goodness, darkness
-ous, -ious, -eous	adjective	having the quality of	spontaneous, pious
-ship	noun	status or condition	partnership, ownership
-tion	noun	action or state	renovation, promotion
-y	adjective	characterized by	smoky, dreamy

Through knowledge of prefixes and suffixes, a student's vocabulary can be instantly expanded with an understanding of **etymology**—the origin of words. This, in turn, can be used to add sentence structure variety to academic writing.

Context Clues

Familiarity with common prefixes, suffixes, and root words assists tremendously in unraveling the meaning of an unfamiliar word and making an educated guess as to its meaning. However, some words do not contain many easily-identifiable clues that point to their meaning. In this case, rather than looking at the elements within the word, it is useful to consider elements around the word—i.e., its context. **Context** refers to the other words and information within the sentence or surrounding sentences that indicate the unknown word's probable meaning. The following sentences provide context for the potentially-unfamiliar word *quixotic*:

> Rebecca had never been one to settle into a predictable, ordinary life. Her quixotic personality led her to leave behind a job with a prestigious law firm in Manhattan and move halfway around the world to pursue her dream of becoming a sushi chef in Tokyo.

A reader unfamiliar with the word *quixotic* doesn't have many clues to use in terms of affixes or root meaning. The suffix *–ic* indicates that the word is an adjective, but that is it. In this case, then, a reader would need to look at surrounding information to obtain some clues about the word. Other adjectives in

134

the passage include *predictable* and *ordinary*, things that Rebecca was definitely not, as indicated by "Rebecca had never been one to settle." Thus, a first clue might be that *quixotic* means the opposite of predictable.

The second sentence doesn't offer any other modifier of *personality* other than *quixotic*, but it does include a story that reveals further information about her personality. She had a stable, respectable job, but she decided to give it up to follow her dream. Combining these two ideas together, then—unpredictable and dream-seeking—gives the reader a general idea of what *quixotic* probably means. In fact, the root of the word is the character Don Quixote, a romantic dreamer who goes on an impulsive adventure.

While context clues are useful for making an approximate definition for newly-encountered words, these types of clues also come in handy when encountering common words that have multiple meanings. The word *reservation* is used differently in each the following sentences:

A. That restaurant is booked solid for the next month; it's impossible to make a reservation unless you know somebody.

B. The hospital plans to open a branch office inside the reservation to better serve Native American patients who cannot easily travel to the main hospital fifty miles away.

C. Janet Clark is a dependable, knowledgeable worker, and I recommend her for the position of team leader without reservation.

All three sentences use the word to express different meanings. In fact, most words in English have more than one meaning—sometimes meanings that are completely different from one another. Thus, context can provide clues as to which meaning is appropriate in a given situation. A quick search in the dictionary reveals several possible meanings for *reservation*:

1. An exception or qualification
2. A tract of public land set aside, such as for the use of American Indian tribes
3. An arrangement for accommodations, such as in a hotel, on a plane, or at a restaurant

Sentence A mentions a restaurant, making the third definition the correct one in this case. In sentence B, some context clues include Native Americans, as well as the implication that a reservation is a place—"inside the reservation," both of which indicate that the second definition should be used here. Finally, sentence C uses *without reservation* to mean "completely" or "without exception," so the first definition can be applied here.

Using context clues in this way can be especially useful for words that have multiple, widely varying meanings. If a word has more than one definition and two of those definitions are the opposite of each other, it is known as an **auto-antonym**—a word that can also be its own antonym. In the case of auto-antonyms, context clues are crucial to determine which definition to employ in a given sentence. For example, the word *sanction* can either mean "to approve or allow" or "a penalty." Approving and penalizing have opposite meanings, so *sanction* is an example of an auto-antonym. The following sentences reflect the distinction in meaning:

A. In response to North Korea's latest nuclear weapons test, world leaders have called for harsher sanctions to punish the country for its actions.

B. The general has sanctioned a withdrawal of troops from the area.

A context clue can be found in sentence A, which mentions "to punish." A punishment is similar to a penalty, so sentence A is using the word *sanction* according to this definition.

Other examples of auto-antonyms include *oversight*—"to supervise something" or "a missed detail"), *resign*—"to quit" or "to sign again, as a contract," and *screen*—"to show" or "to conceal." For these types of words, recognizing context clues is an important way to avoid misinterpreting the sentence's meaning.

Syntax

Syntax refers to the arrangement of words, phrases, and clauses to form a sentence. Knowledge of syntax can also give insight into a word's meaning. The section above considered several examples using the word *reservation* and applied context clues to determine the word's appropriate meaning in each sentence. Here is an example of how the placement of a word can impact its meaning and grammatical function:

A. The development team has reserved the conference room for today.

B. Her quiet and reserved nature is sometimes misinterpreted as unfriendliness when people first meet her.

In addition to using *reserved* to mean different things, each sentence also uses the word to serve a different grammatical function. In sentence A, *reserved* is part of the verb phrase *has reserved*, indicating the meaning "to set aside for a particular use." In sentence B, *reserved* acts as a modifier within the noun phrase "her quiet and reserved nature." Because the word is being used as an adjective to describe a personality characteristic, it calls up a different definition of the word—"restrained or lacking familiarity with others." As this example shows, the function of a word within the overall sentence structure can allude to its meaning. It is also useful to refer to the earlier chart about suffixes and parts of speech as another clue into what grammatical function a word is serving in a sentence.

Analyzing Nuances of Word Meaning and Figures of Speech

By now, it should be apparent that language is not as simple as one word directly correlated to one meaning. Rather, one word can express a vast array of diverse meanings, and similar meanings can be expressed through different words. However, there are very few words that express exactly the same meaning. For this reason, it is important to be able to pick up on the nuances of word meaning.

Many words contain two levels of meaning: connotation and denotation as discussed previously in the informational texts and rhetoric section. A word's **denotation** is its most literal meaning—the definition that can readily be found in the dictionary. A word's **connotation** includes all of its emotional and cultural associations.

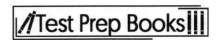

In literary writing, authors rely heavily on connotative meaning to create mood and characterization. The following are two descriptions of a rainstorm:

- The rain slammed against the windowpane, and the wind howled through the fireplace. A pair of hulking oaks next to the house cast eerie shadows as their branches trembled in the wind.

- The rain pattered against the windowpane, and the wind whistled through the fireplace. A pair of stately oaks next to the house cast curious shadows as their branches swayed in the wind.

Description A paints a creepy picture for readers with strongly emotional words like *slammed*, connoting force and violence. *Howled* connotes pain or wildness, and *eerie* and *trembled* connote fear. Overall, the connotative language in this description serves to inspire fear and anxiety.

However, as can be seen in description B, swapping out a few key words for those with different connotations completely changes the feeling of the passage. *Slammed* is replaced with the more cheerful *pattered*, and *hulking* has been swapped out for *stately*. Both words imply something large, but *hulking* is more intimidating whereas *stately* is more respectable. *Curious* and *swayed* seem more playful than the language used in the earlier description. Although both descriptions represent roughly the same situation, the nuances of the emotional language used throughout the passages create a very different sense for readers.

Selective choice of connotative language can also be extremely impactful in other forms of writing, such as editorials or persuasive texts. Through connotative language, writers reveal their biases and opinions while trying to inspire feelings and actions in readers:

1. Parents won't stop complaining about standardized tests.
2. Parents continue to raise concerns about standardized tests.

Readers should be able to identify the nuance in meaning between these two sentences. The first one carries a more negative feeling, implying that parents are being bothersome or whiny. Readers of the second sentence, though, might come away with the feeling that parents are concerned and involved in their children's education. Again, the aggregate of even subtle cues can combine to give a specific emotional impression to readers, so from an early age, students should be aware of how language can be used to influence readers' opinions.

Another form of non-literal expression can be found in **figures of speech**. As with connotative language, figures of speech tend to be shared within a cultural group and may be difficult to pick up on for learners outside of that group. In some cases, a figure of speech may be based on the literal denotation of the words it contains, but in other cases, a figure of speech is far removed from its literal meaning. A case in point is **irony**, where what is said is the exact opposite of what is meant:

The new tax plan is poorly planned, based on faulty economic data, and unable to address the financial struggles of middle class families. Yet legislators remain committed to passing this brilliant proposal.

When the writer refers to the proposal as brilliant, the opposite is implied—the plan is "faulty" and "poorly planned." By using irony, the writer means that the proposal is anything but brilliant by using the word in a non-literal sense.

Another figure of speech is **hyperbole**—extreme exaggeration or overstatement. Statements like, "I love you to the moon and back" or "Let's be friends for a million years" utilize hyperbole to convey a greater depth of emotion, without literally committing oneself to space travel or a life of immortality.

Figures of speech may sometimes use one word in place of another. **Synecdoche**, for example, uses a part of something to refer to its whole. The expression "Don't hurt a hair on her head!" implies protecting more than just an individual hair, but rather her entire body. "The art teacher is training a class of Picassos" uses Picasso, one individual notable artist, to stand in for the entire category of talented artists. Another figure of speech using word replacement is **metonymy**, where a word is replaced with something closely associated to it. For example, news reports may use the word "Washington" to refer to the American government or "the crown" to refer to the British monarch.

Supporting and Illustrating Arguments and Explanations

Identifying Details that Develop a Main Idea

The main idea of a piece is the central topic or theme. To identify the main idea, a reader should consider these questions: "What's the point? What does the author want readers to take away from this text?" Everything within the selection should relate back to the main idea because it is the center of the organizational web of any written work. Particularly in articles and reports, the main idea often appears within the opening paragraphs to orient the reader to what the author wants to say about the subject. A sentence that expresses the main idea is known as a thesis sentence or **thesis statement**.

After the main idea has been introduced, **supporting details** are what develop the main idea—they make up the bulk of the work. Without supporting details, the main idea would simply be a statement, so additional details are needed to give that statement weight and validity. Supporting details can often be identified by recognizing the key words that introduce them. The following example offers several supporting details, with key words underlined:

> Man did not evolve from apes. Though we share a common ancestor, humans and apes originated through very different evolutionary paths. There are several reasons why this is true. The <u>first</u> reason is that, logically, if humans evolved from apes, modern-day apes and humans would not coexist. Evolution occurs when a genetic mutation in a species ensures the survival over the rest of the species, allowing them to pass on their genes and create a new lineage of organisms. <u>Another</u> reason is that hominid fossils only fall into one of two categories—ape-like or human-like—and there are very strong differences between the two. Australopithecines, the hominid fossils originally believed to be ancestral to humans, are ape-like, indicated by their long arms, long and curved fingers, and funnel-shaped chests. Their hand bones suggest that they "knuckle-walked" like modern day chimpanzees and gorillas, something not found in *Homo sapien* fossils. <u>Finally</u>, there is no fossilized evidence to suggest a transition between the ape-like ancestor and the *Homo sapien*, indicating that a sudden mutation may have been responsible. These and many other reasons are indicative that humans and ape-like creatures are evolutionarily different.

The underlined words—*first, another,* and *finally*—are the key words that identify the supporting details. These details can be summarized as follows:

138

- Humans and apes could not coexist.
- Human-like and ape-like fossils are very different.
- No transition is seen between humans and ape-like ancestors.

The supporting details all relate to the central idea that "Man did not evolve from apes," which is the first sentence of the paragraph.

Even though supporting details are more specific than the main idea, they should nevertheless all be directly related to the main idea. Without sufficient supporting details, the writer's main idea will be too weak to be effective.

Developing and Maintaining Style and Tone

Style, Tone, and Mood

Style, *tone*, and *mood* are often thought to be the same thing. Though they're closely related, there are important differences to keep in mind. The easiest way to do this is to remember that style "creates and affects" tone and mood. More specifically, style is *how the writer uses words* to create the desired tone and mood for their writing.

Style
Style can include any number of technical writing choices, and some may have to be analyzed on the test. A few examples of style choices include:

- Sentence Construction: When presenting facts, does the writer use shorter sentences to create a quicker sense of the supporting evidence, or do they use longer sentences to elaborate and explain the information?

- Technical Language: Does the writer use jargon to demonstrate their expertise in the subject, or do they use ordinary language to help the reader understand things in simple terms?

- Formal Language: Does the writer refrain from using contractions such as won't or can't to create a more formal tone, or do they use a colloquial, conversational style to connect to the reader?

- Formatting: Does the writer use a series of shorter paragraphs to help the reader follow a line of argument, or do they use longer paragraphs to examine an issue in great detail and demonstrate their knowledge of the topic?

On the test, examine the writer's style and how their writing choices affect the way the passage comes across.

Tone
Tone refers to the writer's attitude toward the subject matter. Tone is usually explained in terms of a work of fiction. For example, the tone conveys how the writer feels about their characters and the situations in which they're involved. Nonfiction writing is sometimes thought to have no tone at all, but this is incorrect.

A lot of nonfiction writing has a neutral tone, which is an extremely important tone for the writer to take. A neutral tone demonstrates that the writer is presenting a topic impartially and letting the information speak for itself. On the other hand, nonfiction writing can be just as effective and appropriate if the tone isn't neutral. For instance, take the previous examples involving seat belt use. In them, the writer mostly chooses to retain a neutral tone when presenting information. If the writer would instead include their own personal experience of losing a friend or family member in a car accident, the tone would change dramatically. The tone would no longer be neutral. Now it would show that the writer has a personal stake in the content, allowing them to interpret the information in a different way. When analyzing tone, consider what the writer is trying to achieve in the passage, and how they *create* the tone using style.

Mood

Mood refers to the feelings and atmosphere that the writer's words create for the reader. Like tone, many nonfiction pieces can have a neutral mood. To return to the previous example, if the writer would choose to include information about a person they know being killed in a car accident, the passage would suddenly carry an emotional component that is absent in the previous examples. Depending on how they present the information, the writer can create a sad, angry, or even hopeful mood. When analyzing the mood, consider what the writer wants to accomplish and whether the best choice was made to achieve that end.

Consistency

Whatever style, tone, and mood the writer uses, good writing should remain *consistent* throughout. If the writer chooses to include the tragic, personal experience above, it would affect the style, tone, and mood of the entire piece. It would seem out of place for such an example to be used in the middle of a neutral, measured, and analytical piece. To adjust the rest of the piece, the writer needs to make additional choices to remain consistent. For example, the writer might decide to use the word *tragedy* in place of the more neutral *fatality*, or they could describe a series of car-related deaths as an *epidemic*. Adverbs and adjectives such as *devastating* or *horribly* could be included to maintain this consistent attitude toward the content. When analyzing writing, look for sudden shifts in style, tone, and mood, and consider whether the writer would be wiser to maintain the prevailing strategy.

Synthesizing Information from Multiple Sources

Evaluation of Sources

Identifying Relevant Information During Research

Relevant information is that which is pertinent to the topic at hand. Particularly when doing research online, it is easy for students to get overwhelmed with the wealth of information available to them. Before conducting research, then, students need to begin with a clear idea of the question they want to answer.

For example, a student may be interested in learning more about marriage practices in Jane Austen's England. If that student types "marriage" into a search engine, he or she will have to sift through thousands of unrelated sites before finding anything related to that topic. Narrowing down search parameters can aid in locating relevant information.

When using a book, students can consult the table of contents, glossary, or index to discover whether the book contains relevant information before using it as a resource. If the student finds a hefty volume on Jane Austen, he or she can flip to the index in the back, look for the word marriage, and find out how many page references are listed in the book. If there are few or no references to the subject, it is probably not a relevant or useful source.

In evaluating research articles, students may also consult the title, abstract, and keywords before reading the article in its entirety. Referring to the date of publication will also determine whether the research contains up-to-date discoveries, theories, and ideas about the subject, or whether it is outdated.

Evaluating the Credibility of a Print or Digital Source

There are several additional criteria that need to be examined before using a source for a research topic.

The following questions will help determine whether a source is credible:

Author
- Who is he or she?
- Does he or she have the appropriate credentials—e.g., M.D, PhD?
- Is this person authorized to write on the matter through their job or personal experiences?
- Is he or she affiliated with any known credible individuals or organizations?
- Has he or she written anything else?

Publisher
- Who published/produced the work? Is it a well-known journal, like National Geographic, or a tabloid, like The National Enquirer?
- Is the publisher from a scholarly, commercial, or government association?
- Do they publish works related to specific fields?
- Have they published other works?
- If a digital source, what kind of website hosts the text? Does it end in .edu, .org, or .com?

Bias
- Is the writing objective? Does it contain any loaded or emotional language?
- Does the publisher/producer have a known bias, such as Fox News or CNN?
- Does the work include diverse opinions or perspectives?
- Does the author have any known bias—e.g., Michael Moore, Bill O'Reilly, or the Pope? Is he or she affiliated with any organizations or individuals that may have a known bias—e.g., Citizens United or the National Rifle Association?
- Does the magazine, book, journal, or website contain any advertising?

References
- Are there any references?
- Are the references credible? Do they follow the same criteria as stated above?
- Are the references from a related field?
- Accuracy/reliability
- Has the article, book, or digital source been peer reviewed?
- Are all of the conclusions, supporting details, or ideas backed with published evidence?

- If a digital source, is it free of grammatical errors, poor spelling, and improper English?
- Do other published individuals have similar findings?

Coverage
- Are the topic and related material both successfully addressed?
- Does the work add new information or theories to those of their sources?
- Is the target audience appropriate for the intended purpose?

Integrating Multiple Sources and Formats of Information

Students should be able to solve problems and make decisions through the use of multiple informational sources. It is important for students to be able to analyze sources for credibility and relevance, evaluate them for any bias or inaccuracies, and ultimately synthesize them to generate an answer or make a decision. The more diverse the sources, the more comprehensive the answer or decision will be. One area where this is especially important is in Internet research. Students must be able to discern between many sources and choose the most reliable information to integrate. One way for students to glean an answer from multiple sources is through cross-referencing. When a fact is repeated in many credible sources, especially a variety of different types of sources, it can generally be accepted as true. Students should also know the criteria for evaluating a source's credibility, such as author credentials, peer-reviewed status, and timeliness of the information. As other media become more prevalent, such as videos and social media posts, students must also be able to identify what makes these types of sources credible and how to integrate them with more traditional sources.

Integrating Information from Source Material

It can be daunting to integrate so many sources into a research paper while still maintaining fluency and coherency. Most source material is incorporated in the form of quotations or paraphrases, while citing the source at the end of their respective references. There are several guidelines to consider when integrating a source into writing:

- The piece should be written in the author's voice. Quotations, especially long ones, should be limited and spaced evenly throughout the paper.

- All paragraphs should begin with the author's own words and end with their own words; quotations should never start or end a paragraph.

- Quotations and paraphrases should be used to emphasize a point, give weight to an idea, and validate a claim.

- Supporting evidence should be introduced in a sentence or paragraph, and then explained afterwards: *According to Waters (1979)* [signal phrase], *"All in all, we're just another brick in the wall" (p.24). The wall suggests that people are becoming more alienated, and the bricks symbolize a paradoxical connection to that alienation* [Explanation].

- When introducing a source for the first time, the author's name and a smooth transition should be included: *In Pink Floyd's groundbreaking album The Wall, Roger Waters argues that society is causing people to become more alienated.*

142

- There should be an even balance between quotations and paraphrases.

- Quotations or paraphrases should never be taken out of context in a way that alters the original author's intent.

- Quotations should be syntactically and grammatically integrated.

- Quotations should not simply be copied and pasted in the paper, rather, they should be introduced into a paper with natural transitions.

- As argued in Johnson's article…

- Evidence of this point can be found in Johnson's article, where she asserts that…

- The central argument of John's article is…

Quantitative Information

Some writing in the test contains **infographics** such as charts, tables, or graphs. In these cases, interpret the information presented and determine how well it supports the claims made in the text. For example, if the writer makes a case that seat belts save more lives than other automobile safety measures, they might want to include a graph (like the one below) showing the number of lives saved by seat belts versus those saved by air bags.

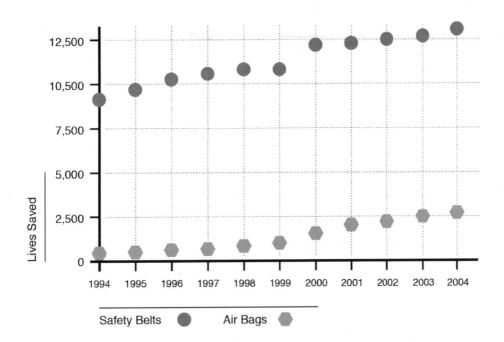

Based on data from the National Highway Traffic Safety Administration

If the graph clearly shows a higher number of lives are saved by seat belts, then it's effective. However, if the graph shows air bags save more lives than seat belts, then it doesn't support the writer's case.

Finally, graphs should be easy to understand. Their information should immediately be clear to the reader at a glance. Here are some basic things to keep in mind when interpreting infographics:

- In a **bar graph**, higher bars represent larger numbers. Lower bars represent smaller numbers.

- **Line graphs** often show trends over time. Points that are higher represent larger numbers than points that are lower. A line that consistently ascends from left to right shows a steady increase over time. A line that consistently descends from left to right shows a steady decrease over time. A line that bounces up and down represents instability or inconsistency in the trend. When interpreting a line graph, determine the point the writer is trying to make, and then see if the graph supports that point.

- **Pie charts** *are used to show proportions or percentages of a whole but are less effective in showing change over time.*

- **Tables** present information in numerical form, not as graphics. When interpreting a table, make sure to look for patterns in the numbers.

There can also be timelines, illustrations, or maps on the test. When interpreting these, keep in mind the writer's intentions and determine whether or not the graphic supports the case.

Conveying Complex Information Clearly and Coherently

Using Clear and Coherent Writing

Organizing a Text Clearly and Coherently
There are five basic elements inherent in effective writing, and each will be discussed throughout the various subheadings of this section.

- **Main idea**: The driving message of the writing, clearly stated or implied

- **Clear organization**: The effective and purposeful arrangement of the content to support the main idea

- **Supporting details/evidence**: Content that gives appropriate depth and weight to the main idea of the story, argument, or information

- **Diction/tone**: The type of language, vocabulary, and word choice used to express the main idea, purposefully aligned to the audience and purpose

- **Adherence to conventions of English**: Correct spelling, grammar, punctuation, and sentence structure, allowing for clear communication of ideas

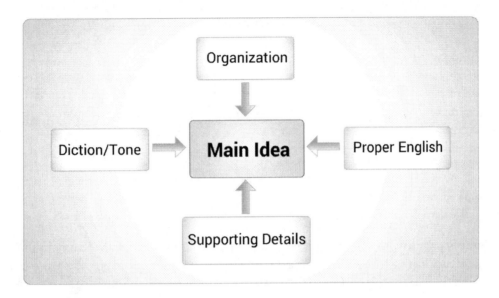

Using Varied and Effective Transitions

Transitions are the glue that holds the writing together. They function to purposefully incorporate new topics and supporting details in a smooth and coherent way. Usually, transitions are found at the beginnings of sentences, but they can also be located in the middle as a way to link clauses together. There are two types of clauses: independent and dependent.

Transition words connect clauses within and between sentences for smoother writing. "I dislike apples. They taste like garbage." is choppier than "I dislike apples because they taste like garbage." Transitions demonstrate the relationship between ideas, allow for more complex sentence structures, and can alert the reader to which type of organizational format the author is using. For example, the above selection on human evolution uses the words *first, another*, and *finally* to indicate that the writer will be listing the reasons why humans and apes are evolutionarily different.

Sophisticated writing also aims to avoid overuse of transitions and ensure that those used are meaningful. Using a variety of transitions makes the writing appear more lively and informed and helps readers follow the progression of ideas.

Justifying Stylistic Choices

Stylistic choices refer to elements such as a writer's diction, sentence structure, and use of figurative language. A writer's **diction** is their word choice and may be elevated, academic, conversational, humorous, or any other style. The choice of diction depends on the purpose of a piece of writing. A textbook or a research paper is likely to use academic diction whereas a blog post will use more conversational expressions.

Sentence structure also affects an author's writing style. Will he or she use short, staccato sentences or longer sentences with complex structure? Effective writing tends to incorporate both styles to increase reader interest or to punctuate ideas.

Figurative language includes the use of simile, metaphor, hyperbole, or allusion, to name but a few examples. Creative or descriptive writing is likely to incorporate more non-literal expressions than academic or informative writing will. Instructors should allow students to experiment with different styles of writing and understand how style affects expression and understanding.

Introducing, Developing, and Concluding a Text Effectively

Almost all coherent written works contain three primary parts: a beginning, middle, and end. The organizational arrangements differ widely across distinct writing modes. Persuasive and expository texts utilize an introduction, body, and conclusion whereas narrative works use an orientation, series of events/conflict, and a resolution.

Every element within a written piece relates back to the main idea, and the beginning of a persuasive or expository text generally conveys the main idea or the purpose. For a narrative piece, the beginning is the section that acquaints the reader with the characters and setting, directing them to the purpose of the writing. The main idea in narrative may be implied or addressed at the end of the piece.

Depending on the primary purpose, the arrangement of the middle will adhere to one of the basic organizational structures described in the information texts and rhetoric section. They are cause and effect, problem and solution, compare and contrast, description/spatial, sequence, and order of importance.

The ending of a text is the metaphorical wrap-up of the writing. A solid ending is crucial for effective writing as it ties together loose ends, resolves the action, highlights the main points, or repeats the central idea. A conclusion ensures that readers come away from a text understanding the author's main idea. The table below highlights the important characteristics of each part of a piece of writing.

Structure	Argumentative/Informative	Narrative
Beginning	Introduction *Purpose, main idea*	Orientation *Introduces characters, setting, necessary background*
Middle	Body *Supporting details, reasons and evidence*	Events/Conflict *Story's events that revolve around a central conflict*
End	Conclusion *Highlights main points, summarizes and paraphrases ideas, reiterates the main idea*	Resolution *The solving of the central conflict*

Conciseness

"Less is more" is a good rule to follow when writing a sentence. Unfortunately, writers often include extra words and phrases that seem necessary at the time but add nothing to the main idea. This confuses the reader and creates unnecessary repetition. Writing that lacks *conciseness* is usually guilty of excessive wordiness and redundant phrases. Here's an example containing both of these issues:

> When legislators decided to begin creating legislation making it mandatory for automobile drivers and passengers to make use of seat belts while in cars, a large number of them made those laws for reasons that were political reasons.

146

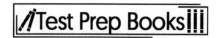

There are several empty or "fluff" words here that take up too much space. These can be eliminated while still maintaining the writer's meaning. For example:

- "decided to begin" could be shortened to "began"
- "making it mandatory for" could be shortened to "requiring"
- "make use of" could be shortened to "use"
- "a large number" could be shortened to "many"

In addition, there are several examples of redundancy that can be eliminated:

- "legislators decided to begin creating legislation" and "made those laws"
- "automobile drivers and passengers" and "while in cars"
- "reasons that were political reasons"

These changes are incorporated as follows:

> When legislators began requiring drivers and passengers to use seat belts, many of them did so for political reasons.

There are many examples of redundant phrases, such as "add an additional," "complete and total," "time schedule," and "transportation vehicle." If asked to identify a redundant phrase on the test, look for words that are close together with the same (or similar) meanings.

Citing Data, Conclusions, and Opinions of Others

Understanding Effective and Ethical Research Practices

Identifying the Components of a Citation

Citation styles vary according to which style guide is consulted. Examples of commonly-used styles include MLA, APA, and Chicago/Turabian. Each citation style includes similar components, although the order and formatting of these components varies.

MLA Style

For an **MLA style citation**, components must be included or excluded depending on the source, so writers should determine which components are applicable to the source being cited. Here are the basic components:

- Author—last name, first name
- Title of source
- Title of container—e.g., a journal title or website
- Other contributors—e.g., editor or translator
- Version
- Number
- Publisher
- Publication date
- Location—e.g., the URL or DOI
- Date of Access—optional

APA Style
The following components can be found in **APA style citations**. Components must be included or excluded depending on the source, so writers should determine which components are applicable to the source being cited.

The basic components are as follows:

- Author—last name, first initial, middle initial
- Publication date
- Title of chapter, article, or text
- Editor— last name, first initial, middle initial
- Version/volume
- Number/issue
- Page numbers
- DOI or URL
- Database—if article is difficult to locate
- City of publication
- State of publication, abbreviated
- Publisher

Chicago/Turabian Style
Chicago/Turabian style citations are also referred to as note systems and are used most frequently in the humanities and the arts. Components must be included or excluded depending on the source, so writers should determine which components are applicable to the source being cited. They contain the following elements:

- Author—last name, first name, middle initial
- Title of chapter or article—in quotation marks
- Title of source
- Editor—first name, last name
- Page numbers
- Version/volume
- Number/issue
- Page numbers
- Date of access
- DOI
- Publication location—city and state abbreviation/country
- Publisher
- Publication Date

Citing Source Material Appropriately
The following information contains examples of the common types of sources used in research as well as the formats for each citation style. First lines of citation entries are presented flush to the left margin, and second/subsequent details are presented with a hanging indent. Some examples of bibliography entries are presented below:

148

Book

- MLA

  Format: Last name, First name, Middle initial. *Title of Source*. Publisher, Publication Date.

  Example: Sampson, Maximus R. *Diaries from an Alien Invasion*. Campbell Press, 1989.

- APA

  Format: Last name, First initial, Middle initial. (Year Published) *Book Title*. City, State: Publisher.

  Example: Sampson, M. R. (1989). *Diaries from an Alien Invasion*. Springfield, IL: Campbell Press.

- Chicago/Turabian

  Format: Last name, First name, Middle initial. *Book Title*. City, State: Publisher, Year of publication.

  Example: Sampson, Maximus R. *Diaries from an Alien Invasion*. Springfield, IL: Campbell Press, 1989.

A Chapter in an Edited Book

- MLA

  Format: Last name, First name, Middle initial. "Title of Source." *Title of Container*, Other Contributors, Publisher, Publication Date, Location.

  Example: Sampson, Maximus R. "The Spaceship." *Diaries from an Alien Invasion*, edited by Allegra M. Brewer, Campbell Press, 1989, pp. 45-62.

- APA

  Format: Last name, First Initial, Middle initial. (Year Published) Chapter title. In First initial, Middle initial, Last Name (Ed.), *Book title* (pp. page numbers). City, State: Publisher.

  Example: Sampson, M. R. (1989). The Spaceship. In A. M. Brewer (Ed.), *Diaries from an Alien Invasion* (pp. 45-62). Springfield, IL: Campbell Press.

- Chicago/Turabian

  Format: Last name, First name, Middle initial. "Chapter Title." In Book Title, edited by Editor's Name (First, Middle In. Last), Page(s). City: Publisher, Year Published.

  Example: Sampson, Maximus R. "The Spaceship," in *Diaries from an Alien Invasion*, edited by Allegra M. Brewer, 45-62. Springfield: Campbell Press, 1989.

Article in a Journal

- MLA

  Format: Last name, First name, Middle initial. "Title of Source." *Title of Journal, Number, Publication* Date, Location.

  Example: Rowe, Jason R. "The Grief Monster." *Strong Living*, vol. 9, no. 9, 2016, pp 25-31.

- APA

  Format: Last name, First initial, Middle initial. (Year Published). Title of article. *Name of Journal, volume*(issue), page(s).

  Example: Rowe, J. R. (2016). The grief monster. *Strong Living, 9*(9), 25-31.

- Chicago/Turabian:

  Format: Last name, First name, Middle initial. "Title of Article." *Name of Journal* volume, issue (Year Published): Page(s).

  Example: Rowe, Jason, R. "The Grief Monster." *Strong Living* 9, no. 9 (2016): 25-31.

Page on a Website

- MLA
  Format: Last name, First name, Middle initial. "Title of Article." *Name of Website*, date published (Day Month Year), URL. Date accessed (Day Month Year).
  Example: Rowe, Jason. "The Grief Monster." *Strong Living Online*, 9 Sept. 2016. http://www.somanylosses.com/the-grief-monster/html. Accessed 13 Sept. 2016.
- APA
  Format: Last name, First initial. Middle initial. (Date Published—Year, Month Day). Page or article title. Retrieved from URL
  Example: Rowe, J. W. (2016, Sept. 9). The grief monster. Retrieved from http://www.somanylosses.com/ the-grief-monster/html
- Chicago/Turabian
  Format: Last Name, First Name, Middle initial. "Page Title." *Website Title*. Last modified Month day, year. Accessed month, day, year. URL.
  Example: Rowe, Jason. "The Grief Monster." Strong Living Online. Last modified September 9, 2016. Accessed September 13, 2016. http://www.somanylosses.com/the-grief-monster/html.

In-Text Citations

Most of the content found in a research paper will be supporting evidence that must be cited in-text, i.e., directly after the sentence that makes the statement. In-text citations contain details that correspond to the first detail in the bibliography entry—usually the author.

- MLA style - In-text citations will contain the author and the page number (if the source has page numbers) for direct quotations. Paraphrased source material may have just the author.
  - According to Johnson, liver cancer treatment is "just beyond our reach" (976).
  - The treatment of liver cancer is not within our reach, currently (Johnson).
  - The narrator opens the story with a paradoxical description: "It was the best of times, it was the worst of times" (Dickens 1).
- APA Style - In text citations will contain the author, the year of publication, and a page marker— if the source is paginated—for direct quotations. Paraphrased source material will include the author and year of publication.
  - According to Johnson (1986), liver cancer treatment is "just beyond our reach" (p. 976).
  - The treatment of liver cancer is not within our reach, currently (Johnson, 1986).
- Chicago Style - Chicago style has two approaches to in-text citation: notes and bibliography or author-date.
  - Notes – There are two options for notes: endnotes—provided in a sequential list at the end of the paper and separate from bibliography—or footnotes provided at the bottom of a page. In either case, the use of superscript indicates the citation number.
    - Johnson states that treatment of liver cancer is "just beyond our reach."[1]
    - Robert W. Johnson, Oncology in the Twenty-first Century (Kentville, Nova Scotia: Kentville Publishing, 1986), 159.
  - Author-Date – The author-date system includes the author's name, publication year, and page number.
    - Johnson states that treatment of liver cancer is "just beyond our reach" (1986, 159).

Establishing a Substantive Claim and Acknowledging Competing Arguments

Support

Once the main idea or proposition is stated, the writer attempts to prove or *support* the claim with text evidence and supporting details. Take for example the sentence, "Seat belts save lives." Though most people can't argue with this statement, its impact on the reader is much greater when supported by additional content. The writer can support this idea by:

- Providing statistics on the rate of highway fatalities alongside statistics for estimated seat belt usage.

- Explaining the science behind a car accident and what happens to a passenger who doesn't use a seat belt.

- Offering anecdotal evidence or true stories from reliable sources on how seat belts prevent fatal injuries in car crashes.

However, using only one form of supporting evidence is not nearly as effective as using a variety to support a claim. Presenting only a list of statistics can be boring to the reader, but providing a true story that's both interesting and humanizing helps. In addition, one example isn't always enough to prove the writer's larger point, so combining it with other examples is extremely effective for the writing. Thus, when reading a passage, don't just look for a single form of supporting evidence.

Another key aspect of supporting evidence is a **reliable source**. Does the writer include the source of the information? If so, is the source well known and trustworthy? Is there a potential for bias? For example, a seat belt study done by a seat belt manufacturer may have its own agenda to promote.

Conceptual and Organizational Skills

Organization

Good writing is not merely a random collection of sentences. No matter how well written, sentences must relate and coordinate appropriately to one another. If not, the writing seems random, haphazard, and disorganized. Therefore, good writing must be *organized* (where each sentence fits a larger context and relates to the sentences around it).

The writer should act as a guide, showing the reader how all the sentences fit together. Consider this example:

> Seat belts save more lives than any other automobile safety feature. Many studies show that airbags save lives as well. Not all cars have airbags. Many older cars don't. Air bags aren't entirely reliable. Studies show that in 15% of accidents, airbags don't deploy as designed. Seat belt malfunctions are extremely rare.

There's nothing wrong with any of these sentences individually, but together they're disjointed and difficult to follow. The best way for the writer to communicate information is through the use of *transition words*. Transition words and phrases tie sentences together, enabling a more natural flow.

Here is an update to the previous example using transition words. These changes make it easier to read and bring clarity to the writer's points:

> Seat belts save more lives than any other automobile safety feature. Many studies show that airbags save lives as well. However, not all cars have airbags. For instance, some older cars don't. Furthermore, air bags aren't entirely reliable. For example, studies show that in 15% of accidents, airbags don't deploy as designed. But, on the other hand, seat belt malfunctions are extremely rare.

Also, be prepared to analyze whether the writer is using the best transition word or phrase for the situation. Take this sentence for example: "As a result, seat belt malfunctions are extremely rare." This sentence doesn't make sense in the context above because the writer is trying to show the *contrast* between seat belts and airbags, not the causality.

Introducing, Developing, and Concluding a Text Effectively

Almost all coherent written works contain three primary parts: a beginning, middle, and end. The organizational arrangements differ widely across distinct writing modes. Persuasive and expository texts utilize an introduction, body, and conclusion whereas narrative works use an orientation, series of events/conflict, and a resolution.

Every element within a written piece relates back to the main idea, and the beginning of a persuasive or expository text generally conveys the main idea or the purpose. For a narrative piece, the beginning is the section that acquaints the reader with the characters and setting, directing them to the purpose of the writing. The main idea in narrative may be implied or addressed at the end of the piece.

Depending on the primary purpose, the arrangement of the middle will adhere to one of the basic organizational structures described in the information texts and rhetoric section. They are cause and effect, problem and solution, compare and contrast, description/spatial, sequence, and order of importance.

The ending of a text is the metaphorical wrap-up of the writing. A solid ending is crucial for effective writing as it ties together loose ends, resolves the action, highlights the main points, or repeats the central idea. A conclusion ensures that readers come away from a text understanding the author's main idea. The table below highlights the important characteristics of each part of a piece of writing.

Structure	Argumentative/Informative	Narrative
Beginning	Introduction *Purpose, main idea*	Orientation *Introduces characters, setting, necessary background*
Middle	Body *Supporting details, reasons and evidence*	Events/Conflict *Story's events that revolve around a central conflict*
End	Conclusion *Highlights main points, summarizes and paraphrases ideas, reiterates the main idea*	Resolution *The solving of the central conflict*

Logical Sequence

Even if the writer includes plenty of information to support their point, the writing is only effective when the information is in a logical order. **Logical sequencing** is really just common sense, but it's also an important writing technique. First, the writer should introduce the main idea, whether for a paragraph, a section, or the entire piece. Second, they should present evidence to support the main idea by using transitional language. This shows the reader how the information relates to the main idea and to the sentences around it. The writer should then take time to interpret the information, making sure necessary connections are obvious to the reader. Finally, the writer can summarize the information in a closing section.

Although most writing follows this pattern, it isn't a set rule. Sometimes writers change the order for effect. For example, the writer can begin with a surprising piece of supporting information to grab the reader's attention, and then transition to the main idea. Thus, if a passage doesn't follow the logical order, don't immediately assume it's wrong. However, most writing usually settles into a logical sequence after a nontraditional beginning.

Elements of Effective Writing

The following are characteristics that make writing readable and effective:

- Ideas
- Organization
- Voice
- Word choice
- Sentence fluency
- Proper Writing Conventions
- Presentation

153

Ideas
This refers to the content of the writing. Writers should focus on the topic shown in the picture or prompt. They should narrow down and focus their idea, remembering that they only have fifteen minutes to plan and write! Then they learn to develop the idea and choose the details that best shows the idea to others.

Organization
Many writers are inclined to jump into their writing without a clear direction for where it is going. Organization helps plan out the writing so that it's successful. Your writing should have an introduction, a body, and a conclusion.

Introduction (beginning): Writers should invite the reader into their work with a good introduction. They should restate the prompt in their own words so that readers know what they are going to read about.

Body (middle): The body is where the main thoughts and ideas are put together. Thoughtful transitions between ideas and key points help keep readers interested. Writers should create logical and purposeful sequences of ideas.

Conclusion (end): Writers should include a powerful conclusion to their piece that summarizes the information but leaves the reader with something to think about.

Voice
Voice is how the writer uses words and how they use sentence structure to sound like themselves! It shows that the writing is meaningful and that the author cares about it. It is what makes the writing uniquely the author's own. It is how the reader begins to know the author and what they "sound like."

Word Choice
The right word choice helps the author connect with their audience. If the work is narrative, the words tell a story. If the work is descriptive, the words can almost make you taste, touch, and feel what you are reading! If the work is an opinion, the words give new ideas and invite thought. Writers should choose detailed vocabulary and language that is clear and lively.

Sentence Fluency
When sentences are built to fit together and move with one another to create writing that is easy to read aloud, the author has written with fluency. Sentences and paragraphs start and stop in just the right places so that the writing moves well. Sentences should have a lot of different of structures and lengths.

Proper Writing Conventions
Writers should make their writing clear and understandable through the use of proper grammar, spelling, capitalization, and punctuation.

Presentation
Writers should try to make their work inviting to the reader. Writers show they care about their writing when it is neat and readable.

Word Choice Skills

Effective Language Use

Language can be analyzed in a variety of ways. But one of the primary ways is its effectiveness in communicating and especially convincing others.

Rhetoric is a literary technique used to make the writing (or speaking) more effective or persuasive. Rhetoric makes use of other effective language devices such as irony, metaphors, allusion, and repetition. An example of the rhetorical use of repetition would be: "Let go, I say, let go!!!".

Figures of Speech

A **figure of speech** (sometimes called an *idiom*) is a rhetorical device. It's a phrase that's not intended to be taken literally.

When the writer uses a figure of speech, their intention must be clear if it's to be used effectively. Some phrases can be interpreted in a number of ways, causing confusion for the reader. In the PSAT Writing and Language Test, questions may ask for an alternative to a problematic word or phrase. Look for clues to the writer's true intention to determine the best replacement. Likewise, some figures of speech may seem out of place in a more formal piece of writing. To show this, here is the previous seat belt example but with one slight change:

> Seat belts save more lives than any other automobile safety feature. Many studies show that airbags save lives as well. However, not all cars have airbags. For instance, some older cars don't. In addition, air bags aren't entirely reliable. For example, studies show that in 15% of accidents, airbags don't deploy as designed. But, on the other hand, seat belt malfunctions happen once in a blue moon.

Most people know that "once in a blue moon" refers to something that rarely happens. However, because the rest of the paragraph is straightforward and direct, using this figurative phrase distracts the reader. In this example, the earlier version is much more effective.

Now it's important to take a moment and review the meaning of the word *literally*. This is because it's one of the most misunderstood and misused words in the English language. *Literally* means that something is exactly what it says it is, and there can be no interpretation or exaggeration. Unfortunately, *literally* is often used for emphasis as in the following example:

> This morning, I literally couldn't get out of bed.

This sentence meant to say that the person was extremely tired and wasn't able to get up. However, the sentence can't *literally* be true unless that person was tied down to the bed, paralyzed, or affected by a strange situation that the writer (most likely) didn't intend.

Here's another example:

> I literally died laughing.

The writer tried to say that something was very funny. However, unless they're writing this from beyond the grave, it can't *literally* be true.

155

Rhetorical Fallacies

A **rhetorical fallacy** is an argument that doesn't make sense. It usually involves distracting the reader from the issue at hand in some way. There are many kinds of rhetorical fallacies. Here are just a few, along with examples of each:

- **Ad Hominem**: Makes an irrelevant attack against the person making the claim, rather than addressing the claim itself.

- Senator Wilson opposed the new seat belt legislation, but should we really listen to someone who's been divorced four times?

- **Exaggeration**: Represents an idea or person in an obviously excessive manner.

- Senator Wilson opposed the new seat belt legislation. Maybe she thinks if more people die in car accidents, it will help with overpopulation.

- **Stereotyping** (or Categorical Claim): Claims that all people of a certain group are the same in some way.

- Senator Wilson still opposes the new seat belt legislation. You know women can never admit when they're wrong.

When examining a possible rhetorical fallacy, carefully consider the point the writer is trying to make and if the argument directly relates to that point. If something feels wrong, there's a good chance that a fallacy is at play. The PERT doesn't expect the fallacy to be named using specific terms like those above. However, questions can include identifying why something is a fallacy or suggesting a sounder argument.

Syntax

Syntax is the order of words in a sentence. While most of the writing on the test has proper syntax, there may be questions on ways to vary the syntax for effectiveness. One of the easiest writing mistakes to spot is *repetitive sentence structure*. For example:

> Seat belts are important. They save lives. People don't like to use them. We have to pass seat belt laws. Then more people will wear seat belts. More lives will be saved.

What's the first thing that comes to mind when reading this example? The short, choppy, and repetitive sentences! In fact, most people notice this syntax issue more than the content itself. By combining some sentences and changing the syntax of others, the writer can create a more effective writing passage:

> Seat belts are important because they save lives. Since people don't like to use seat belts, though, more laws requiring their usage need to be passed. Only then will more people wear them and only then will more lives be saved.

Many rhetorical devices can be used to vary syntax (more than can possibly be named here). These often have intimidating names like *anadiplosis*, *metastasis*, and *paremptosis*. The test questions don't ask for definitions of these tricky techniques, but they can ask how the writer plays with the words and

156

what effect that has on the writing. For example, *anadiplosis* is when the last word (or phrase) from a sentence is used to begin the next sentence:

> Cars are driven by people. People cause accidents. Accidents cost taxpayers money.

The test doesn't ask for this technique by name but be prepared to recognize what the writer is doing and why they're using the technique in this situation. In this example, the writer is probably using *anadiplosis* to demonstrate causation.

Precision

People often think of **precision** in terms of math, but precise word choice is another key to successful writing. Since language itself is imprecise, it's important for the writer to find the exact word or words to convey the full, intended meaning of a given situation. For example:

> The number of deaths has gone down since seat belt laws started.

There are several problems with this sentence. First, the word *deaths* is too general. From the context, it's assumed that the writer is referring only to *deaths* caused by car accidents. However, without clarification, the sentence lacks impact and is probably untrue. The phrase "gone down" might be accurate, but a more precise word could provide more information and greater accuracy. Did the numbers show a slow and steady decrease of highway fatalities or a sudden drop? If the latter is true, the writer is missing a chance to make their point more dramatically. Instead of "gone down" they could substitute *plummeted*, *fallen drastically*, or *rapidly diminished* to bring the information to life. Also, the phrase "seat belt laws" is unclear. Does it refer to laws requiring cars to include seat belts or to laws requiring drivers and passengers to use them? Finally, *started* is not a strong verb. Words like *enacted* or *adopted* are more direct and make the content more real. When put together, these changes create a far more powerful sentence:

> The number of highway fatalities has plummeted since laws requiring seat belt usage were enacted.

However, it's important to note that precise word choice can sometimes be taken too far. If the writer of the sentence above takes precision to an extreme, it might result in the following:

> The incidence of high-speed, automobile accident related fatalities has decreased 75% and continued to remain at historical lows since the initial set of federal legislations requiring seat belt use were enacted in 1992.

This sentence is extremely precise, but it takes so long to achieve that precision that it suffers from a lack of clarity. Precise writing is about finding the right balance between information and flow. This is also an issue of *conciseness* (discussed in the next section).

The last thing to consider with precision is a word choice that's not only unclear or uninteresting, but also confusing or misleading. For example:

> The number of highway fatalities has become hugely lower since laws requiring seat belt use were enacted.

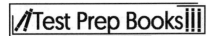

In this case, the reader might be confused by the word *hugely*. Huge means large, but here the writer uses *hugely* to describe something small. Though most readers can decipher this, doing so disconnects them from the flow of the writing and makes the writer's point less effective.

On the test, there can be questions asking for alternatives to the writer's word choice. In answering these questions, always consider the context and look for a balance between precision and flow.

Frequently Confused Words

There are a handful of words in the English language that writers often confuse with other words because they sound similar or identical. Errors involving these words are hard to spot because they *sound* right even when they're wrong. Also, because these mistakes are so pervasive, many people think they're correct. Here are a few examples that may be encountered on the test:

They're vs. Their vs. There

This set of words is probably the all-time winner of misuse. The word *they're* is a contraction of "they are." Remember that contractions combine two words, using an apostrophe to replace any eliminated letters. If a question asks whether the writer is using the word *they're* correctly, change the word to "they are" and reread the sentence. Look at the following example:

Legislators can be proud of they're work on this issue.

This sentence *sounds* correct, but replace the contraction *they're* with "they are" to see what happens:

Legislators can be proud of they are work on this issue.

The result doesn't make sense, which shows that it's an incorrect use of the word *they're*. Did the writer mean to use the word *their* instead? The word *their* indicates possession because it shows that something *belongs* to something else. Now put the word *their* into the sentence:

Legislators can be proud of their work on this issue.

To check the answer, find the word that comes right after the word *their* (which in this case is *work*). Pose this question: whose *work* is it? If the question can be answered in the sentence, then the word signifies possession. In the sentence above, it's the legislators' work. Therefore, the writer is using the word *their* correctly.

If the words *they're* and *their* don't make sense in the sentence, then the correct word is almost always *there*. The word *there* can be used in many different ways, so it's easy to remember to use it when *they're* and *their* don't work. Now test these methods with the following sentences:

Their going to have a hard time passing these laws.

Enforcement officials will have there hands full.

They're are many issues to consider when discussing car safety.

In the first sentence, asking the question "Whose going is it?" doesn't make sense. Thus the word *their* is wrong. However, when replaced with the conjunction *they're* (or *they are*), the sentence works. Thus the correct word for the first sentence should be *they're*.

158

In the second sentence, ask this question: "Whose hands are full?" The answer (*enforcement officials*) is correct in the sentence. Therefore, the word *their* should replace *there* in this sentence.

In the third sentence, changing the word *they're* to "they are" ("They are are many issues") doesn't make sense. Ask this question: "Whose are is it?" This makes even less sense, since neither of the words *they're* or *their* makes sense. Therefore, the correct word must be *there*.

Who's vs. Whose

Who's is a contraction of "who is" while the word *whose* indicates possession. Look at the following sentence:

> Who's job is it to protect America's drivers?

The easiest way to check for correct usage is to replace the word *who's* with "who is" and see if the sentence makes sense:

> Who is job is it to protect America's drivers?

By changing the contraction to "Who is" the sentence no longer makes sense. Therefore, the correct word must be *whose*.

Your vs. You're

The word *your* indicates possession, while *you're* is a contraction for "you are." Look at the following example:

> Your going to have to write your congressman if you want to see action.

Again, the easiest way to check correct usage is to replace the word *Your* with "You are" and see if the sentence still makes sense.

> You are going to have to write your congressman if you want to see action.

By replacing Your with "You are," the sentence still makes sense. Thus, in this case, the writer should have used "You're."

Its vs. It's

Its is a word that indicates possession, while the word *it's* is a contraction of "it is." Once again, the easiest way to check for correct usage is to replace the word with "it is" and see if the sentence makes sense. Look at the following sentence:

> It's going to take a lot of work to pass this law.

Replacing *it's* with "it is" results in this: "It is going to take a lot of work to pass this law." This makes sense, so the contraction (*it's*) is correct. Now look at another example:

> The car company will have to redesign it's vehicles.

Replacing *it's* with "it is" results in this: "The car company will have to redesign it is vehicles." This sentence doesn't make sense, so the contraction (*it's*) is incorrect.

Than vs. Then

Than is used in sentences that involve comparisons, while *then* is used to indicate an order of events. Consider the following sentence:

> Japan has more traffic fatalities than the U.S.

The use of the word *than* is correct because it compares Japan to the U.S. Now look at another example:

> Laws must be passed, and then we'll see a change in behavior.

Here the use of the word *then* is correct because one thing happens after the other.

Affect vs. Effect

Affect is a verb that means to change something, while *effect* is a noun that indicates such a change. Look at the following sentence:

> There are thousands of people affected by the new law.

This sentence is correct because *affected* is a verb that tells what's happening. Now look at this sentence:

> The law will have a dramatic effect.

This sentence is also correct because *effect* is a noun and the thing that happens.

Note that a noun version of *affect* is occasionally used. It means "emotion" or "desire," usually in a psychological sense.

Two vs. Too vs. To

Two is the number (2). *Too* refers to an amount of something, or it can mean *also*. *To* is used for everything else. Look at the following sentence:

> Two senators still haven't signed the bill.

This is correct because there are *two* (2) senators. Here's another example:

> There are too many questions about this issue.

In this sentence, the word *too* refers to an amount ("too many questions"). Now here's another example:

> Senator Wilson is supporting this legislation, too.

In this sentence, the word *also* can be substituted for the word *too*, so it's also correct. Finally, one last example:

> I look forward to signing this bill into law.

In this sentence, the tests for *two* and *too* don't work. Thus the word *to* fits the bill!

Other Common Writing Confusions

In addition to all of the above, there are other words that writers often misuse. This doesn't happen because the words sound alike, but because the writer is not aware of the proper way to use them.

Logical Comparison

Writers often make comparisons in their writing. However, it's easy to make mistakes in sentences that involve comparisons, and those mistakes are difficult to spot. Try to find the error in the following sentence:

> Senator Wilson's proposed seat belt legislation was similar to Senator Abernathy.

Can't find it? First, ask what two things are actually being compared. It seems like the writer *wants* to compare two different types of legislation, but the sentence actually compares legislation ("Senator Wilson's proposed seat belt legislation") to a person ("Senator Abernathy"). This is a strange and illogical comparison to make.

So how can the writer correct this mistake? The answer is to make sure that the second half of the sentence logically refers back to the first half. The most obvious way to do this is to repeat words:

> Senator Wilson's proposed seat belt legislation was similar to Senator Abernathy's seat belt legislation.

Now the sentence is logically correct, but it's a little wordy and awkward. A better solution is to eliminate the word-for-word repetition by using suitable replacement words:

> Senator Wilson's proposed seat belt legislation was similar to that of Senator Abernathy.

> Senator Wilson's proposed seat belt legislation was similar to the bill offered by Senator Abernathy.

Here's another similar example:

> More lives in the U.S. are saved by seat belts than Japan.

The writer probably means to compare lives saved by seat belts in the U.S. to lives saved by seat belts in Japan. Unfortunately, the sentence's meaning is garbled by an illogical comparison, and instead refers to U.S. lives saved *by Japan* rather than *in Japan*. To resolve this issue, first repeat the words and phrases needed to make an identical comparison:

> More lives in the U.S. are saved by seat belts than lives in Japan are saved by seat belts.

Then, use a replacement word to clean up the repetitive text:

> More lives in the U.S. are saved by seat belts than in Japan.

161

Sentence Structure Skills

Sentence Structure

Fragments and Run-Ons

A **sentence fragment** is a failed attempt to create a complete sentence because it's missing a required noun or verb. Fragments don't function properly because there isn't enough information to understand the writer's intended meaning. For example:

> Seat belt use corresponds to a lower rate of hospital visits, reducing strain on an already overburdened healthcare system. Insurance claims as well.

Look at the last sentence: *Insurance claims as well*. What does this mean? This is a fragment because it has a noun but no verb, and it leaves the reader guessing what the writer means about insurance claims. Many readers can probably infer what the writer means, but this distracts them from the flow of the writer's argument. Choosing a suitable replacement for a sentence fragment may be one of the questions on the test. The fragment is probably related to the surrounding content, so look at the overall point the writer is trying to make and choose the answer that best fits that idea.

Remember that sometimes a fragment can *look* like a complete sentence or have all the nouns and verbs it needs to make sense. Consider the following two examples:

> Seat belt use corresponds to a lower rate of hospital visits.

> Although seat belt use corresponds to a lower rate of hospital visits.

Both examples above have nouns and verbs, but only the first sentence is correct. The second sentence is a fragment, even though it's actually longer. The key is the writer's use of the word *although*. Starting a sentence with *although* turns that part into a *subordinate clause* (more on that next). Keep in mind that one doesn't have to remember that it's called a subordinate clause on the test. Just be able to recognize that the words form an incomplete thought and identify the problem as a sentence fragment.

A *run-on sentence* is, in some ways, the opposite of a fragment. It contains two or more sentences that have been improperly forced together into one. An example of a run-on sentence looks something like this:

> Seat belt use corresponds to a lower rate of hospital visits it also leads to fewer insurance claims.

Here, there are two separate ideas in one sentence. It's difficult for the reader to follow the writer's thinking because there is no transition from one idea to the next. On the test, choose the best way to correct the run-on sentence.

Here are two possibilities for the sentence above:

> Seat belt use corresponds to a lower rate of hospital visits. It also leads to fewer insurance claims.

162

Seat belt use corresponds to a lower rate of hospital visits, but it also leads to fewer insurance claims.

Both solutions are grammatically correct, so which one is the best choice? That depends on the point that the writer is trying to make. Always read the surrounding text to determine what the writer wants to demonstrate, and choose the option that best supports that thought.

Subordination and Coordination

With terms like "coordinate clause" and "subordinating conjunction," grammar terminology can scare people! So, just for a minute, forget about the terms and look at how the sentences work.

Sometimes a sentence has two ideas that work together. For example, say the writer wants to make the following points:

Seat belt laws have saved an estimated 50,000 lives.

More lives are saved by seat belts every year.

These two ideas are directly related and appear to be of equal importance. Therefore they can be joined with a simple "and" as follows:

Seat belt laws have saved an estimated 50,000 lives, and more lives are saved by seat belts every year.

The word *and* in the sentence helps the two ideas work together or, in other words, it "coordinates" them. It also serves as a junction where the two ideas come together, better known as a **conjunction**. Therefore the word *and* is known as a **coordinating conjunction** (a word that helps bring two equal ideas together). Now that the ideas are joined together by a conjunction, they are known as **clauses**. Other coordinating conjunctions include *or*, *but*, and *so*.

Sometimes, however, two ideas in a sentence are *not* of equal importance:

Seat belt laws have saved an estimated 50,000 lives.

Many more lives could be saved with stronger federal seat belt laws.

In this case, combining the two with a coordinating conjunction (*and*) creates an awkward sentence:

Seat belt laws have saved an estimated 50,000 lives, and many more lives could be saved with stronger federal seat belt laws.

Now the writer uses a word to show the reader which clause is the most important (or the "boss") of the sentence:

Although seat belt laws have saved an estimated 50,000 lives, many more lives could be saved with stronger federal seat belt laws.

In this example, the second clause is the key point that the writer wants to make, and the first clause works to set up that point. Since the first clause "works for" the second, it's called the **subordinate clause**. The word *although* tells the reader that this idea isn't as important as the clause that follows. This word is called the **subordinating conjunction**. Other subordinating conjunctions include *after*,

163

because, *if*, *since*, *unless*, and many more. As mentioned before, it's easy to spot subordinate clauses because they don't stand on their own (as shown in this previous example):

> Although seat belt laws have saved an estimated 50,000 lives

This is not a complete thought. It needs the other clause (called the *independent clause*) to make sense. On the test, when asked to choose the best subordinating conjunction for a sentence, look at the surrounding text. Choose the word that best allows the sentence to support the writer's argument.

Parallel Structure

Parallel structure usually has to do with lists. Look at the following sentence and spot the mistake:

> Increased seat belt legislation has been supported by the automotive industry, the insurance industry, and doctors.

Many people don't see anything wrong, but the word *doctors* breaks the sentence's parallel structure. The previous items in the list refer to an industry as a singular noun, so every item in the list must follow that same format:

> Increased seat belt legislation has been supported by the automotive industry, the insurance industry, and the healthcare industry.

Another common mistake in parallel structure might look like this:

> Before the accident, Maria enjoyed swimming, running, and played soccer.

Here, the words "played soccer" break the parallel structure. To correct it, the writer must change the final item in the list to match the format of the previous two:

> Before the accident, Maria enjoyed swimming, running, and playing soccer.

Consider the following:

> Incorrect: At the recital, the boys and girls were dancing, singing, and played musical instruments.
> Correct: At the recital, the boys and girls were dancing, singing, and playing musical instruments.

Notice that in the second example, *played* is not in the same verb tense as the other verbs, nor is it compatible with the helping verb *were*. To test for parallel structure in lists, try reading each item as if it were the only item in the list.

> The boys and girls were dancing.
> The boys and girls were singing.
> The boys and girls were played musical instruments.

Suddenly, the error in the sentence becomes very clear. Here's another example:

> Incorrect: After the accident, I informed the police *that Mrs. Holmes backed* into my car, *that Mrs. Holmes got out* of her car to look at the damage, and *she was driving* off without leaving a note.

Correct: After the accident, I informed the police *that Mrs. Holmes backed* into my car, *that Mrs. Holmes got out* of her car to look at the damage, and *that Mrs. Holmes drove off* without leaving a note.

Correct: After the accident, I informed the police that Mrs. Holmes *backed* into my car, *got out* of her car to look at the damage, and *drove off* without leaving a note.

Note that there are two ways to fix the nonparallel structure of the first sentence. The key to parallelism is consistent structure.

Various Sentence Structures

Sentence Fluency

It's time to take what's been studied and put it all together in order to construct well-written sentences and paragraphs that have correct structure. Learning and utilizing the mechanics of structure will encourage effective, professional results, and adding some creativity will elevate one's writing to a higher level.

First, let's review the basic elements of sentences. A **sentence** is a set of words that make up a grammatical unit. The words must have certain elements and be spoken or written in a specific order to constitute a complete sentence that makes sense.

1. A sentence must have a *subject* (a noun or noun phrase). The subject tells whom or what the sentence is addressing (i.e. what it is about).

2. A sentence must have an *action* or *state of being* (*a verb*). To reiterate: A verb forms the main part of the predicate of a sentence. This means that it explains what the noun is doing.

3. A sentence must convey a complete thought.

When examining writing, be mindful of grammar, structure, spelling, and patterns. Sentences can come in varying sizes and shapes; so, the point of grammatical correctness is not to stamp out creativity or diversity in writing. Rather, grammatical correctness ensures that writing will be enjoyable and clear. One of the most common methods for catching errors is to mouth the words as you read them. Many typos are fixed automatically by our brain, but mouthing the words often circumvents this instinct and helps one read what's actually on the page. Often, grammar errors are caught not by memorization of grammar rules but by the training of one's mind to know whether something *sounds* right or not.

Types of Sentences

There isn't an overabundance of absolutes in grammar, but here is one: every sentence in the English language falls into one of four categories.

- **Declarative**: a simple statement that ends with a period

  The price of milk per gallon is the same as the price of gasoline.

- **Imperative**: a command, instruction, or request that ends with a period

  Buy milk when you stop to fill up your car with gas.

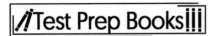
- **Interrogative**: a question that ends with a question mark

     Will you buy the milk?

- **Exclamatory**: a statement or command that expresses emotions like anger, urgency, or surprise and ends with an exclamation mark

     Buy the milk now!

Declarative sentences are the most common type, probably because they are comprised of the most general content, without any of the bells and whistles that the other three types contain. They are, simply, declarations or statements of any degree of seriousness, importance, or information.

Imperative sentences often seem to be missing a subject. The subject is there, though; it is just not visible or audible because it is *implied*. Look at the imperative example sentence.

     Buy the milk when you fill up your car with gas.

You is the implied subject, the one to whom the command is issued. This is sometimes called *the understood you* because it is understood that *you* is the subject of the sentence.

Interrogative sentences—those that ask questions—are defined as such from the idea of the word *interrogation*, the action of questions being asked of suspects by investigators. Although that is serious business, interrogative sentences apply to all kinds of questions.

To exclaim is at the root of *exclamatory* sentences. These are made with strong emotions behind them. The only technical difference between a declarative or imperative sentence and an exclamatory one is the exclamation mark at the end. The example declarative and imperative sentences can both become an exclamatory one simply by putting an exclamation mark at the end of the sentences.

     The price of milk per gallon is the same as the price of gasoline!
     Buy milk when you stop to fill up your car with gas!

After all, someone might be really excited by the price of gas or milk, or they could be mad at the person that will be buying the milk! However, as stated before, exclamation marks in abundance defeat their own purpose! After a while, they begin to cause fatigue! When used only for their intended purpose, they can have their expected and desired effect.

Lengths
The ideal sentence length—the number of words in a sentence—depends upon the sentence's purpose.

It's okay for a sentence to be brief, and it's fine for a sentence to be lengthy. It's just important to make sure that long sentences do not become run-on sentences or too long to keep up with.

To keep writing interesting, vary sentence lengths, using a mixture of short, medium and long sentences.

Transitions
Transitions *are the glue used to make organized thoughts adhere to one another.* Transitions are the glue that helps put ideas together seamlessly, within sentences and paragraphs, between them, and (in longer documents) even between sections. Transitions may be single words, sentences, or whole

166

paragraphs (as in the prior example). Transitions help readers to digest and understand what to feel about what has gone on and clue readers in on what is going on, what will be, and how they might react to all these factors. Transitions are like good clues left at a crime scene.

Examples of Transitional Words and Phrases

Transitions have many emphases as can be seen below.

- To show emphasis: truly, in fact
- To show examples: for example, namely, specifically
- To show similarities: also, likewise
- To show dissimilarities: on the other hand, even if, in contrast
- To show progression of time: later, previously, subsequently
- To show sequence or order: next, finally
- To show cause and effect: therefore, so
- To show place or position: above, nearby, there
- To provide evidence: furthermore, then
- To summarize: finally, summarizing

Sentence Structures

A *simple sentence* has one independent clause.

I am going to win.

A **compound sentence** has two independent clauses. A conjunction—*for, and, nor, but, or, yet, so*—links them together. Note that each of the independent clauses has a subject and a verb.

I am going to win, but the odds are against me.

A **complex sentence** has one independent clause and one or more dependent clauses.

I am going to win, even though I don't deserve it.

Even though I don't deserve it is a dependent clause. It does not stand on its own. Some conjunctions that link an independent and a dependent clause are *although, because, before, after, that, when, which,* and *while.*

A **compound-complex sentence** has at least three clauses, two of which are independent and at least one that is a dependent clause.

While trying to dance, I tripped over my partner's feet, but I regained my balance quickly.

The dependent clause is *While trying to dance.*

Grammar, Spelling, Capitalization and Punctuation Skills

Conventions of Standard English Spelling

Spelling might or might not be important to some, or maybe it just doesn't come naturally, but those who are willing to discover some new ideas and consider their benefits can learn to spell better and improve their writing. Misspellings reduce a writer's credibility and can create misunderstandings. Spell checkers built into word processors are not a substitute for accuracy. They are neither foolproof nor without error. In addition, a writer's misspelling of one word may also be a word. For example, a writer intending to spell *herd* might accidentally type *s* instead of *d* and unintentionally spell *hers*. Since *her*s is a word, it would not be marked as a misspelling by a spell checker. In short, use spell check, but don't rely on it.

Guidelines for Spelling

Saying and listening to a word serves as the beginning of knowing how to spell it. Keep these subsequent guidelines in mind, remembering there are often exceptions because the English language is replete with them.

Guideline #1: Syllables must have at least one vowel. In fact, every syllable in every English word has a vowel.

- d*o*g
- h*a*yst*a*ck
- *a*nsw*e*r*i*ng
- *a*bst*e*nt*io*u*s
- s*i*mpl*e*

Guideline #2: The long and short of it. When the vowel has a short vowel sound as in *mad* or *bed,* only the single vowel is needed. If the word has a long vowel sound, add another vowel, either alongside it or separated by a consonant: bed/*bead*; mad/*made.* When the second vowel is separated by two consonants— *madder*—it does not affect the first vowel's sound.

Guideline #3: Suffixes. Refer to the examples listed above.

Guideline #4: Which comes first; the *i* or the *e*? Remember the saying, "*I* before *e* except after *c* or when sounding as *a* as in *neighbor* or *weigh*." Keep in mind that these are only guidelines and that there are always exceptions to every rule.

Guideline #5: Vowels in the right order. Another helpful rhyme is, "When two vowels go walking, the first one does the talking." When two vowels are in a row, the first one often has a long vowel sound and the other is silent. An example is *team.*

If you have difficulty spelling words, determine a strategy to help. Work on spelling by playing word games like Scrabble or Words with Friends. Consider using phonics, which is sounding words out by slowly and surely stating each syllable. Try repeating and memorizing spellings as well as picturing words in your head. Try making up silly memory aids. See what works best.

Homophones

Homophones are two or more words that have no particular relationship to one another except their identical pronunciations. Homophones make spelling English words fun and challenging like these:

Common Homophones		
affect, effect	cell, sell	it's, its
allot, a lot	do, due, dew	knew, new
barbecue, barbeque	dual, duel	libel, liable
bite, byte	eminent, imminent	principal, principle
brake, break	flew, flu, flue	their, there, they're
capital, capitol	gauge, gage	to, too, two
cash, cache	holy, wholly	yoke, yolk

Irregular Plurals

Irregular plurals are words that aren't made plural the usual way.

- Most nouns are made plural by adding –s (books, televisions, skyscrapers).
- Most nouns ending in *ch, sh, s, x,* or *z* are made plural by adding –es (churches, marshes).
- Most nouns ending in a vowel + *y* are made plural by adding –s (days, toys).
- Most nouns ending in a consonant + *y,* are made plural by the -y becoming -ies (baby becomes *babies*).
- Most nouns ending in an *o* are made plural by adding –s (pianos, photos).
- Some nouns ending in an *o,* though, may be made plural by adding –es (example: potatoes, volcanoes), and, of note, there is no known rhyme or reason for this!
- Most nouns ending in an *f* or *fe* are made plural by the -f or -fe becoming -ves! (example: wolf becomes *wolves*).
- Some words function as both the singular and plural form of the word (fish, deer).
- Other exceptions include *man* becomes *men, mouse* becomes *mice, goose* becomes *geese,* and *foot* becomes *feet.*

Contractions

The basic rule for making **contractions** is one area of spelling that is pretty straightforward: combine the two words by inserting an apostrophe (') in the space where a letter is omitted. For example, to combine *you* and *are*, drop the *a* and put the apostrophe in its place: *you're.*

> he + is = he's
> you + all = y'all (informal but often misspelled)

Note that *it's*, when spelled with an apostrophe, is always the contraction for *it is*. The possessive form of the word is written without an apostrophe as *its.*

Correcting Misspelled Words

A good place to start looking at commonly misspelled words here is with the word *misspelled*. While it looks peculiar, look at it this way: *mis* (the prefix meaning *wrongly*) + *spelled = misspelled.*

Let's look at some commonly misspelled words.

Commonly Misspelled Words					
accept	benign	existence	jewelry	parallel	separate
acceptable	bicycle	experience	judgment	pastime	sergeant
accidentally	brief	extraordinary	library	permissible	similar
accommodate	business	familiar	license	perseverance	supersede
accompany	calendar	February	maintenance	personnel	surprise
acknowledgement	campaign	fiery	maneuver	persuade	symmetry
acquaintance	candidate	finally	mathematics	possess	temperature
acquire	category	forehead	mattress	precede	tragedy
address	cemetery	foreign	millennium	prevalent	transferred
aesthetic	changeable	foremost	miniature	privilege	truly
aisle	committee	forfeit	mischievous	pronunciation	usage
altogether	conceive	glamorous	misspell	protein	valuable
amateur	congratulations	government	mortgage	publicly	vengeance
apparent	courtesy	grateful	necessary	questionnaire	villain
appropriate	deceive	handkerchief	neither	recede	Wednesday
arctic	desperate	harass	nickel	receive	weird
asphalt	discipline	hygiene	niece	recommend	
associate	disappoint	hypocrisy	ninety	referral	
attendance	dissatisfied	ignorance	noticeable	relevant	
auxiliary	eligible	incredible	obedience	restaurant	
available	embarrass	intelligence	occasion	rhetoric	
balloon	especially	intercede	occurrence	rhythm	
believe	exaggerate	interest	omitted	schedule	
beneficial	exceed	irresistible	operate	sentence	

Capitalization

Here's a non-exhaustive list of things that should be capitalized.

- The first word of every sentence
- The first word of every line of poetry
- The first letter of proper nouns (World War II)
- Holidays (Valentine's Day)
- The days of the week and months of the year (Tuesday, March)
- The first word, last word, and all major words in the titles of books, movies, songs, and other creative works (In the novel, *To Kill a Mockingbird*, note that *a* is lowercase since it's not a major word, but *to* is capitalized since it's the first word of the title.)
- Titles when preceding a proper noun (President Roberto Gonzales, Aunt Judy)

When simply using a word such as president or secretary, though, the word is not capitalized.

Officers of the new business must include a *president* and *treasurer*.

Seasons—spring, fall, etc.—are not capitalized.

North, *south*, *east*, and *west* are capitalized when referring to regions but are not when being used for directions. In general, if it's preceded by *the* it should be capitalized.

I'm from the South.
I drove south.

Conventions of Standard English Punctuation

Ellipses

An **ellipsis (…)** consists of three handy little dots that can speak volumes on behalf of irrelevant material. Writers use them in place of words, lines, phrases, list content, or paragraphs that might just as easily have been omitted from a passage of writing. This can be done to save space or to focus only on the specifically relevant material.

Exercise is good for some unexpected reasons. Watkins writes, "Exercise has many benefits such as…reducing cancer risk."

In the example above, the ellipsis takes the place of the other benefits of exercise that are more expected.

The ellipsis may also be used to show a pause in sentence flow.

"I'm wondering…how this could happen," Dylan said in a soft voice.

Commas

A **comma (,)** is the punctuation mark that signifies a pause—breath—between parts of a sentence. It denotes a break of flow. As with so many aspects of writing structure, authors will benefit by reading their writing aloud or mouthing the words. This can be particularly helpful if one is uncertain about whether the comma is needed.

In a complex sentence—one that contains a subordinate (dependent) clause or clauses—the use of a comma is dictated by where the subordinate clause is located. If the subordinate clause is located before the main clause, a comma is needed between the two clauses.

I will not pay for the steak, *because I don't have that much money*.

Generally, if the subordinate clause is placed after the main clause, no punctuation is needed.

I did well on my exam because I studied two hours the night before.

Notice how the last clause is dependent because it requires the earlier independent clauses to make sense.

Use a comma on both sides of an interrupting phrase.

I will pay for the ice cream, *chocolate and vanilla*, and then will eat it all myself.

The words forming the phrase in italics are nonessential (extra) information. To determine if a phrase is nonessential, try reading the sentence without the phrase and see if it's still coherent.

A comma is not necessary in this next sentence because no interruption—nonessential or extra information—has occurred. Read sentences aloud when uncertain.

I will pay for his chocolate and vanilla ice cream and then will eat it all myself.

If the nonessential phrase comes at the beginning of a sentence, a comma should only go at the end of the phrase. If the phrase comes at the end of a sentence, a comma should only go at the beginning of the phrase.

Other types of interruptions include the following:

- interjections: Oh no, I am not going.
- abbreviations: Barry Potter, M.D., specializes in heart disorders.
- direct addresses: Yes, Claudia, I am tired and going to bed.
- parenthetical phrases: His wife, lovely as she was, was not helpful.
- transitional phrases: Also, it is not possible.

The second comma in the following sentence is called an Oxford comma.

I will pay for ice cream, syrup, and pop.

It is a comma used after the second-to-last item in a series of three or more items. It comes before the word *or* or *and*. Not everyone uses the Oxford comma; it is optional, but many believe it is needed. The comma functions as a tool to reduce confusion in writing. So, if omitting the Oxford comma would cause confusion, then it's best to include it.

Commas are used in math to mark the place of thousands in numerals, breaking them up so they are easier to read. Other uses for commas are in dates (*March 19, 2016*), letter greetings (*Dear Sally,*), and in between cities and states (*Louisville, KY*).

Semicolons

The **semicolon (;)** might be described as a heavy-handed comma. Take a look at these two examples:

I will pay for the ice cream, but I will not pay for the steak.
I will pay for the ice cream; I will not pay for the steak.

What's the difference? The first example has a comma and a conjunction separating the two independent clauses. The second example does not have a conjunction, but there are two independent clauses in the sentence. So something more than a comma is required. In this case, a semicolon is used.

Two independent clauses can only be joined in a sentence by either a comma and conjunction or a semicolon. If one of those tools is not used, the sentence will be a run-on. Remember that while the clauses are independent, they need to be closely related in order to be contained in one sentence.

Another use for the semicolon is to separate items in a list when the items themselves require commas.

The family lived in Phoenix, Arizona; Oklahoma City, Oklahoma; and Raleigh, North Carolina.

172

Colons

Colons have many miscellaneous functions. Colons can be used to precede further information or a list. In these cases, a colon should only follow an independent clause.

> Humans take in sensory information through five basic senses: sight, hearing, smell, touch, and taste.

The meal includes the following components:

- Caesar salad
- spaghetti
- garlic bread
- cake

The family got what they needed: a reliable vehicle.

While a comma is more common, a colon can also precede a formal quotation.

> He said to the crowd: "Let's begin!"

The colon is used after the greeting in a formal letter.

> Dear Sir:
> To Whom It May Concern:

In the writing of time, the colon separates the minutes from the hour (*4:45 p.m.*). The colon can also be used to indicate a ratio between two numbers (*50:1*).

Hyphens

The **hyphen (-)** is a little hash mark that can be used to join words to show that they are linked.

Hyphenate two words that work together as a single adjective (a compound adjective).

> honey-covered biscuits

Some words always require hyphens, even if not serving as an adjective.

> merry-go-round

Hyphens always go after certain prefixes like *anti-* & *all-*.

Hyphens should also be used when the absence of the hyphen would cause a strange vowel combination (*semi-engineer*) or confusion. For example, *re-collect* should be used to describe something being gathered twice rather than being written as *recollect*, which means to remember.

Parentheses and Dashes

Parentheses are half-round brackets that look like this: *( )*. They set off a word, phrase, or sentence that is an afterthought, explanation, or side note relevant to the surrounding text but not essential. A pair of commas is often used to set off this sort of information, but parentheses are generally used for information that would not fit well within a sentence or that the writer deems not important enough to be structurally part of the sentence.

> The picture of the heart (see above) shows the major parts you should memorize.
> Mount Everest is one of three mountains in the world that are over 28,000 feet high (K2 and Kanchenjunga are the other two).

See how the sentences above are complete without the parenthetical statements? In the first example, *see above* would not have fit well within the flow of the sentence. The second parenthetical statement could have been a separate sentence, but the writer deemed the information not pertinent to the topic.

The **em-dash (—)** is a mark longer than a hyphen used as a punctuation mark in sentences and to set apart a relevant thought. Even after plucking out the line separated by the dash marks, the sentence will be intact and make sense.

> Looking out the airplane window at the landmarks—Lake Clarke, Thompson Community College, and the bridge—she couldn't help but feel excited to be home.

The dashes use is similar to that of parentheses or a pair of commas. So, what's the difference? Many believe that using dashes makes the clause within them stand out while using parentheses is subtler. It's advised to not use dashes when commas could be used instead.

Quotation Marks

Here are some instances where *quotation marks* should be used:

- Dialogue for characters in narratives. When characters speak, the first word should always be capitalized, and the punctuation goes inside the quotes. For example:
- Janie said, "The tree fell on my car during the hurricane."
- Around titles of songs, short stories, essays, and chapters in books
- To emphasize a certain word
- To refer to a word as the word itself

Apostrophes

This punctuation mark, the **apostrophe (')**, is a versatile little mark. It has a few different functions:

- Quotes: Apostrophes are used when a second quote is needed within a quote.
- In my letter to my friend, I wrote, "The girl had to get a new purse, and guess what Mary did? She said, 'I'd like to go with you to the store.' I knew Mary would buy it for her."
- Contractions: Another use for an apostrophe in the quote above is a contraction. *I'd* is used for *I would*.
- Possession: An apostrophe followed by the letter *s* shows possession (*Mary's* purse). If the possessive word is plural, the apostrophe generally just follows the word.
- The trees' leaves are all over the ground.

Apostrophes are often misused. For the purpose of the test, there are three things to know about using apostrophes:

- Use apostrophes to show possession
- Senator Wilson's bill just passed committee.
- Use apostrophes in contractions to replace eliminated letters
- Does not → Doesn't

Note: It's common to see acronyms made plural using apostrophes (RV's, DVD's, TV's), but these are incorrect. Acronyms function as words, so they are pluralized the same way (RVs, DVDs, TVs).

On the test, when an apostrophe-related question is asked, determine if it shows possession or is part of a contraction. If neither answer fits, then the apostrophe probably doesn't belong there.

Practice Quiz

Directions for questions 1 and 2:

Select the best version of the underlined part of the sentence. The first choice is the same as the original sentence. If you think the original sentence is best, choose the first answer.

1. It is necessary for instructors to offer tutoring <u>to any students who need extra help in the class.</u>
    a. to any students who need extra help in the class.
    b. for any students that need extra help in the class.
    c. with any students who need extra help in the class.
    d. for any students needing any extra help in their class.

2. <u>Because many people</u> feel there are too many distractions to get any work done, I actually enjoy working from home.
    a. Because many people
    b. While many people
    c. Maybe many people
    d. With most people

3. Polls show that more and more people in the US distrust the government and view it as dysfunctional and corrupt. Every election, the same people are voted back into office.

Which word or words would best link these sentences?
    a. Not surprisingly,
    b. Understandably,
    c. And yet,
    d. Therefore,

4. The following sentence contains what kind of error?
    This summer, I'm planning to travel to Italy, take a Mediterranean cruise, going to Pompeii, and eat a lot of Italian food.

    a. Parallelism
    b. Sentence fragment
    c. Misplaced modifier
    d. Subject-verb agreement

5. The student at a high school, after witnessing some wrongdoing on behalf of others, needed to talk to several _____ based on his _____ .
    a. principals; principles
    b. principles; principals
    c. princapals; princaples
    d. princaples; princapals

See answers on next page.

Answer Explanations

1. A: Choice *A* uses the best, most concise word choice. Choice *B* uses the pronoun *that* to refer to people instead of *who*. *Choice C* incorrectly uses the preposition *with*. Choice *D* uses the preposition *for* and the additional word *any*, making the sentence wordy and less clear.

2. B: Choice *B* uses the best choice of words to create a subordinate and independent clause. In Choice *A*, *because* makes it seem like this is the reason they enjoy working from home, which is incorrect. In Choice *C*, the word *maybe* creates two independent clauses, which are not joined properly with a comma. Choice *D* uses *with*, which does not make grammatical sense.

3. C: The second sentence tells of an unexpected outcome of the first sentence. Choice *A*, Choice *B*, and Choice *D* indicate a logical progression, which does not match this surprise. Only Choice *C* indicates this unexpected twist.

4. A: Parallelism refers to consistent use of sentence structure or word form. In this case, the list within the sentence does not utilize parallelism; three of the verbs appear in their base form—*travel, take,* and *eat*—but one appears as a gerund—*going*. A parallel version of this sentence would be "This summer, I'm planning to travel to Italy, take a Mediterranean cruise, go to Pompeii, and eat a lot of Italian food." Choice *B* is incorrect because this description is a complete sentence. Choice *C* is incorrect as a misplaced modifier is a modifier that is not located appropriately in relation to the word or words they modify. Choice *D* is incorrect because subject-verb agreement refers to the appropriate conjugation of a verb in relation to its subject.

5. A: *Principals* are the leaders of a school. *Principles* indicate values, morals, or ideology. For Choice *B*, the words are reversed. For Choices *C* and *D*, both answers are misspelled, regardless of position.

Practice Test #1

Math

1. What is the value of $x^2 - 2xy + 2y^2$ when $x = 2, y = 3$?
   a. 8
   b. 10
   c. 12
   d. 14

2. $(2x - 4y)^2 =$
   a. $4x^2 - 16xy + 16y^2$

   b. $4x^2 - 8xy + 16y^2$

   c. $4x^2 - 16xy - 16y^2$

   d. $2x^2 - 8xy + 8y^2$

3. If $x > 3$, then $\frac{x^2 - 6x + 9}{x^2 - x - 6} =$
   a. $\frac{x+2}{x-3}$
   b. $\frac{x-2}{x-3}$
   c. $\frac{x-3}{x+3}$
   d. $\frac{x-3}{x+2}$

4. If $x^2 - x - 3 = 0$, what is the value of $\left(x - \frac{1}{2}\right)^2$?
   a. $\frac{13}{2}$

   b. $\frac{13}{4}$

   c. 13

   d. $\frac{169}{4}$

5. If $4x - 3 = 5$, what is the value of x?
   a. 1
   b. 2
   c. 3
   d. 4

178

6. Solve for x, if $x^2 - 2x - 8 = 0$.
   a. $2 \pm \frac{\sqrt{30}}{2}$
   b. $2 \pm 4\sqrt{2}$
   c. 1 ± 3
   d. $4 \pm \sqrt{2}$

7. Which of the following is a factor of both $x^2 + 4x + 4$ and $x^2 - x - 6$?
   a. $x - 3$
   b. $x + 2$
   c. $x - 2$
   d. $x + 3$

8. Write the expression for six less than three times the sum of twice a number and one.
   a. $2x + 1 - 6$
   b. $3x + 1 - 6$
   c. $3(x + 1) - 6$
   d. $3(2x + 1) - 6$

9. On Monday, Robert mopped the floor in 4 hours. On Tuesday, he did it in 3 hours. If on Monday, his average rate of mopping was p sq. ft. per hour, what was his average rate on Tuesday?
   a. $\frac{4}{3}p$ sq. ft. per hour
   b. $\frac{3}{4}p$ sq. ft. per hour
   c. $\frac{5}{4}p$ sq. ft. per hour
   d. $p + 1$ sq. ft. per hour

10. Which of the following inequalities is equivalent to $3 - \frac{1}{2}x \geq 2$?
    a. $x \geq 2$
    b. $x \leq 2$
    c. $x \geq 1$
    d. $x \leq 1$

11. For which of the following are $x = 4$ and $x = -4$ solutions?
    a. $x^2 + 16 = 0$
    b. $x^2 + 4x - 4 = 0$
    c. $x^2 - 2x - 2 = 0$
    d. $x^2 - 16 = 0$

12. If x is not zero, then $\dfrac{3}{x} + \dfrac{5u}{2x} - \dfrac{u}{4} =$

   a. $\dfrac{12+10u-ux}{4x}$

   b. $\dfrac{3+5u-ux}{x}$

   c. $\dfrac{12x+10u+ux}{4x}$

   d. $\dfrac{12+10u-u}{4x}$

13. Which of the following is the result of simplifying the expression:

$$\frac{4a^{-1}b^3}{a^4b^{-2}} \times \frac{3a}{b}$$

   a. $12a^3b^5$

   b. $12\dfrac{b^4}{a^4}$

   c. $\dfrac{12}{a^4}$

   d. $7\dfrac{b^4}{a}$

14. Which of the following augmented matrices represents the system of equations below?
$$2x - 3y + z = -5$$
$$4x - y - 2z = -7$$
$$-x + 2z = -1$$

   a. $\begin{bmatrix} 2 & -3 & 1 & -5 \\ 4 & -1 & -2 & -7 \\ -1 & 0 & 2 & -1 \end{bmatrix}$

   b. $\begin{bmatrix} 2 & 4 & -1 \\ -3 & -1 & 0 \\ 1 & -2 & 2 \\ -5 & -7 & -1 \end{bmatrix}$

   c. $\begin{bmatrix} 2 & 4 & -1 & -5 \\ -3 & -1 & 0 & -7 \\ 2 & -2 & 2 & -1 \end{bmatrix}$

   d. $\begin{bmatrix} 2 & -3 & 1 \\ 4 & -1 & -2 \\ -1 & 0 & 2 \end{bmatrix}$

15. What are the zeros of the function: $f(x) = x^3 + 4x^2 + 4x$?

   a. -2

   b. 0, -2

   c. 2

   d. 0, 2

16. What is the solution to the following system of equations?
$$x^2 - 2x + y = 8$$
$$x - y = -2$$

a. $(-2, 3)$
b. There is no solution.
c. $(-2, 0) (1, 3)$
d. $(-2, 0) (3, 5)$

17. Which of the following shows the correct result of simplifying the following expression?
$$(7n + 3n^3 + 3) + (8n + 5n^3 + 2n^4)$$

a. $9n^4 + 15n - 2$
b. $2n^4 + 5n^3 + 15n - 2$
c. $9n^4 + 8n^3 + 15n$
d. $2n^4 + 8n^3 + 15n + 3$

18. What is the product of the following expression?
$$(4x - 8)(5x^2 + x + 6)$$

a. $20x^3 - 36x^2 + 16x - 48$
b. $6x^3 - 41x^2 + 12x + 15$
c. $20x^3 + 11x^2 - 37x - 12$
d. $2x^3 - 11x^2 - 32x + 20$

19. How could the following equation be factored to find the zeros?
$$y = x^3 - 3x^2 - 4x$$

a. $0 = x^2(x - 4), x = 0, 4$
b. $0 = 3x(x + 1)(x + 4), x = 0, -1, -4$
c. $0 = x(x + 1)(x + 6), x = 0, -1, -6$
d. $0 = x(x + 1)(x - 4), x = 0, -1, 4$

20. What is the solution for the following equation?
$$\frac{x^2 + x - 30}{x - 5} = 11$$

a. $x = -6$
b. There is no solution.
c. $x = 16$
d. $x = 5$

21. What is the domain for the function $y = \sqrt{x}$?
a. All real numbers
b. $x \geq 0$
c. $x > 0$
d. $y \geq 0$

181

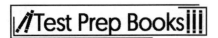
22. In the *xy*-plane, the graph of $y = x^2 + 2$ and the circle with center $(0, 1)$ and radius 1 have how many points of intersection?
    a. 0
    b. 1
    c. 2
    d. 3

23. A line goes through the point $(-4, 0)$ and the point $(0, 2)$. What is the slope of the line?
    a. 2

    b. 4

    c. $\frac{3}{2}$

    d. $\frac{1}{2}$

24. A root of $x^2 - 2x - 2$ is
    a. $1 + \sqrt{3}$

    b. $1 + 2\sqrt{2}$

    c. $2 + 2\sqrt{3}$

    d. $2 - 2\sqrt{3}$

25. Which of the following expressions is equivalent to this equation?

$$\frac{2xy^2 + 4x - 8y}{16xy}$$

    a. $\frac{y}{8} + \frac{1}{4y} - \frac{1}{2x}$
    b. $8xy + 4y - 2x$
    c. $xy^2 + \frac{x}{4y} - \frac{1}{2x}$
    d. $\frac{y}{8} + 4y - 8y$

26. What is the answer to $\frac{3+3i}{3-3i}$?
    a. 18
    b. $18i$
    c. i
    d. $9i$

27. Four people split a bill. The first person pays for $\frac{1}{5}$, the second person pays for $\frac{1}{4}$, and the third person pays for $\frac{1}{3}$. What fraction of the bill does the fourth person pay?

    a. $\frac{13}{60}$

    b. $\frac{47}{60}$

    c. $\frac{1}{4}$

    d. $\frac{4}{15}$

28. If a car can travel 300 miles in 4 hours, how far can it go in an hour and a half?

    a. 100 miles
    b. 112.5 miles
    c. 135.5 miles
    d. 150 miles

29. If $\frac{5}{2} \div \frac{1}{3} = n$, then n is between:

    a. 5 and 7
    b. 7 and 9
    c. 9 and 11
    d. 3 and 5

30. A closet is filled with red, blue, and green shirts. If $\frac{1}{3}$ of the shirts are green and $\frac{2}{5}$ are red, what fraction of the shirts are blue?

    a. $\frac{4}{15}$

    b. $\frac{1}{5}$

    c. $\frac{7}{15}$

    d. $\frac{1}{2}$

Reading

Questions 1-6 are based upon the following passage:

My gentleness and good behaviour had gained so far on the emperor and his court, and indeed upon the army and people in general, that I began to conceive hopes of getting my liberty in a short time. I took all possible methods to cultivate this favourable disposition. The natives came, by degrees, to be less apprehensive of any danger from me. I would sometimes lie down, and let five or six of them dance on my hand; and at last the boys and girls would venture to come and play at hide-and-seek in my hair. I had now made a good progress in understanding and speaking the language. The emperor had a mind one day to entertain me with several of the country shows, wherein they exceed all nations I have known, both for dexterity and magnificence. I was diverted

183

with none so much as that of the rope-dancers, performed upon a slender white thread, extended about two feet, and twelve inches from the ground. Upon which I shall desire liberty, with the reader's patience, to enlarge a little.

This diversion is only practised by those persons who are candidates for great employments, and high favour at court. They are trained in this art from their youth, and are not always of noble birth, or liberal education. When a great office is vacant, either by death or disgrace (which often happens,) five or six of those candidates petition the emperor to entertain his majesty and the court with a dance on the rope; and whoever jumps the highest, without falling, succeeds in the office. Very often the chief ministers themselves are commanded to show their skill, and to convince the emperor that they have not lost their faculty. Flimnap, the treasurer, is allowed to cut a caper on the straight rope, at least an inch higher than any other lord in the whole empire. I have seen him do the summerset several times together, upon a trencher fixed on a rope which is no thicker than a common packthread in England. My friend Reldresal, principal secretary for private affairs, is, in my opinion, if I am not partial, the second after the treasurer; the rest of the great officers are much upon a par.

This excerpt is an adaptation of Jonathan Swift's *Gulliver's Travels into Several Remote Nations of the World.*

1. Which of the following statements best summarizes the central purpose of this text?
    a. Gulliver details his fondness for the archaic yet interesting practices of his captors.
    b. Gulliver conjectures about the intentions of the aristocratic sector of society.
    c. Gulliver becomes acquainted with the people and practices of his new surroundings.
    d. Gulliver's differences cause him to become penitent around new acquaintances.

2. What is the word *principal* referring to in the following text?
    My friend Reldresal, principal secretary for private affairs, is, in my opinion, if I am not partial, the second after the treasurer; the rest of the great officers are much upon a par.

    a. Primary or chief
    b. An acolyte
    c. An individual who provides nurturing
    d. One in a subordinate position

3. What can the reader infer from this passage?
    I would sometimes lie down, and let five or six of them dance on my hand; and at last the boys and girls would venture to come and play at hide-and-seek in my hair.

    a. The children tortured Gulliver.
    b. Gulliver traveled because he wanted to meet new people.
    c. Gulliver is considerably larger than the children who are playing around him.
    d. Gulliver has a genuine love and enthusiasm for people of all sizes.

4. What is the significance of the word *mind* in the following passage?

> The emperor had a mind one day to entertain me with several of the country shows, wherein they exceed all nations I have known, both for dexterity and magnificence.

a. The ability to think
b. A collective vote
c. A definitive decision
d. A mythological question

5. Which of the following assertions does NOT support the fact that games are a commonplace event in this culture?

a. My gentleness and good behavior . . . short time.
b. They are trained in this art from their youth . . . liberal education.
c. Very often the chief ministers themselves are commanded to show their skill . . . not lost their faculty.
d. Flimnap, the treasurer, is allowed to cut a caper on the straight rope . . . higher than any other lord in the whole empire.

6. How do Flimnap and Reldresal demonstrate the community's emphasis on physical strength and leadership abilities?

a. Only children used Gulliver's hands as a playground.
b. The two men who exhibited superior abilities held prominent positions in the community.
c. Only common townspeople, not leaders, walk the straight rope.
d. No one could jump higher than Gulliver.

Questions 7-12 are based upon the following passage:

> "Did you ever come across a protégé of his—one Hyde?" He asked.
>
> "Hyde?" repeated Lanyon. "No. Never heard of him. Since my time."
>
> That was the amount of information that the lawyer carried back with him to the great, dark bed on which he tossed to and fro until the small hours of the morning began to grow large. It was a night of little ease to his toiling mind, toiling in mere darkness and besieged by questions.
>
> Six o'clock struck on the bells of the church that was so conveniently near to Mr. Utterson's dwelling, and still he was digging at the problem. Hitherto it had touched him on the intellectual side alone; but now his imagination also was engaged, or rather enslaved; and as he lay and tossed in the gross darkness of the night in the curtained room, Mr. Enfield's tale went by before his mind in a scroll of lighted pictures. He would be aware of the great field of lamps in a nocturnal city; then of the figure of a man walking swiftly; then of a child running from the doctor's; and then these met, and that human Juggernaut trod the child down and passed on regardless of her screams. Or else he would see a room in a rich house, where his friend lay asleep, dreaming and smiling at his dreams; and then the door of that room would be opened, the curtains of the bed plucked apart, the sleeper recalled, and, lo! There would stand by his side a figure to whom power was given, and even at that dead hour he must rise and do its bidding. The figure in these two phrases haunted the lawyer all night; and if at anytime

185

he dozed over, it was but to see it glide more stealthily through sleeping houses, or move the more swiftly, and still the more smoothly, even to dizziness, through wider labyrinths of lamplighted city, and at every street corner crush a child and leave her screaming. And still the figure had no face by which he might know it; even in his dreams it had no face, or one that baffled him and melted before his eyes; and thus there it was that there sprung up and grew apace in the lawyer's mind a singularly strong, almost an inordinate, curiosity to behold the features of the real Mr. Hyde. If he could but once set eyes on him, he thought the mystery would lighten and perhaps roll altogether away, as was the habit of mysterious things when well examined. He might see a reason for his friend's strange preference or bondage, and even for the startling clauses of the will. And at least it would be a face worth seeing: the face of a man who was without bowels of mercy: a face which had but to show itself to raise up, in the mind of the unimpressionable Enfield, a spirit of enduring hatred.

From that time forward, Mr. Utterson began to haunt the door in the by-street of shops. In the morning before office hours, at noon when business was plenty of time scarce, at night under the face of the full city moon, by all lights and at all hours of solitude or concourse, the lawyer was to be found on his chosen post.

"If he be Mr. Hyde," he had thought, "I should be Mr. Seek."

This excerpt is an adaptation of Robert Louis Stevenson's *The Strange Case of Dr. Jekyll and Mr. Hyde.*

7. What is the purpose of the use of repetition in the following passage?
   It was a night of little ease to his toiling mind, toiling in mere darkness and besieged by questions.

   a. It serves as a demonstration of the mental state of Mr. Lanyon.
   b. It is reminiscent of the church bells that are mentioned in the story.
   c. It mimics Mr. Utterson's ambivalence.
   d. It emphasizes Mr. Utterson's anguish in failing to identify Hyde's whereabouts.

8. What is the setting of the story in this passage?
   a. In the city
   b. On the countryside
   c. In a jail
   d. In a mental health facility

9. What can one infer about the meaning of the word "Juggernaut" from the author's use of it in the passage?
   a. It is an apparition that appears at daybreak.
   b. It scares children.
   c. It is associated with space travel.
   d. Mr. Utterson finds it soothing.

10. What is the definition of the word *haunt* in the following passage?
    From that time forward, Mr. Utterson began to haunt the door in the by-street of shops. In the morning before office hours, at noon when business was plenty of time scarce, at night under

186

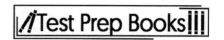

the face of the full city moon, by all lights and at all hours of solitude or concourse, the lawyer was to be found on his chosen post.

a. To levitate
b. To constantly visit
c. To terrorize
d. To daunt

11. The phrase *labyrinths of lamplighted city* contains an example of what?
a. Hyperbole
b. Simile
c. Juxtaposition
d. Alliteration

12. What can one reasonably conclude from the final comment of this passage?
"If he be Mr. Hyde," he had thought, "I should be Mr. Seek."

a. The speaker is considering a name change.
b. The speaker is experiencing an identity crisis.
c. The speaker has mistakenly been looking for the wrong person.
d. The speaker intends to continue to look for Hyde.

Questions 13-18 are based upon the following passage:

Fellow citizens—Pardon me, and allow me to ask, why am I called upon to speak here today? What have I, or those I represent, to do with your national independence? Are the great principles of political freedom and of natural justice, embodied in that Declaration of Independence, extended to us? And am I therefore called upon to bring our humble offering to the national altar, and to confess the benefits, and express devout gratitude for the blessings, resulting from your independence to us?

Would to God, both for your sakes and ours, ours that an affirmative answer could be truthfully returned to these questions! Then would my task be light, and my burden easy and delightful. For who is there so cold that a nation's sympathy could not warm him? Who so obdurate and dead to the claims of gratitude that would not thankfully acknowledge such priceless benefits? Who so stolid and selfish, that would not give his voice to swell the hallelujahs of a nation's jubilee, when the chains of servitude had been torn from his limbs? I am not that man. In a case like that, the dumb may eloquently speak, and the lame man leap as an hart.

But, such is not the state of the case. I say it with a sad sense of the disparity between us. I am not included within the pale of this glorious anniversary. Oh pity! Your high independence only reveals the immeasurable distance between us. The blessings in which you this day rejoice, I do not enjoy in common. The rich inheritance of justice, liberty, prosperity, and independence, bequeathed by your fathers, is shared by *you*, not by *me*. This Fourth of July is *yours,* not *mine.* You may rejoice, *I* must mourn. To drag a man in fetters into the grand illuminated temple of liberty, and call upon him to join you in joyous anthems, were inhuman mockery and sacrilegious irony. Do you mean, citizens, to mock me, by asking me to speak today? If so there is a parallel to your

187

conduct. And let me warn you that it is dangerous to copy the example of a nation whose crimes, towering up to heaven, were thrown down by the breath of the Almighty, burying that nation and irrecoverable ruin! I can today take up the plaintive lament of a peeled and woe-smitten people.

By the rivers of Babylon, there we sat down. Yea! We wept when we remembered Zion. We hanged our harps upon the willows in the midst thereof. For there, they that carried us away captive, required of us a song; and they who wasted us required of us mirth, saying, "Sing us one of the songs of Zion." How can we sing the Lord's song in a strange land? If I forget thee, O Jerusalem, let my right hand forget her cunning. If I do not remember thee, let my tongue cleave to the roof of my mouth.

This excerpt is adapted from "What to the Slave is the Fourth of July?" Rochester, New York July 5, 1852.

13. What is the tone of the first paragraph of this passage?
   a. Exasperated
   b. Inclusive
   c. Contemplative
   d. Nonchalant

14. Which word CANNOT be used synonymously with the term *obdurate* as it is conveyed in the text below?
   Who so obdurate and dead to the claims of gratitude, that would not thankfully acknowledge such priceless benefits?

   a. Steadfast
   b. Stubborn
   c. Contented
   d. Unwavering

15. What is the central purpose of this text?
   a. To demonstrate the author's extensive knowledge of the Bible
   b. To address the hypocrisy of the Fourth of July holiday
   c. To convince wealthy landowners to adopt new holiday rituals
   d. To explain why minorities often relished the notion of segregation in government institutions

16. Which statement serves as evidence of the previous question?
   a. By the rivers of Babylon . . . down.
   b. Fellow citizens . . . today.
   c. I can . . . woe-smitten people.
   d. The rich inheritance of justice . . . *not by me.*

17. The statement below features an example of which of the following literary devices?
Oh pity! Your high independence only reveals the immeasurable distance between us.

a. Assonance
b. Parallelism
c. Amplification
d. Hyperbole

18. The speaker's use of biblical references, such as "rivers of Babylon" and the "songs of Zion," helps the reader to do all of the following EXCEPT:
a. Identify with the speaker through the use of common text
b. Convince the audience that injustices have been committed by referencing another group of people who have been previously affected by slavery
c. Display the equivocation of the speaker and those that he represents
d. Appeal to the listener's sense of humanity

Questions 19-24 are based upon the following passage:

Four score and seven years ago our fathers brought forth on this continent, a new nation, conceived in liberty, and dedicated to the proposition that all men are created equal.

Now we are engaged in a great civil war, testing whether that nation, or any nation so conceived and so dedicated, can long endure. We are met on a great battlefield of that war. We have come to dedicate a portion of that field, as a final resting place for those who here gave their lives that this nation might live. It is altogether fitting and proper that we should do this.

But, in a larger sense, we cannot dedicate, we cannot consecrate, we cannot hallow this ground.. The brave men, living and dead, who struggled here, have consecrated it, far above our poor power to add or detract. The world will little note, nor long remember what we say here, but it can never forget what they did here. It is for us the living, rather, to be dedicated here to the unfinished work which they who fought here have thus far so nobly advanced. It is rather for us to be here and dedicated to the great task remaining before us—that from these honored dead we take increased devotion to that cause for which they gave the last full measure of devotion—that we here highly resolve that these dead shall not have died in vain—that this nation, under God, shall have a new birth of freedom—and that government of people, by the people, for the people, shall not perish from the earth.

This excerpt is an adapted from Abraham Lincoln's Address Delivered at the Dedication of the Cemetery at Gettysburg, November 19, 1863.

19. The best description for the phrase *four score and seven years ago* is which of the following?
a. A unit of measurement
b. A period of time
c. A literary movement
d. A statement of political reform

20. What is the setting of this text?
    a. A battleship off of the coast of France
    b. A desert plain on the Sahara Desert
    c. A battlefield in North America
    d. The residence of Abraham Lincoln

21. Which war is Abraham Lincoln referring to in the following passage?
    Now we are engaged in a great civil war, testing whether that nation, or any nation so conceived and so dedicated, can long endure.

    a. World War I
    b. The War of the Spanish Succession
    c. World War II
    d. The American Civil War

22. What message is the author trying to convey through this address?
    a. The audience should perpetuate the ideals of freedom that the soldiers died fighting for.
    b. The audience should honor the dead by establishing an annual memorial service.
    c. The audience should form a militia that would overturn the current political structure.
    d. The audience should forget the lives that were lost and discredit the soldiers.

23. Which rhetorical device is being used in the following passage?
    . . . we here highly resolve that these dead shall not have died in vain—that this nation, under God, shall have a new birth of freedom—and that government of people, by the people, for the people, shall not perish from the earth.

    a. Antimetabole
    b. Antiphrasis
    c. Anaphora
    d. Epiphora

24. What is the effect of Lincoln's statement in the following passage?
    But, in a larger sense, we cannot dedicate, we cannot consecrate, we cannot hallow this ground.. The brave men, living and dead, who struggled here, have consecrated it, far above our poor power to add or detract.

    a. His comparison emphasizes the great sacrifice of the soldiers who fought in the war.
    b. His comparison serves as a reminder of the inadequacies of his audience.
    c. His comparison serves as a catalyst for guilt and shame among audience members.
    d. His comparison attempts to illuminate the great differences between soldiers and civilians.

Questions 25-30 are based upon the following two passages:

Passage A

From such verses the Poems in these volumes will be found distinguished at least by one mark of difference, that each of them has a worthy *purpose.* Not that I always began to write with a distinct purpose formerly conceived; but habits of meditation have, I trust, so prompted and regulated my feelings, that my descriptions of such objects as strongly excite those feelings, will

190

be found to carry along with them a *purpose.* If this opinion be erroneous, I can have little right to the name of a Poet. For all good poetry is the spontaneous overflow of powerful feelings: and though this be true, Poems to which any value can be attached were never produced on any variety of subjects but by a man who, being possessed of more than usual organic sensibility, had also thought long and deeply. For our continued influxes of feeling are modified and directed by our thoughts, which are indeed the representatives of all our past feelings; and, as by contemplating the relation of these general representatives to each other, we discover what is really important to men, so, by the repetition and continuance of this act, our feelings will be connected with important subjects, till at length, if we be originally possessed of much sensibility, such habits of mind will be produced, that, by obeying blindly and mechanically the impulses of those habits, we shall describe objects, and utter sentiments, of such a nature, and in such connexion with each other, that the understanding of the Reader must necessarily be in some degree enlightened, and his affections strengthened and purified.

This excerpt is adapted from *Preface to Lyrical Ballads* by William Wordsworth (1800).

Passage B

If you compare several representative passages of the greatest poetry you see how great is the variety of types of combination, and also how completely any semi-ethical criterion of "sublimity" misses the mark. For it is not the "greatness," the intensity, of the emotions, the components, but the intensity of the artistic process, the pressure, so to speak, under which the fusion takes place, that counts. The episode of Paolo and Francesca employs a definite emotion, but the intensity of the poetry is something quite different from whatever intensity in the supposed experience it may give the impression of. It is no more intense, furthermore, than Canto XXVI, the voyage of Ulysses, which has not the direct dependence upon an emotion. Great variety is possible in the process of transmution of emotion: the murder of Agamemnon, or the agony of Othello, gives an artistic effect apparently closer to a possible original than the scenes from Dante. In the *Agamemnon,* the artistic emotion approximates to the emotion of an actual spectator; in *Othello* to the emotion of the protagonist himself. But the difference between art and the event is always absolute; the combination which is the murder of Agamemnon is probably as complex as that which is the voyage of Ulysses. In either case there has been a fusion of elements. The ode of Keats contains a number of feelings which have nothing particular to do with the nightingale, but which the nightingale, partly, perhaps, because of its attractive name, and partly because of its reputation, served to bring together.

This excerpt is adapted from *Tradition and the Individual Talent* by T.S. Eliot (1921).

25. Which one of the following most accurately characterizes the relationship between the two passages?
   a. Passage A offers an explanation of the purpose of poetry, while passage B offers an explanation of the results of poetry.
   b. Passage A is concerned with the context of poetry involving nature, while passage B is concerned with the context of poetry involving urban life.
   c. Passage A focuses on lyric poetry, while passage B is concerned with epic poetry.
   d. Passage A argues that the source of great poetry comes from emotions within, while passage B argues that great poetry is based off the skill and expertise of the poet.

26. What does the author of passage B mean by the last sentence?
    a. The author is explaining that the feelings portrayed in Keats' ode are brought forth and signified by the symbolism of the nightingale used within the language of the poem.
    b. The author means that Keats' poetry is more valuable than epic verse because the feelings expressed in his poetry are backed by literary talent.
    c. The author means that the figure of the nightingale serves a myriad of purposes; here, for a symbolic use of a range of emotions such as grief, fear, and sorrow.
    d. The author is trying to argue that the reputation of the poet serves to bring about the feelings of the reader; or, that the ethos of the writing is closely related to the pathos in the audience.

27. The author of passage A thinks which of the following about thoughts and feelings as they relate to poetry?
    a. That the thoughts of the poet are the primary source of inspiration, and that feeling is a secondary motivation for the poet. Once the poet gets their thoughts onto paper, the feelings of the poet will come after.
    b. That thoughts and feelings are one and the same thing; that they happen simultaneously, and that this merging creates the perfect condition to write a poem.
    c. That feelings from the past will accumulate into representations of thought. The poet is then responsible for putting these direct thoughts onto paper, creating a poem. Therefore, the original source of poetry is from the past feelings of the poet.
    d. That thoughts and feelings are overrated; namely, that critics of the past have put too much emphasis on thoughts and feelings as they relate to poetry.

28. The authors of the passages differ in their explanations of great poetry in that the author of passage B:
    a. argues that the intensity of the emotion felt while writing the poem counts for more than the effort put into a poem.
    b. argues that the effort put into a poem counts for more than the intensity of the emotion felt while writing the poem.
    c. argues that the purpose of poetry is for the reader to feel an emotional connection with the author.
    d. argues that good poetry is produced by poets who think long and deeply about their subjects before they write about it.

Below there is a blank in each question. Choose the word or phrase in the answer choice that best fits the meaning of the sentence as a whole.

29. Before she put a down payment on the house, the would-be buyer had to make sure the house was properly _____ first.
    a. Vacated
    b. Dilapidated
    c. Inspected
    d. Insulated

30. The time had come when Deirdre knew she had to _____ her position at her company in order to go back to school and earn a degree.
   a. Relinquish
   b. Rearrange
   c. Reciprocate
   d. Receive

Writing

Read the selection about traveling in an RV and answer Questions 1-7.

1   I have to admit that when my father bought a recreational vehicle (RV), I thought he was making a huge mistake. I didn't really know anything about RVs, but I knew that my dad was as big a "city slicker" as there was. (1) In fact, I even thought he might have gone a little bit crazy. On trips to the beach, he preferred to swim at the pool, and whenever he went hiking, he avoided touching any plants for fear that they might be poison ivy. Why would this man, with an almost irrational fear of the outdoors, want a 40-foot camping behemoth?

2   (2) The RV was a great purchase for our family and brought us all closer together. Every morning (3) we would wake up, eat breakfast, and broke camp. We laughed at our own comical attempts to back The Beast into spaces that seemed impossibly small. (4) We rejoiced as "hackers." When things inevitably went wrong and we couldn't solve the problems on our own, we discovered the incredible helpfulness and friendliness of the RV community. (5) We even made some new friends in the process.

3   (6) Above all, it allowed us to share adventures. While traveling across America, which we could not have experienced in cars and hotels. Enjoying a campfire on a chilly summer evening with the mountains of Glacier National Park in the background, or waking up early in the morning to see the sun rising over the distant spires of Arches National Park are memories that will always stay with me and our entire family. (7) Those are also memories that my siblings and me have now shared with our own children.

For questions 1-7, which of the following would be the best choice for each sentence?

1. Which of the following would be the best choice for this sentence (reproduced below)?

   (1) In fact, I even thought he might have gone a little bit crazy.

   a. Leave it where it is now.
   b. Move the sentence so that it comes before the preceding sentence.
   c. Move the sentence to the end of the first paragraph.
   d. Omit the sentence.

2. Which of the following would be the best choice for this sentence (reproduced below)?

(2) <u>The RV</u> was a great purchase for our family and brought us all closer together.

a. NO CHANGE
b. Not surprisingly, the RV
c. Furthermore, the RV
d. As it turns out, the RV

3. Which of the following would be the best choice for this sentence (reproduced below)?

Every morning (3) <u>we would wake up, eat breakfast, and broke camp.</u>

a. NO CHANGE
b. we would wake up, eat breakfast, and break camp.
c. would we wake up, eat breakfast, and break camp?
d. we are waking up, eating breakfast, and breaking camp.

4. Which of the following would be the best choice for this sentence (reproduced below)?

(4) <u>We rejoiced as "hackers."</u>

a. NO CHANGE
b. To a nagging problem of technology, we rejoiced as "hackers."
c. We rejoiced when we figured out how to "hack" a solution to a nagging technological problem.
d. To "hack" our way to a solution, we had to rejoice.

5. Which of the following would be the best choice for this sentence (reproduced below)?

(5) <u>We even made some new friends in the process.</u>

a. NO CHANGE
b. In the process was the friends we were making.
c. We are even making some new friends in the process.
d. We will make new friends in the process.

6. Which of the following would be the best choice for this sentence (reproduced below)?

(6) <u>Above all, it allowed us to share adventures. While traveling across America,</u> which we could not have experienced in cars and hotels.

a. NO CHANGE
b. Above all, it allowed us to share adventures while traveling across America
c. Above all, it allowed us to share adventures; while traveling across America
d. Above all, it allowed us to share adventures—while traveling across America

194

7. Which of the following would be the best choice for this sentence (reproduced below)?

(7) <u>Those are also memories that my siblings and me</u> have now shared with our own children.

a. NO CHANGE
b. Those are also memories that me and my siblings
c. Those are also memories that my siblings and I
d. Those are also memories that I and my siblings

Read the following section about Fred Hampton and answer Questions 8-20.

1   Fred Hampton desired to see lasting social change for African American people through nonviolent means and community recognition. (8) <u>In the meantime,</u> he became an African American activist during the American Civil Rights Movement and led the Chicago chapter of the Black Panther Party.

Hampton's Education

2   Hampton was born and raised (9) <u>in Maywood of Chicago, Illinois in 1948.</u> Gifted academically and a natural athlete, he became a stellar baseball player in high school. (10) <u>After graduating from Proviso East High School in 1966, he later went on to study law at Triton Junior College. While studying at Triton, Hampton joined and became a leader of the National Association for the Advancement of Colored People (NAACP). As a result of his leadership, the NAACP gained more than 500 members.</u> Hampton worked relentlessly to acquire recreational facilities in the neighborhood and improve the educational resources provided to the impoverished black community of Maywood.

The Black Panthers

3   The Black Panther Party (BPP) (11) <u>was another that</u> formed around the same time as and was similar in function to the NAACP. Hampton was quickly attracted to the (12) <u>Black Panther Party's approach</u> to the fight for equal rights for African Americans. Hampton eventually joined the chapter and relocated to downtown Chicago to be closer to its headquarters.

4   His charismatic personality, organizational abilities, sheer determination, and rhetorical skills (13) <u>enable him to quickly rise</u> through the chapter's ranks. Hampton soon became the leader of the Chicago chapter of the BPP where he organized rallies, taught political education classes, and established a free medical clinic. (14) <u>He also took part in the community police supervision project. He played an instrumental role</u> in the BPP breakfast program for impoverished African American children.

5   Hampton's (15) <u>greatest</u> <u>acheivement</u> as the <u>leader</u> of the BPP may be his fight against street gang violence in Chicago. In 1969, (16) <u>Hampton was held by a press conference</u> where he made the gangs agree to a nonaggression pact known as the Rainbow Coalition. As a result of the pact, a multiracial alliance between blacks, Puerto Ricans, and poor youth was developed.

Assassination

195

6   (17) As the Black Panther Party's popularity and influence grew, the Federal Bureau of Investigation (FBI) placed the group under constant surveillance. In an attempt to neutralize the party, the FBI launched several harassment campaigns against the BPP, raided its headquarters in Chicago three times, and arrested over one hundred of the group's members. Hampton was shot during such a raid that occurred on the morning of December 4th 1969.

7   (18) In 1976; seven years after the event, it was revealed that William O'Neal, Hampton's trusted bodyguard, was an undercover FBI agent. (19) O'Neal will provide the FBI with detailed floor plans of the BPP's headquarters, identifying the exact location of Hampton's bed. It was because of these floor plans that the police were able to target and kill Hampton.

8   The assassination of Hampton fueled outrage amongst the African American community. It was not until years after the assassination that the police admitted wrongdoing. (20) The Chicago City Council now are commemorating December 4th as Fred Hampton Day.

8. Which of the following would be the best choice for this sentence (reproduced below)?

(8) In the meantime, he became an African American activist during the American Civil Rights Movement and led the Chicago chapter of the Black Panther Party.

a. NO CHANGE
b. Unfortunately,
c. Finally,
d. As a result,

9. Which of the following would be the best choice for this sentence (reproduced below)?

Hampton was born and raised (9) in Maywood of Chicago, Illinois in 1948.

a. NO CHANGE
b. in Maywood, of Chicago, Illinois in 1948.
c. in Maywood of Chicago, Illinois, in 1948.
d. in Chicago, Illinois of Maywood in 1948.

10. Which of these sentences, if any, should begin a new paragraph?

(10) After graduating from Proviso East High School in 1966, he later went on to study law at Triton Junior College. While studying at Triton, Hampton joined and became a leader of the National Association for the Advancement of Colored People (NAACP). As a result of his leadership, the NAACP gained more than 500 members.

a. NO CHANGE
b. After graduating from Proviso East High School in 1966, he later went on to study law at Triton Junior College.
c. While studying at Triton, Hampton joined and became a leader of the National Association for the Advancement of Colored People (NAACP).
d. As a result of his leadership, the NAACP gained more than 500 members.

11. Which of the following facts would be the most relevant to include here?

The Black Panther Party (BPP) (11) was another that formed around the same time as and was similar in function to the NAACP.

a. NO CHANGE; best as written
b. was another activist group that
c. had a lot of members that
d. was another school that

12. Which of the following would be the best choice for this sentence (reproduced below)?

Hampton was quickly attracted to the (12) Black Panther Party's approach to the fight for equal rights for African Americans.

a. NO CHANGE
b. Black Panther Parties approach
c. Black Panther Partys' approach
d. Black Panther Parties' approach

13. Which of the following would be the best choice for this sentence (reproduced below)?

His charismatic personality, organizational abilities, sheer determination, and rhetorical skills (13) enable him to quickly rise through the chapter's ranks.

a. NO CHANGE
b. are enabling him to quickly rise
c. enabled him to quickly rise
d. will enable him to quickly rise

14. Which of the following would be the best choice for this sentence (reproduced below)?

(14) He also took part in the community police supervision project. He played an instrumental role in the BPP breakfast program for impoverished African American children.

a. NO CHANGE
b. He also took part in the community police supervision project but played an instrumental role
c. He also took part in the community police supervision project, he played an instrumental role
d. He also took part in the community police supervision project and played an instrumental role

197

15. Which of these, if any, is misspelled?

Hampton's (15) <u>greatest</u> <u>acheivement</u> as the <u>leader</u> of the BPP may be his fight against street gang violence in Chicago.

a. None of these are misspelled.
b. greatest
c. acheivement
d. leader

16. Which of the following would be the best choice for this sentence (reproduced below)?

In 1969, (16) <u>Hampton was held by a press conference</u> where he made the gangs agree to a nonaggression pact known as the Rainbow Coalition.

a. NO CHANGE
b. Hampton held a press conference
c. Hampton, holding a press conference
d. Hampton to hold a press conference

17. Which of the following would be the best choice for this sentence (reproduced below)?

(17) <u>As the Black Panther Party's popularity and influence grew, the Federal Bureau of Investigation (FBI) placed the group under constant surveillance.</u>

a. NO CHANGE
b. The Federal Bureau of Investigation (FBI) placed the group under constant surveillance as the Black Panther Party's popularity and influence grew.
c. Placing the group under constant surveillance, the Black Panther Party's popularity and influence grew.
d. As their influence and popularity grew, the FBI placed the group under constant surveillance.

18. Which of the following would be the best choice for this sentence (reproduced below)?

(18) <u>In 1976; seven years after the event,</u> it was revealed that William O'Neal, Hampton's trusted bodyguard, was an undercover FBI agent.

a. NO CHANGE
b. In 1976, seven years after the event,
c. In 1976 seven years after the event,
d. In 1976. Seven years after the event,

198

19. Which of the following would be the best choice for this sentence (reproduced below)?

(19) <u>O'Neal will provide</u> the FBI with detailed floor plans of the BPP's headquarters, identifying the exact location of Hampton's bed.

a. NO CHANGE
b. O'Neal provides
c. O'Neal provided
d. O'Neal, providing

20. Which of the following would be the best choice for this sentence (reproduced below)?

(20) <u>The Chicago City Council now are commemorating December 4th as Fred Hampton Day.</u>

a. NO CHANGE
b. Fred Hampton Day by the Chicago City Council, December 4, is now commemorated.
c. Now commemorated December 4th is Fred Hampton Day.
d. The Chicago City Council now commemorates December 4th as Fred Hampton Day.

Directions for questions 21–25

Select the best version of the underlined part of the sentence. The first choice is the same as the original sentence. If you think the original sentence is best, choose the first answer.

21. <u>An important issues stemming from this meeting</u> is that we won't have enough time to meet all of the objectives.
a. An important issues stemming from this meeting
b. Important issue stemming from this meeting
c. An important issue stemming from this meeting
d. Important issues stemming from this meeting

22. The rising popularity of the clean eating movement can be attributed <u>to the fact that experts say added sugars and chemicals in our food are to blame for the obesity epidemic.</u>
a. to the fact that experts say added sugars and chemicals in our food are to blame for the obesity epidemic.
b. in the facts that experts say added sugars and chemicals in our food are to blame for the obesity epidemic.
c. to the fact that experts saying added sugars and chemicals in our food are to blame for the obesity epidemic.
d. with the facts that experts say added sugars and chemicals in our food are to blame for the obesity epidemic.

23. She's looking for a suitcase that can fit all of her <u>clothes, shoes, accessory, and makeup.</u>
a. clothes, shoes, accessory, and makeup.
b. clothes, shoes, accessories, and makeup.
c. clothes, shoes, accessories, and makeups.
d. clothes, shoe, accessory, and makeup.

199

24. Shawn started taking guitar lessons <u>while he wanted to become a better musician.</u>
    a. while he wanted to become a better musician.
    b. because he wants to become a better musician.
    c. even though he wanted to become a better musician.
    d. because he wanted to become a better musician.

25. <u>Considering the recent rains we have had, it's a wonder</u> the plants haven't drowned.
    a. Considering the recent rains we have had, it's a wonder
    b. Consider the recent rains we have had, it's a wonder
    c. Considering for how much recent rain we have had, its a wonder
    d. Considering, the recent rains we have had, its a wonder

Directions for questions 26–28

Rewrite the sentence in your head following the directions given below. Keep in mind that your new sentence should be well written and should have essentially the same meaning as the original sentence.

26. Although she was nervous speaking in front of a crowd, the author read her narrative with poise and confidence.

Rewrite, beginning with

<u>The author had poise and confidence while reading</u>

The next words will be
    a. because she was nervous speaking in front of a crowd.
    b. but she was nervous speaking in front of a crowd.
    c. even though she was nervous speaking in front of a crowd.
    d. before she was nervous speaking in front of a crowd.

27. There was a storm surge and loss of electricity during the hurricane.

Rewrite, beginning with

<u>While the hurricane occurred,</u>

The next words will be
    a. there was a storm surge after the electricity went out.
    b. the storm surge caused the electricity to go out.
    c. the electricity surged into the storm.
    d. the electricity went out, and there was a storm surge.

28. When one elephant in a herd is sick, the rest of the herd will help it walk and bring it food.

Rewrite, beginning with

<u>An elephant herd will</u>

The next words will be
   a. be too sick and tired to walk
   b. help and support
   c. gather food when they're sick
   d. be unable to walk without food

29. A student is starting a research assignment on Japanese-American internment camps during World War II, but she is unsure of how to gather relevant resources. Which of the following would be the most helpful advice for the student?
   a. Conduct a broad internet search to get a wide view of the subject.
   b. Consult an American history textbook.
   c. Find websites about Japanese culture such as fashion and politics.
   d. Locate texts in the library related to World War II in America and look for references to internment camps in the index.

30. Which of the following should be evaluated to ensure the credibility of a source?
   a. The publisher, the author, and the references
   b. The subject, the title, and the audience
   c. The organization, stylistic choices, and transition words
   d. The length, the tone, and the contributions of multiple authors

Answer Explanations #1

Math

1. B: Start with the original equation: $x^2 - 2xy + 2y$, then replace each instance of x with a 2, and each instance of y with a 3 to get:

$$2^2 - 2 \times 2 \times 3 + 2 \times 3^2 = 4 - 12 + 18 = 10$$

2. A: To expand a squared binomial, it's necessary to use the First, Outer, Inner, Last (FOIL) Method.

$$(2x - 4y)^2$$

$$(2x)(2x) + (2x)(-4y) + (-4y)(2x) + (-4y)(-4y)$$

$$4x^2 - 8xy - 8xy + 16y^2$$

$$4x^2 - 16xy + 16y^2$$

3. D: Factor the numerator into $x^2 - 6x + 9 = (x - 3)^2$, since:

$$-3 - 3 = -6, (-3)(-3) = 9$$

Factor the denominator into $x^2 - x - 6 = (x - 3)(x + 2)$, since:

$$-3 + 2 = -1, (-3)(2) = -6$$

This means the rational function can be rewritten as:

$$\frac{x^2 - 6x + 9}{x^2 - x - 6} = \frac{(x - 3)^2}{(x - 3)(x + 2)}$$

Using the restriction of $x > 3$, do not worry about any of these terms being 0, and cancel an $x - 3$ from the numerator and the denominator, leaving $\frac{x-3}{x+2}$.

4. B: The first step is to use the quadratic formula on the first equation ($x^2 - x - 3 = 0$) to solve for x. In this case, a is 1, b is -1, and c is -3, yielding:

$$x = \frac{-b \pm \sqrt{b^2 - 4ac}}{2a}$$

$$x = \frac{1 \pm \sqrt{1 - 4 \times 1(-3)}}{2}$$

$$x = \frac{1}{2} \pm \frac{\sqrt{13}}{2}$$

Therefore, $x - \frac{1}{2}$, which is in our second equation, equals $\pm \frac{\sqrt{13}}{2}$. We are looking for $\left(x - \frac{1}{2}\right)^2$ though, so we square the $\pm \frac{\sqrt{13}}{2}$. Doing so causes the $\pm$ to cancel and we are left with:

$$\left(x - \frac{1}{2}\right)^2 = \left(\frac{\sqrt{13}}{2}\right)^2 = \frac{13}{4}$$

5. B: Add 3 to both sides to get $4x = 8$. Then divide both sides by 4 to get $x = 2$.

6. C: The quadratic formula can be used to solve this problem. Given the equation, use the values $a = 1$, $b = -2$, and $c = 8$.

$$x = \frac{-b \pm \sqrt{b^2 - 4ac}}{2a} = \frac{-(-2) \pm \sqrt{(-2)^2 - 4(1)(-8)}}{2(1)}$$

From here, simplify to solve for x.

$$x = \frac{2 \pm \sqrt{4 + 32}}{2} = \frac{2 \pm \sqrt{36}}{2} = \frac{2 \pm 6}{2} = 1 \pm 3$$

7. B: To factor $x^2 + 4x + 4$, the numbers needed are those that add to 4 and multiply to 4. Therefore, both numbers must be 2, and the expression factors to:

$$x^2 + 4x + 4 = (x + 2)^2$$

Similarly, the second expression factors to $x^2 - x - 6 = (x - 3)(x + 2)$, so that they have $x + 2$ in common.

8. D: The expression is three times the sum of twice a number and 1, which is $3(2x + 1)$. Then, 6 is subtracted from this expression.

9. A: Robert accomplished his task on Tuesday in $\frac{3}{4}$ the time compared to Monday. He must have worked $\frac{4}{3}$ as fast.

10. B: To simplify this inequality, subtract 3 from both sides to get $-\frac{1}{2}x \geq -1$. Then, multiply both sides by -2 (remembering this flips the direction of the inequality) to get $x \leq 2$.

11. D: There are two ways to approach this problem. Each value can be substituted into each equation. A can be eliminated, since $4^2 + 16 = 32$. Choice B can be eliminated, since:

$$4^2 + 4 \times 4 - 4 = 28$$

Choice C can be eliminated, since

$$4^2 - 2 \times 4 - 2 = 6$$

However, Choice D does work because plugging in either value into $x^2 - 16$ yields a mathematically true statement:

$$(\pm 4)^2 - 16 = 16 - 16 = 0$$

12. A: The common denominator here will be $4x$. Rewrite these fractions as:

$$\frac{3}{x} + \frac{5u}{2x} - \frac{u}{4} = \frac{12}{4x} + \frac{10u}{4x} - \frac{ux}{4x} = \frac{12x + 10u - ux}{4x}$$

13. B: To simplify the given equation, the first step is to make all exponents positive by moving them to the opposite place in the fraction. This expression becomes:

$$\frac{4b^3 b^2}{a^1 a^4} \times \frac{3a}{b}$$

Then the rules for exponents can be used to simplify. Multiplying the same bases means the exponents can be added. Dividing the same bases means the exponents are subtracted. Thus, after multiplying the exponents in the first fraction, the equation becomes:

$$\frac{4b^5}{a^5} \times \frac{3a}{b}$$

Therefore, we can first multiply to get:

$$\frac{12ab^5}{a^5 b}$$

Then, simplifying yields:

$$12\frac{b^4}{a^4}$$

14. A: The augmented matrix that represents the system of equations has dimensions 4×3 because there are three equations with three unknowns. The coefficients of the variables make up the first three columns, and the last column is made up of the numbers to the right of the equals sign. This system can be solved by reducing the matrix to row-echelon form, where the last column gives the solution for the unknown variables.

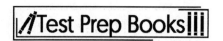

15. B: There are two zeros for the given function. They are $x = 0, -2$. The zeros can be found several ways, but this particular equation can be factored into:

$$f(x) = x(x^2 + 4x + 4) = x(x + 2)(x + 2)$$

By setting each factor equal to zero and solving for x, there are two solutions: $x = 0$ and $x = -2$. On a graph, these zeros can be seen where the line crosses the x-axis.

16. D: This system of equations involves one quadratic function and one linear function, as seen from the degree of each equation. One way to solve this is through substitution.

Solving for y in the second equation yields:

$$y = x + 2$$

Plugging this equation in for the y of the quadratic equation yields:

$$x^2 - 2x + x + 2 = 8$$

Simplifying the equation, it becomes:

$$x^2 - x + 2 = 8$$

Setting this equal to zero and factoring, it becomes:

$$x^2 - x - 6 = 0 = (x - 3)(x + 2)$$

Solving these two factors for x gives the zeros:

$$x = 3, -2$$

To find the y-value for the point, each number can be plugged in to either original equation. Solving each one for y yields the points $(3, 5)$ and $(-2, 0)$.

17. D: The expression is simplified by collecting like terms. Terms with the same variable and exponent are like terms, and their coefficients can be added.

18. A: Finding the product means distributing one polynomial to the other so that each term in the first is multiplied by each term in the second. Then, like terms can be collected. Multiplying the factors yields the expression:

$$20x^3 + 4x^2 + 24x - 40x^2 - 8x - 48$$

Collecting like terms means adding the x^2 terms and adding the x-terms. The final answer after simplifying the expression is:

$$20x^3 - 36x^2 + 16x - 48$$

19. D: Finding the zeros for a function by factoring is done by setting the equation equal to zero, then completely factoring. Since there is a common x for each term in the provided equation, that should be factored out first. Then the quadratic that is left can be factored into two binomials, which are $(x + 1)(x - 4)$. Setting each factor equal to zero and solving for x yields three zeros.

205

20. B: The equation can be solved by factoring the numerator into $(x + 6)(x - 5)$. Since that same factor $(x - 5)$ exists on top and bottom, that factor cancels. This leaves the equation $x + 6 = 11$. Solving the equation gives the answer $x = 5$. When this value is plugged into the equation, it yields a zero in the denominator of the fraction. Since this is undefined, there is no solution.

21. B: The domain is all possible input values, or x-values. For this equation, the domain is every number greater than or equal to zero. There are no negative numbers in the domain because taking the square root of a negative number results in an imaginary number.

22. B: The graph of $y = x^2 + 2$ has a vertex at $(0, 2)$ on the y-axis. The circle with a center at $(0, 1)$ also lies on the y-axis. With a radius of 1, the circle touches the parabola at one point: the vertex of the parabola $(0, 2)$.

23. D: The slope is given by the change in y divided by the change in x. The change in y is $2 - 0 = 2$, and the change in x is $0 - (-4) = 4$. The slope is $\frac{2}{4} = \frac{1}{2}$.

24. A: Check each value, but it is easiest to use the quadratic formula, which gives:

$$x = \frac{2 \pm \sqrt{(-2)^2 - 4(1)(-2)}}{2} = 1 \pm \frac{\sqrt{12}}{2}$$

$$1 \pm \frac{2\sqrt{3}}{2} = 1 \pm \sqrt{3}$$

The only one of these which appears as an answer choice is $1 + \sqrt{3}$.

25. A: First, separate each element of the numerator with the denominator as follows:

$$\frac{2xy^2}{16xy} + \frac{4x}{16xy} - \frac{8y}{16xy}$$

Simplify each expression accordingly, reaching Choice A:

$$\frac{y}{8} + \frac{1}{4y} - \frac{1}{2x}$$

26. C: First, factor out the 3's: $\frac{1+i}{1-i}$. Then, multiply the top and bottom by its complex conjugate, $1 + i$:

$$\frac{(1 + i)(1 + i)}{(1 - i)(1 + i)} = \frac{1 + 2i + i^2}{1 - i^2}$$

Since i is the square root of -1, this goes to:

$$\frac{1 + 2i + (-1)}{1 - (-1)}$$

This equates to $\frac{2i}{2}$. Cancelling out the 2's leaves i. Choice A is not the correct answer because that only represents the denominator that is part of a fraction that needs to be simplified. Choice B is not the correct answer because that only represents the numerator that is part of a fraction that needs to be

206

simplified. Choice *D* is not the final answer because it shows only part of the result from the FOIL method.

27. A: To find the fraction of the bill that the first three people pay, the fractions need to be added, which means finding the common denominator. The common denominator will be 60.

$$\frac{1}{5}+\frac{1}{4}+\frac{1}{3}=\frac{12}{60}+\frac{15}{60}+\frac{20}{60}=\frac{47}{60}$$

The remainder of the bill is:

$$1-\frac{47}{60}=\frac{60}{60}-\frac{47}{60}=\frac{13}{60}$$

28. B: 300 miles in 4 hours is $300 \div 4 = 75$ miles per hour. In 1.5 hours, the car will go 1.5×75 miles, or 112.5 miles.

29. B:

$$\frac{5}{2} \div \frac{1}{3}$$

$$\frac{5}{2} \times \frac{3}{1}$$

$$\frac{15}{2} = 7.5$$

30. A: The total fraction taken up by green and red shirts will be:

$$\frac{1}{3}+\frac{2}{5}=\frac{5}{15}+\frac{6}{15}=\frac{11}{15}$$

The remaining fraction is:

$$1-\frac{11}{15}$$

$$\frac{15}{15}-\frac{11}{15}=\frac{4}{15}$$

Reading

1. C: Gulliver becomes acquainted with the people and practices of his new surroundings. Choice *C* is the correct answer because it most extensively summarizes the entire passage. While Choices *A* and *B* are reasonable possibilities, they reference portions of Gulliver's experiences, not the whole. Choice *D* is incorrect because Gulliver doesn't express repentance or sorrow in this particular passage.

2. A: *Principal* refers to *chief* or *primary* within the context of this text. Choice *A* is the answer that most closely aligns with this definition. Choices *B* and *D* make reference to a helper or followers while Choice *C* doesn't meet the description of Reldresal from the passage.

3. C: One can reasonably infer that Gulliver is considerably larger than the children who were playing around him because multiple children could fit into his hand. Choice *B* is incorrect because there is no indication of stress in Gulliver's tone. Choices *A* and *D* aren't the best answer because though Gulliver seems fond of his new acquaintances, he didn't travel there with the intentions of meeting new people or to express a definite love for them in this particular portion of the text.

4. C: The emperor made a *definitive decision* to expose Gulliver to their native customs. In this instance, the word *mind* was not related to a vote, question, or cognitive ability.

5. A: Choice *A* is correct. This assertion does *not* support the fact that games are a commonplace event in this culture because it mentions conduct, not games. Choices *B*, *C*, and *D* are incorrect because these do support the fact that games were a commonplace event.

6. B: Choice *B* is the only option that mentions the correlation between physical ability and leadership positions. Choices *A* and *D* are unrelated to physical strength and leadership abilities. Choice *C* does not make a deduction that would lead to the correct answer—it only comments upon the abilities of common townspeople.

7. D: It emphasizes Mr. Utterson's anguish in failing to identify Hyde's whereabouts. Context clues indicate that Choice *D* is correct because the passage provides great detail of Mr. Utterson's feelings about locating Hyde. Choice *A* does not fit because there is no mention of Mr. Lanyon's mental state. Choice *B* is incorrect; although the text does make mention of bells, Choice *B* is not the *best* answer overall. Choice *C* is incorrect because the passage clearly states that Mr. Utterson was determined, not unsure.

8. A: In the city. The word *city* appears in the passage several times, thus establishing the location for the reader.

9. B: It scares children. The passage states that the Juggernaut causes the children to scream. Choices *A* and *D* don't apply because the text doesn't mention either of these instances specifically. Choice *C* is incorrect because there is nothing in the text that mentions space travel.

10. B: To constantly visit. The mention of *morning*, *noon*, and *night* make it clear that the word *haunt* refers to frequent appearances at various times. Choice *A* doesn't work because the text makes no mention of levitating. Choices *C* and *D* are not correct because the text makes mention of Mr. Utterson's anguish and disheartenment because of his failure to find Hyde but does not make mention of Mr. Utterson's feelings negatively affecting anyone else.

11. D: This is an example of alliteration. Choice *D* is the correct answer because of the repetition of the *L*-words. Hyperbole is an exaggeration, so Choice *A* doesn't work. No comparison is being made, so no simile or juxtaposition is being used, thus eliminating Choices B and C.

12. D: The speaker intends to continue to look for Hyde. Choices *A* and *B* are not possible answers because the text doesn't refer to any name changes or an identity crisis, despite Mr. Utterson's extreme obsession with finding Hyde. The text also makes no mention of a mistaken identity when referring to Hyde, so Choice *C* is also incorrect.

13. A: The tone is exasperated. While contemplative is an option because of the inquisitive nature of the text, Choice *A* is correct because the speaker is frustrated by the thought of being included when he felt

208

that the fellow members of his race were being excluded. The speaker is not nonchalant, nor accepting of the circumstances which he describes.

14. C: Choice C, *contented*, is the only word that has different meaning. Furthermore, the speaker expresses objection and disdain throughout the entire text.

15. B: To address the hypocrisy of the Fourth of July holiday. While the speaker makes biblical references, it is not the main focus of the passage, thus eliminating Choice A as an answer. The passage also makes no mention of wealthy landowners and doesn't speak of any positive response to the historical events, so Choices C and D are not correct.

16. D: Choice D is the correct answer because it clearly makes reference to justice being denied.

17. D: Hyperbole. Choices A and B are unrelated. Assonance is the repetition of sounds and commonly occurs in poetry. Parallelism refers to two statements that correlate in some manner. Choice C is incorrect because amplification normally refers to clarification of meaning by broadening the sentence structure, while hyperbole refers to a phrase or statement that is being exaggerated.

18. C: Choice C is correct because the speaker is clear about his intention and stance throughout the text; thus, it's not true that he makes biblical references to display his own equivocation and that of those that he represents. Choice A could be true, but the words "common text" is arguable because not everyone will understand the reference. Choice B is also partially true, as another group of people affected by slavery are being referenced. However, the speaker is not trying to convince the audience that injustices have been committed, as it is already understood there have been injustices committed. Choice D is also close to the correct answer, but it is not the best answer choice possible.

19. B: A period of time. It is apparent that Lincoln is referring to a period of time within the context of the passage because of how the sentence is structured with the word *ago*.

20. C: Lincoln's reference to *the brave men, living and dead, who struggled here,* proves that he is referring to a battlefield. Choices A and B are incorrect, as a *civil war* is mentioned and not a war with France or a war in the Sahara Desert. Choice D is incorrect because it does not make sense to consecrate a President's ground instead of a battlefield ground for soldiers who died during the American Civil War.

21. D: Abraham Lincoln is a former president of the United States, and he referenced a "civil war" during his address.

22. A: The audience should perpetuate the ideals of freedom that the soldiers died fighting for. Lincoln doesn't address any of the topics outlined in Choices B, C, or D. Therefore, Choice A is the correct answer.

23. D: Choice D is the correct answer because of the repetition of the word *people* at the end of the passage. Choice A, *antimetatabole*, is the repetition of words in a succession. Choice B, *antiphrasis*, is a form of denial of an assertion in a text. Choice C, *anaphora*, is the repetition that occurs at the beginning of sentences.

24. A: Choice A is correct because Lincoln's intention was to memorialize the soldiers who had fallen as a result of war as well as celebrate those who had put their lives in danger for the sake of their country.

Choices *B* and *D* are incorrect because Lincoln's speech was supposed to foster a sense of pride among the members of the audience while connecting them to the soldiers' experiences.

25. D: Passage A argues that the source of great poetry comes from emotions within, while passage B argues that great poetry is based off the skill and expertise of the poet. Choice *A* is incorrect; both passages attempt to explain how great poetry is created, not its aim or its results. The "purpose" passage A talks about are the author's individual poems, but the main idea of the passage is contained in the middle, starting with "For all good poetry." Choice *B* is incorrect; neither passages make any mention of nature or urban life. Choice *C* is incorrect; passage B does use epic poetry for most of its examples, but it is not solely concerned with epic poetry. It recalls Keats' "Ode to a Nightingale" at the very end. This is not the best answer choice.

26. A: The author is explaining that the feelings portrayed in Keats' ode are brought forth and signified by the symbolism of the nightingale used within the language of the poem. Eliot is relating it back to the original point of the passage: that great poetry doesn't simply come from powerful emotion, but that it is that emotion coupled with the literary devices of the poet that makes great poetry. Some of the other choices have similar wording to the last sentence, but they are not the best answer choice.

27. C: That feelings from the past will accumulate into representations of thought. The poet is then responsible for putting these direct thoughts onto paper, creating a poem. Therefore, the original source of poetry is from the past feelings of the poet. This is explained by the author beginning with the sentence "For our continued influxes of feeling . . . " The author is very clear about feelings from the past accumulating into representations of thought, so all the other answer choices are incorrect.

28. B: The author of passage B argues that the effort put into a poem counts for more than the intensity of the emotion felt while writing the poem. Choice *A* is the opposite of what passage B argues. Choices *C* and *D* are more closely related to the ideas of passage A.

29. C: The best word here is inspected, which means *approved* or *investigated*. Choice *A*, vacated, means to leave empty. While this is a possible choice, it is not the best choice because it is assumed that the house would be vacated before it was bought. Choice *B*, dilapidated, means destroyed. Someone buying a house does not want the house to be left destroyed, so this is incorrect. Choice *D*, insulated, means that the house would be properly enclosed against the loss of heat or the intrusion of sound. Although this is a possible answer, this would be included in an inspection. Therefore, Choice *D* is incorrect.

30. A: Relinquish most closely means to give up or let go. Deirdre knew she had to give up her position in order to go back to school. Choice *B*, rearrange, means to shift or change. Choice *C*, reciprocate, means to exchange or swap. Choice *D*, receive, means to accept.

Writing

1. B: Move the sentence so that it comes before the preceding sentence. For this question, place the underlined sentence in each prospective choice's position. To keep it as-is is incorrect because the father "going crazy" doesn't logically follow the fact that he was a "city slicker." Choice *C* is incorrect because the sentence in question is not a concluding sentence and does not transition smoothly into the second paragraph. Choice *D* is incorrect because the sentence doesn't necessarily need to be omitted since it logically follows the very first sentence in the passage.

210

2. D: Choice *D* is correct because "As it turns out" indicates a contrast from the previous sentiment, that the RV was a great purchase. Choice *A* is incorrect because the sentence needs an effective transition from the paragraph before. Choice *B* is incorrect because the text indicates it *is* surprising that the RV was a great purchase because the author was skeptical beforehand. Choice *C* is incorrect because the transition "Furthermore" does not indicate a contrast.

3. B: This sentence calls for parallel structure. Choice *B* is correct because the verbs "wake," "eat," and "break" are consistent in tense and parts of speech. Choice *A* is incorrect because the words "wake" and "eat" are present tense while the word "broke" is in past tense. Choice *C* is incorrect because this turns the sentence into a question, which doesn't make sense within the context. Choice *D* is incorrect because it breaks tense with the rest of the passage. "Waking," "eating," and "breaking" are all present participles, and the context around the sentence is in past tense.

4. C: Choice *C* is correct because it is clear and fits within the context of the passage. Choice *A* is incorrect because "We rejoiced as 'hackers'" does not give a reason why hacking was rejoiced. Choice *B* is incorrect because it does not mention a solution being found and is therefore not specific enough. Choice *D* is incorrect because the meaning is eschewed by the helping verb "had to rejoice," and the sentence suggests that rejoicing was necessary to "hack" a solution.

5. A: The original sentence is correct because the verb tense as well as the meaning aligns with the rest of the passage. Choice *B* is incorrect because the order of the words makes the sentence more confusing than it otherwise would be. Choice *C* is incorrect because "We are even making" is in present tense. Choice *D* is incorrect because "We will make" is future tense. The surrounding text of the sentence is in past tense.

6. B: Choice *B* is correct because there is no punctuation needed if a dependent clause ("while traveling across America") is located behind the independent clause ("it allowed us to share adventures"). Choice *A* is incorrect because there are two dependent clauses connected and no independent clause, and a complete sentence requires at least one independent clause. Choice *C* is incorrect because of the same reason as Choice *A*. Semicolons have the same function as periods: there must be an independent clause on either side of the semicolon. Choice *D* is incorrect because the dash simply interrupts the complete sentence.

7. C: The rules for "me" and "I" is that one should use "I" when it is the subject pronoun of a sentence, and "me" when it is the object pronoun of the sentence. Break the sentence up to see if "I" or "me" should be used. To say "Those are memories that I have now shared" is correct, rather than "Those are memories that me have now shared." Choice *D* is incorrect because "my siblings" should come before "I."

8. D: Choice *D* is correct because Fred Hampton becoming an activist was a direct result of him wanting to see lasting social change for Black people. Choice *A* doesn't make sense because "In the meantime" denotes something happening at the same time as another thing. Choice *B* is incorrect because the text's tone does not indicate that becoming a civil rights activist is an unfortunate path. Choice *C* is incorrect because "Finally" indicates something that comes last in a series of events, and the word in question is at the beginning of the introductory paragraph.

9. C: Choice *C* is correct because there should be a comma between the city and state, as well as after the word "Illinois." Commas should be used to separate all geographical items within a sentence. Choice

A is incorrect because it does not include the comma after "Illinois." Choice *B* is incorrect because the comma after "Maywood" interrupts the phrase, "Maywood of Chicago." Finally, Choice *D* is incorrect because the order of the sentence designates that Chicago, Illinois is in Maywood, which is incorrect.

10. C: This is a difficult question. The paragraph is incorrect as-is because it is too long and thus loses the reader halfway through. Choice *C* is correct because if the new paragraph began with "While studying at Triton," we would see a smooth transition from one paragraph to the next. We can also see how the two paragraphs are logically split in two. The first half of the paragraph talks about where he studied. The second half of the paragraph talks about the NAACP and the result of his leadership in the association. If we look at the passage as a whole, we can see that there are two main topics that should be broken into two separate paragraphs.

11. B: The BPP "was another activist group that . . ." We can figure out this answer by looking at context clues. We know that the BPP is "similar in function" to the NAACP. To find out what the NAACP's function is, we must look at the previous sentences. We know from above that the NAACP is an activist group, so we can assume that the BPP is also an activist group.

12. A: Choice *A* is correct because the Black Panther Party is one entity; therefore, the possession should show the "Party's approach" with the apostrophe between the "y" and the "s." Choice *B* is incorrect because the word "Parties" should not be plural. Choice *C* is incorrect because the apostrophe indicates that the word "Partys" is plural. The plural of "party" is "parties." Choice *D* is incorrect because, again, the word "parties" should not be plural; instead, it is one unified party.

13. C: Choice *C* is correct because the passage is told in past tense, and "enabled" is a past tense verb. Choice *A*, "enable," is present tense. Choice *B*, "are enabling," is a present participle, which suggests a continuing action. Choice *D*, "will enable," is future tense.

14. D: Choice *D* is correct because the conjunction "and" is the best way to combine the two independent clauses. Choice *A* is incorrect because the word "he" becomes repetitive since the two clauses can be joined together. Choice *B* is incorrect because the conjunction "but" indicates a contrast, and there is no contrast between the two clauses. Choice *C* is incorrect because the introduction of the comma after "project" with no conjunction creates a comma splice.

15. C: The word "acheivement" is misspelled. Remember the rules for "*i* before *e* except after *c*." Choices *B* and *D*, "greatest" and "leader," are both spelled correctly.

16. B: Choice *B* is correct because it provides the correct verb tense and verb form. Choice *A* is incorrect; Hampton was not "held by a press conference"—rather, he held a press conference. The passage indicates that he "made the gangs agree to a nonaggression pact," implying that it was Hampton who was doing the speaking for this conference. Choice *C* is incorrect because, with this use of the sentence, it would create a fragment because the verb "holding" has no helping verb in front of it. Choice *D* is incorrect because it adds an infinitive ("to hold") where a past tense form of a verb should be.

17. A: Choice *A* is correct because it provides the most clarity. Choice *B* is incorrect because it doesn't name the group until the end, so the phrase "the group" is vague. Choice *C* is incorrect because it indicates that the BPP's popularity grew as a result of placing the group under constant surveillance, which is incorrect. Choice *D* is incorrect because there is a misplaced modifier; this sentence actually says that the FBI's influence and popularity grew, which is incorrect.

18. B: Choice *B* is correct. Choice *A* is incorrect because there should be an independent clause on either side of a semicolon, and the phrase "In 1976" is not an independent clause. Choice *C* is incorrect because there should be a comma after introductory phrases in general, such as "In 1976," and Choice *C* omits a comma. Choice *D* is incorrect because the sentence "In 1976." is a fragment.

19. C: Choice *C* is correct because the past tense verb "provided" fits in with the rest of the verb tense throughout the passage. Choice *A*, "will provide," is future tense. Choice *B*, "provides," is present tense. Choice *D*, "providing," is a present participle, which means the action is continuous.

20. D: The correct answer is Choice *D* because this statement provides the most clarity. Choice *A* is incorrect because the noun "Chicago City Council" acts as one, so the verb "are" should be singular, not plural. Choice *B* is incorrect because it is perhaps the most confusingly worded out of all the answer choices; the phrase "December 4" interrupts the sentence without any indication of purpose. Choice *C* is incorrect because it is too vague and leaves out *who* does the commemorating.

21. C: In this answer, the article and subject agree, and the subject and predicate agree. Choice *A* is incorrect because the article (*an*) and the noun (*issues*) do not agree in number. Choice *B* is incorrect because an article is needed before *important issue*. Choice *D* is incorrect because the plural subject *issues* does not agree with the singular verb *is*.

22. A: Choices *B* and *D* both use the expression *attributed to the fact* incorrectly. It can only be attributed *to* the fact, not *with* or *in* the fact. Choice *C* incorrectly uses a gerund, *saying*, when it should use the present tense of the verb *say*.

23. B: Choice *B* is correct because it uses correct parallel structure of plural nouns. *A* is incorrect because the word *accessory* is in singular form. Choice *C* is incorrect because it pluralizes *makeup*, which is already in plural form. Choice *D* is incorrect because it again uses the singular *accessory*, and it uses the singular *shoe*.

24. D: In a cause/effect relationship, it is correct to use the word because in the clausal part of the sentence. This can eliminate both Choices *A and* C which don't clearly show the cause/effect relationship. Choice *B* is incorrect because it uses the present tense, when the first part of the sentence is in the past tense. It makes grammatical sense for both parts of the sentence to be in present tense.

25. A: In Choice *B*, the present tense form of the verb *consider* creates an independent clause joined to another independent clause with only a comma, which is a comma splice and grammatically incorrect. Both *C* and *D* use the possessive form of *its*, when it should be the contraction *it's* for *it is*. Choice *D* also includes incorrect comma placement.

26. C: The original sentence states that despite the author being nervous, she was able to read with poise and confidence, which is stated in Choice *C*. Choice *A* changes the meaning by adding *because*; however, the author didn't read with confidence *because* she was nervous, but *despite* being nervous. Choice *B* is closer to the original meaning; however, it loses the emphasis of her succeeding *despite* her condition. Choice *D* adds the word *before*, which doesn't make much sense on its own, much less in relation to the original sentence.

27. D: The original sentence states that there was a storm surge and loss of electricity during the hurricane, making Choice *D* correct. Choices *A* and *B* arrange the storm surge and the loss of electricity within a cause-and-effect statement, which changes the meaning of the original sentence. Choice *C* changes *surge* from a noun into a verb and creates an entirely different situation.

28. B: The original sentence states that an elephant herd will help and support another herd member if it is sick, so Choice *B* is correct. Choice *A* is incorrect because it states the whole herd will be too sick and too tired to walk instead of a single elephant. Choice *C* is incorrect because the original sentence does not say that the herd gathers food when *they* are sick, but when a single member of the herd is sick. Although Choice *D* might be correct in a general sense, it does not relate to the meaning of the original sentence and is therefore incorrect.

29. D: Relevant information refers to information that is closely related to the subject being researched. Students might get overwhelmed by information when they first begin researching, so they should learn how to narrow down search terms for their field of study. Both Choices *A* and *B* are incorrect because they start with a range that is far too wide; the student will spend too much time sifting through unrelated information to gather only a few related facts. Choice *C* introduces a more limited range, but it is not closely related to the topic that is being researched. Finally, Choice *D* is correct because the student is choosing books that are more closely related to the topic and is using the index or table of contents to evaluate whether the source contains the necessary information.

30. A: The publisher, author, and references are elements of a resource that determine credibility. If the publisher has published more than one work, the author has written more than one piece on the subject, or the work references other recognized research, the credibility of a source will be stronger. Choice *B* is incorrect because the subject and title may be used to determine relevancy, not credibility, and the audience does not have much to do with the credibility of a source. Choice *C* is incorrect because the organization, stylistic choices, and transition words are all components of an effectively-written piece, but they have less to do with credibility, other than to ensure that the author knows how to write. The length and tone of a piece are a matter of author's preference, and a work does not have to be written by multiple people to be considered a credible source.

Practice Test #2

Math

1. The variable y is directly proportional to x. If $y = 3$ when $x = 5$, then what is y when $x = 20$?
    a. 10
    b. 12
    c. 14
    d. 16

2. There are $4x + 1$ treats in each party favor bag. If a total of $60x + 15$ treats are distributed, how many bags are given out?
    a. 15
    b. 16
    c. 20
    d. 22

3. Apples cost $2 each, while bananas cost $3 each. Maria purchased 10 fruits in total and spent $22. How many apples did she buy?
    a. 5
    b. 6
    c. 7
    d. 8

4. Five students take a test. The scores of the first four students are 80, 85, 75, and 60. If the median score is 80, which of the following could NOT be the score of the fifth student?
    a. 60
    b. 80
    c. 85
    d. 100

5. Ten students take a test. Five students get a 50. Four students get a 70. If the average score is 55, what was the last student's score?
    a. 20
    b. 40
    c. 50
    d. 60

6. A company invests $50,000 in a building where they can produce saws. If the cost of producing one saw is $40, then which function expresses the amount of money the company pays? The variable y is the money paid, and x is the number of saws produced.
    a. $y = 50{,}000x + 40$
    b. $y + 40 = x - 50{,}000$
    c. $y = 40x - 50{,}000$
    d. $y = 40x + 50{,}000$

215

7. David's car drove 72 miles in 90 minutes. How fast did he drive in feet per second?
    a. 0.8 feet per second
    b. 48.9 feet per second
    c. 0.009 feet per second
    d. 70.4 feet per second

8. A train traveling 50 miles per hour takes a trip lasting 3 hours. If a map has a scale of 1 inch per 10 miles, how many inches apart are the train's starting point and ending point on the map?
    a. 14
    b. 12
    c. 13
    d. 15

9. If $g(x) = x^3 - 3x^2 - 2x + 6$ and $f(x) = 2$, then what is $g(f(x))$?
    a. -26
    b. 6
    c. $2x^3 - 6x^2 - 4x + 12$
    d. -2

10. How do you solve $V = lwh$ for h?
    a. $lwV = h$

    b. $h = \dfrac{V}{lw}$

    c. $h = \dfrac{Vl}{w}$

    d. $h = \dfrac{Vw}{l}$

11. The phone bill is calculated each month using the equation $c = 50g + 75$. The cost of the phone bill per month is represented by c, and g represents the gigabytes of data used that month. What is the value and interpretation of the slope of this equation?
    a. 75 dollars per day
    b. 75 gigabytes per day
    c. 50 dollars per day
    d. 50 dollars per gigabyte

12. What is the slope of this line?

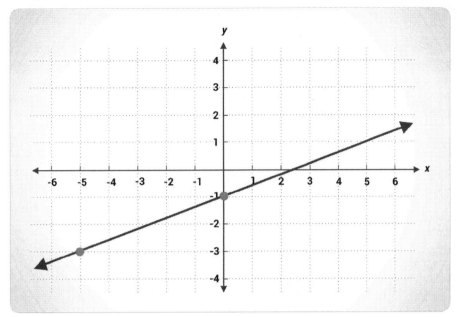

    a. 2

    b. $\frac{5}{2}$

    c. $\frac{1}{2}$

    d. $\frac{2}{5}$

13. Which of the following is NOT a way to write 40 percent of N?

    a. $(0.4)N$

    b. $\frac{2}{5}N$

    c. $40N$

    d. $\frac{4N}{10}$

14. Kassidy drove for 3 hours at a speed of 60 miles per hour. Using the distance formula, $d = r \times t$ ($distance = rate \times time$), how far did Kassidy travel?

    a. 20 miles

    b. 180 miles

    c. 65 miles

    d. 120 miles

15. After a 20% sale discount, Frank purchased a new refrigerator for $850. How much did he save from the original price?
    a. $170
    b. $212.50
    c. $105.75
    d. $200

16. Greg buys a $10 lunch with 5% sales tax. He leaves a $2 tip after his bill. How much money does he spend?
    a. $12.50
    b. $12
    c. $13
    d. $13.25

17. Which equation is not a function?
    a. $y = |x|$
    b. $y = \sqrt{x}$
    c. $x = 3$
    d. $y = 4$

18. Which fractions are equivalent, or would fill the same portion on a number line?
    a. $\frac{2}{4}$ and $\frac{3}{8}$
    b. $\frac{7}{3}$ and $2\frac{1}{3}$
    c. $\frac{3}{6}$ and $\frac{3}{5}$
    d. $1\frac{1}{4}$ and $\frac{7}{8}$

19. In Jim's school, there are 3 girls for every 2 boys. There are 650 students in total. Using this information, how many students are girls?
    a. 260
    b. 130
    c. 65
    d. 390

20. In an office, there are 50 workers. A total of 60% of the workers are women, and the chances of a woman wearing a skirt is 50%. If no men wear skirts, how many workers are wearing skirts?
    a. 12
    b. 15
    c. 16
    d. 20

21. Kelly is selling cookies to raise money for the choir. She has 500 cookies to sell. She sells 45% of the cookies to the sixth graders. At the second lunch, she sells 40% of what's left to the seventh graders. If she sells 60% of the remaining cookies to the eighth graders, how many cookies does Kelly have left at the end of all lunches?

    a. 66
    b. 62
    c. 68
    d. 52

22. Katie works at a clothing company and sold 192 shirts over the weekend. One-third of the shirts that were sold were patterned and the rest were solid. Which mathematical expression would calculate the number of solid shirts Katie sold over the weekend?

    a. $192 \times \frac{1}{3}$
    b. $192 \div \frac{1}{3}$
    c. $192 \times (1 - \frac{1}{3})$
    d. $192 \div 3$

23. If Danny takes 48 minutes to walk 3 miles, how long should it take him to walk 5 miles maintaining the same speed?

    a. 32 min
    b. 64 min
    c. 80 min
    d. 96 min

24. The value of 6×12 is the same as:

    a. $2 \times 4 \times 4 \times 2$
    b. $7 \times 4 \times 3$
    c. $6 \times 6 \times 3$
    d. $3 \times 3 \times 4 \times 2$

25. What is the value of b in this equation?

$$5b - 4 = 2b + 17$$

    a. 13
    b. 24
    c. 7
    d. 21

26. A school has 15 teachers and 20 teaching assistants. They have 200 students. What is the ratio of faculty to students?

    a. $3 : 20$
    b. $4 : 17$
    c. $3 : 2$
    d. $7 : 40$

219

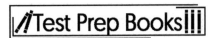

27. A student gets an 85% on a test with 20 questions. How many answers did the student solve correctly?

    a. 15
    b. 16
    c. 17
    d. 18

28. If Sarah reads at an average rate of 21 pages in four nights, how long will it take her to read 140 pages?

    a. 6 nights
    b. 26 nights
    c. 8 nights
    d. 27 nights

29. Johnny earns $2,334.50 from his job each month. He pays $1,437 for monthly expenses. Johnny is planning a vacation in 3 months that he estimates will cost $1,750 total. How much will Johnny have left over from three months of saving once he pays for his vacation?

    a. $948.50
    b. $584.50
    c. $852.50
    d. $942.50

30. Solve the following:

$$3 \times 8 - (2 + 1)^2 + 8$$

    a. 23
    b. 7
    c. 24
    d. 17

Reading

Questions 1–3 refer to the following paragraph:

The Brookside area is an older part of Kansas City, developed mainly in the 1920s and 30s, and is considered one of the nation's first "planned" communities with shops, restaurants, parks, and churches all within a quick walk. A stroll down any street reveals charming two-story Tudor and Colonial homes with smaller bungalows sprinkled throughout the beautiful tree-lined streets. It is common to see lemonade stands on the corners and baseball games in the numerous "pocket" parks tucked neatly behind rows of well-manicured houses. The Brookside shops on 63rd street between Wornall Road and Oak Street are a hub of commerce and entertainment where residents freely shop and dine with their pets (and children) in tow. This is also a common "hangout" spot for younger teenagers because it is easily accessible by bike for most. In short, it is an idyllic neighborhood just minutes from downtown Kansas City.

1. Which of the following states the main idea of this paragraph?
   a. The Brookside shops are a popular hangout for teenagers.
   b. There are a number of pocket parks in the Brookside neighborhood.
   c. Brookside is a great place to live.
   d. Brookside has a high crime rate.

2. In what kind of publication might you read the above paragraph?
   a. Fictional novel
   b. Community profile
   c. Newspaper article
   d. Movie review

3. According to this paragraph, which of the following is unique to this neighborhood?
   a. It is old.
   b. It is in Kansas City.
   c. It has shopping.
   d. It is one of the nation's first planned communities.

Questions 4–6 are based on the following passage:

> At its easternmost part, Long Island opens like the upper and under jaws of some prodigious alligator; the upper and larger one terminating in Montauk Point. The bay that lies in here, and part of which forms the splendid harbor of Greenport, where the Long Island Railroad ends, is called Peconic Bay; and a beautiful and varied water is it, fertile in fish and feathered game. I, who am by no means a skillful fisherman, go down for an hour of a morning on one of the docks, or almost anywhere along shore, and catch a mess of black-fish, which you couldn't buy in New York for a dollar—large fat fellows, with meat on their bones that it takes a pretty long fork to stick through. They have a way here of splitting these fat black-fish and poggies, and broiling them on the coals, beef-steak-fashion, which I recommend your Broadway cooks to copy.

This excerpt is adapted from Walt Whitman's "Letters from a Traveling Bachelor," published in the *New York Sunday Dispatch* on 14 October 1849.

4. Whitman's comparison of the easternmost part of Long Island to an alligator is an example of which literary device?
   a. Hyperbole
   b. Simile
   c. Personification
   d. Alliteration

5. Which of the following is the best summary of this passage?
   a. Walt Whitman was impressed with the quantity and quality of fish he found in Peconic Bay.
   b. Walt Whitman prefers the fish found in restaurants in New York.
   c. Walt Whitman was a Broadway chef.
   d. Walt Whitman is frustrated because he is not a very skilled fisherman.

6. Using the context clues in the passage, what is the meaning of the word *prodigious* in the first line?
   a. Out of place
   b. Great in extent, size, or degree
   c. Mean-spirited
   d. Extremely intelligent

Questions 7–10 are based on the following passage.

Early in my career, a master teacher shared this thought with me: "Education is the last bastion of civility." While I did not completely understand the scope of those words at the time, I have since come to realize the depth, breadth, truth, and significance of what he said. Education provides society with a vehicle for raising its children to be civil, decent, human beings with something valuable to contribute to the world. It is really what makes us human and what distinguishes us as civilized creatures.

Being "civilized" humans means being "whole" humans. Education must address the mind, body, and soul of students. It would be detrimental to society if our schools were myopic in their focus, only meeting the needs of the mind. As humans, we are multi-dimensional, multi-faceted beings who need more than head knowledge to survive. The human heart and psyche have to be fed in order for the mind to develop properly, and the body must be maintained and exercised to help fuel the working of the brain.

Education is a basic human right, and it allows us to sustain a democratic society in which participation is fundamental to its success. It should inspire students to seek better solutions to world problems and to dream of a more equitable society. Education should never discriminate on any basis, and it should create individuals who are self-sufficient, patriotic, and tolerant of other's ideas.

All children can learn, although not all children learn in the same manner. All children learn best, however, when their basic physical needs are met, and they feel safe, secure, and loved. Students are much more responsive to a teacher who values them and shows them respect as individual people. Teachers must model at all times the way they expect students to treat them and their peers. If teachers set high expectations for their students, the students will rise to that high level. Teachers must make the well-being of their students their primary focus and must not be afraid to let their students learn from their own mistakes.

In the modern age of technology, a teacher's focus is no longer the "what" of the content, but more importantly, the "why." Students are bombarded with information and have access to ANY information they need right at their fingertips. Teachers have to work harder than ever before to help students identify salient information and to think critically about the information they encounter. Students have to read between the lines, identify bias, and determine who they can trust in the milieu of ads, data, and texts presented to them.

Schools must work in consort with families in this important mission. While children spend most of their time in school, they are dramatically and indelibly shaped by the influences of their family and culture. Teachers must not only respect this fact but must strive to include parents in the education of their children and must work to keep parents informed of progress and problems. Communication between classroom and home is essential for a child's success.

Humans have always aspired to be more, do more, and to better ourselves and our communities. This is where education lies, right at the heart of humanity's desire to be all that we can be. Education helps us strive for higher goals and better treatment of ourselves and others. I shudder to think what would become of us if education ceased to be the "last bastion of civility." We must be unapologetic about expecting excellence from our students—our very existence depends upon it.

This excerpt is adapted from *"Education is Essential to Civilization."*

7. Which of the following best summarizes the author's main point?
    a. Education as we know it is over-valued in modern society, and we should find alternative solutions.
    b. The survival of the human race depends on the educational system, and it is worth fighting for to make it better.
    c. The government should do away with all public schools and require parents to home school their children instead.
    d. While education is important, some children simply are not capable of succeeding in a traditional classroom.

8. Based on this passage, which of the following can be inferred about the author?
    a. The author feels passionately about education.
    b. The author does not feel strongly about his point.
    c. The author is angry at the educational system.
    d. The author is unsure about the importance of education.

9. Based on this passage, which of the following conclusions could be drawn about the author?
    a. The author would not support raising taxes to help fund much needed reforms in education.
    b. The author would support raising taxes to help fund much needed reforms in education, as long as those reforms were implemented in higher socio-economic areas first.
    c. The author would support raising taxes to help fund much needed reforms in education for all children in all schools.
    d. The author would support raising taxes only in certain states to help fund much needed reforms in education.

10. According to the passage, which of the following is not mentioned as an important factor in education today?
    a. Parent involvement
    b. Communication between parents and teachers
    c. Impact of technology
    d. Cost of textbooks

11. In her famous poem "Because I Could Not Stop for Death," Emily Dickinson writes, "Because I could not stop for Death / He kindly stopped for me." Her mention of death is an example of which of the following?
    a. Hyperbole
    b. Personification
    c. Allusion
    d. Alliteration

12. In the poem quoted above, what does the slash mark between the words "Death" and "He" represent?
    a. The break between two stanzas
    b. The end of one sentence and the start of another
    c. The break between two lines of poetry
    d. The shift from one speaker to another

Use the following three quotations from Thomas Jefferson to answer questions 13 and 14.

"The tree of liberty must be refreshed from time to time with the blood of patriots and tyrants."

"In matters of style, swim with the current; in matters of principle, stand like a rock."

"I hold it, that a little rebellion, now and then, is a good thing, and as necessary in the political world as storms in the physical."

13. What is Jefferson's opinion on conflict?
    a. It is unavoidable and necessary.
    b. It must be avoided at all costs.
    c. Staying true to your principles is never worth the price you might pay.
    d. It will lead to ultimate destruction.

14. The "tree of liberty" is an example of which of the following?
    a. Personification
    b. Allusion
    c. Analogy
    d. Idiom

Use the following excerpt for questions 15 and 16:

Evidently, our country has overlooked both the importance of learning history and the appreciation of it. But why is this a huge problem? Other than historians, who really cares how the War of 1812 began, or who Alexander the Great's tutor was? Well, not many, as it turns out. So, *is* history really that important? Yes! History is *critical* to help us understand the underlying forces that shape decisive events, to prevent us from making the same mistakes twice, and to give us context for current events.

15. The above is an example of which type of writing?
    a. Expository
    b. Persuasive
    c. Narrative
    d. Poetry

16. In the above passage, what does the use of italics type for the word "critical" indicate?
    a. Dialogue
    b. Volume
    c. Emphasis
    d. Misspelling

17. Which of the following sentences contains an opinion statement?
    a. In 1819, the Supreme Court ruled that Congress could create a national bank.
    b. Marshall also ruled that the states did not have the right to tax the bank or any other agency created by the federal government.
    c. John Marshall was one of the most intelligent chief justices in the United States.
    d. The chief justice is the head of the judicial branch of the government.

18. Which of the following sentences is a factual statement?
    a. Many nutritionists believe a low carbohydrate, high protein diet is the healthiest diet.
    b. Legislation should be passed mandating that cell phones be banned in all public-school classrooms.
    c. Spanish is an easier language to learn than Japanese.
    d. College students would benefit greatly from participating in intramural sports on their campuses.

Questions 19 and 20 refer to the following quote from Martin Luther King Jr.'s Nobel Peace Prize acceptance speech in Oslo on December 10, 1964:

> "I refuse to accept the view that mankind is so tragically bound to the starless midnight of racism and war that the bright daybreak of peace and brotherhood can never become a reality . . . I believe that unarmed truth and unconditional love will have the final word."

19. Which of the following statements is NOT accurate based on this quote?
    a. Martin Luther King Jr. felt that the fight against racism was ultimately hopeless due to mankind's primitive instincts.
    b. Martin Luther King Jr. was eternally optimistic about mankind's ability to overcome racism.
    c. Martin Luther King Jr. believed that the war against racism could be won with truth and love.
    d. Martin Luther King Jr. believed that the goodness of mankind would prevail.

20. By referring to the "starless midnight of racism," Martin Luther King means:
    a. Racism involves prejudices against people with dark skin.
    b. Racism is evil and blinds people to the truth.
    c. It is easier to be racist on a starless night.
    d. The problem of racism is not as bad during the day.

Questions 21–24 refer to the following passage:

Although many Missourians know that Harry S. Truman and Walt Disney hailed from their great state, probably far fewer know that it was also home to the remarkable George Washington Carver. At the end of the Civil War, Moses Carver, the slave owner who owned George's parents, decided to keep George and his brother and raise them on his farm. As a child, George was driven to learn and he loved painting. He even went on to study art while in college but was encouraged to pursue botany instead. He spent much of his life helping others by showing them better ways to farm; his ideas improved agricultural productivity in many countries. One of his most notable contributions to the newly emerging class of Black farmers was to teach them the negative effects of agricultural monoculture, i.e. growing the same crops in the same fields year after year, depleting the soil of much needed nutrients and resulting in a lesser yielding crop. Carver was an innovator, always thinking of new and better ways to do things, and is most famous for his over three hundred uses for the peanut. Toward the end of his career, Carver returned to his first love of art. Through his artwork, he hoped to inspire people to see the beauty around them and to do great things themselves. When Carver died, he left his money to help fund ongoing agricultural research. Today, people still visit and study at the George Washington Carver Foundation at Tuskegee Institute.

21. Which of the following describes the kind of writing used in the above passage?
    a. Narrative
    b. Persuasive
    c. Technical
    d. Expository

22. According to the passage, what was George Washington Carver's first love?
    a. Plants
    b. Art
    c. Animals
    d. Soil

23. According to the passage, what is the best definition for agricultural monoculture?
    a. The practice of producing or growing a single crop or plant species over a wide area and for a large number of consecutive years
    b. The practice of growing a diversity of crops and rotating them from year to year
    c. The practice of growing crops organically to avoid the use of pesticides
    d. The practice of charging an inflated price for cheap crops to obtain a greater profit margin

24. Which of the following is the best summary of this passage?
    a. George Washington Carver was born at a time when scientific discovery was at a virtual standstill.
    b. Because he was African American, there were not many opportunities for George Washington Carver.
    c. George Washington Carver was an intelligent man whose research and discoveries had an impact worldwide.
    d. George Washington Carver was far more successful as an artist than he was as a scientist.

Questions 25–29 are based upon the following passage:

Insects as a whole are preeminently creatures of the land and the air. This is shown not only by the possession of wings by a vast majority of the class, but by the mode of breathing to which reference has already been made, a system of branching air-tubes carrying atmospheric air with its combustion-supporting oxygen to all the insect's tissues. The air gains access to these tubes through a number of paired air-holes or spiracles, arranged segmentally in series.

It is of great interest to find that, nevertheless, a number of insects spend much of their time under water. This is true of not a few in the perfect winged state, as for example aquatic beetles and water-bugs ('boatmen' and 'scorpions') which have some way of protecting their spiracles when submerged, and, possessing usually the power of flight, can pass on occasion from pond or stream to upper air. But it is advisable in connection with our present subject to dwell especially on some insects that remain continually under water till they are ready to undergo their final moult and attain the winged state, which they pass entirely in the air. The preparatory instars of such insects are aquatic; the adult instar is aerial. All may-flies, dragon-flies, and caddis-flies, many beetles and two-winged flies, and a few moths thus divide their life-story between the water and the air. For the present we confine attention to the Stone-flies, the May-flies, and the Dragon-flies, three well-known orders of insects respectively called by systematists the Plecoptera, the Ephemeroptera, and the Odonata.

In the case of many insects that have aquatic larvae, the latter are provided with some arrangement for enabling them to reach atmospheric air through the surface-film of the water. But the larva of a stone-fly, a dragon-fly, or a may-fly is adapted more completely than these for aquatic life; it can, by means of gills of some kind, breathe the air dissolved in water.

This excerpt is adapted from *The Life-Story of Insects*, by Geo H. Carpenter.

25. Which statement best details the central idea in this passage?
    a. It introduces certain insects that transition from water to air.
    b. It delves into entomology, especially where gills are concerned.
    c. It defines what constitutes as insects' breathing.
    d. It invites readers to have a hand in the preservation of insects.

26. Which definition most closely relates to the usage of the word *moult* in the passage?
    a. An adventure of sorts, especially underwater
    b. Mating act between two insects
    c. The act of shedding part or all of the outer shell
    d. Death of an organism that ends in a revival of life

27. What is the purpose of the first paragraph in relation to the second paragraph?
    a. The first paragraph serves as a cause, and the second paragraph serves as an effect.
    b. The first paragraph serves as a contrast to the second.
    c. The first paragraph is a description for the argument in the second paragraph.
    d. The first and second paragraphs are merely presented in a sequence.

227

28. What does the following sentence most nearly mean?
    The preparatory instars of such insects are aquatic; the adult instar is aerial.

    a. The volume of water is necessary to prep the insect for transition rather than the volume of the air.
    b. The abdomen of the insect is designed like a star in the water as well as the air.
    c. The early stages in between periods of molting are acted out in the water, while the last stage is in the air.
    d. These insects breathe first in the water through gills yet continue to use the same organs to breathe in the air.

29. Which of the statements reflect information that one could reasonably infer based on the author's tone?
    a. The author's tone is persuasive and attempts to call the audience to action.
    b. The author's tone is passionate due to excitement over the subject and personal narrative.
    c. The author's tone is informative and exhibits interest in the subject of the study.
    d. The author's tone is somber, depicting some anger at the state of insect larvae.

30. "Excuse me, Sir," the host of the party declared, "this matter is not *any* of your business." The use of italics in this sentence indicates which of the following?
    a. Dialogue
    b. Thoughts
    c. Emphasis
    d. Volume

Writing

Questions 1–9 are based on the following passage:

While all dogs (1) descend through gray wolves, it's easy to notice that dog breeds come in a variety of shapes and sizes. With such a (2) drastic range of traits, appearances and body types dogs are one of the most variable and adaptable species on the planet. (3) But why so many differences. The answer is that humans have actually played a major role in altering the biology of dogs. (4) This was done through a process called selective breeding.

(5) Selective breeding which is also called artificial selection is the processes in which animals with desired traits are bred in order to produce offspring that share the same traits. In natural selection, (6) animals must adapt to their environments increase their chance of survival. Over time, certain traits develop in animals that enable them to thrive in these environments. Those animals with more of these traits, or better versions of these traits, gain an (7) advantage over others of their species. Therefore, the animal's chances to mate are increased and these useful (8) genes are passed into their offspring. With dog breeding, humans select traits that are desired and encourage more of these desired traits in other dogs by breeding dogs that already have them.

The reason for different breeds of dogs is that there were specific needs that humans wanted to fill with their animals. For example, scent hounds are known for their extraordinary ability to track game through scent. These breeds are also known for their endurance in seeking deer and

228

other prey. Therefore, early hunters took dogs that displayed these abilities and bred them to encourage these traits. Later, these generations took on characteristics that aided these desired traits. (9) <u>For example, Bloodhounds</u> have broad snouts and droopy ears that fall to the ground when they smell. These physical qualities not only define the look of the Bloodhound, but also contribute to their amazing tracking ability. The broad snout is able to define and hold onto scents longer than many other breeds. The long, floppy ears serve to collect and hold the scents the earth holds so that the smells are clearer and able to be distinguished.

1. Which of the following would be the best choice for this sentence (reproduced below)?

While all dogs (1) <u>descend through gray wolves</u>, it's easy to notice that dog breeds come in a variety of shapes and sizes.

a. NO CHANGE
b. descend by gray wolves
c. descend from gray wolves
d. descended through gray wolves

2. Which of the following would be the best choice for this sentence (reproduced below)?

With such a (2) <u>drastic range of traits, appearances and body types</u>, dogs are one of the most variable and adaptable species on the planet.

a. NO CHANGE
b. drastic range of traits, appearances, and body types,
c. drastic range of traits and appearances and body types,
d. drastic range of traits, appearances, as well as body types,

3. Which of the following would be the best choice for this sentence (reproduced below)?

(3) <u>But why so many differences.</u>

a. NO CHANGE
b. But are there so many differences?
c. But why so many differences are there.
d. But why so many differences?

4. Which of the following would be the best choice for this sentence (reproduced below)?

(4) <u>This was done through a process called selective breeding.</u>

a. NO CHANGE
b. This was done, through a process called selective breeding.
c. This was done, through a process, called selective breeding.
d. This was done through selective breeding, a process.

5. Which of the following would be the best choice for this sentence (reproduced below)?

(5) Selective breeding which is also called artificial selection is the processes in which animals with desired traits are bred in order to produce offspring that share the same traits.

a. NO CHANGE
b. Selective breeding, which is also called artificial selection is the processes
c. Selective breeding which is also called, artificial selection, is the processes
d. Selective breeding, which is also called artificial selection, is the processes

6. Which of the following would be the best choice for this sentence (reproduced below)?

In natural selection, (6) animals must adapt to their environments increase their chance of survival.

a. NO CHANGE
b. animals must adapt to their environments to increase their chance of survival.
c. animals must adapt to their environments, increase their chance of survival.
d. animals must adapt to their environments, increasing their chance of survival.

7. Which of the following would be the best choice for this sentence (reproduced below)?

Those animals with more of these traits, or better versions of these traits, gain an (7) advantage over others of their species.

a. NO CHANGE
b. advantage over others, of their species.
c. advantages over others of their species.
d. advantage over others.

8. Which of the following would be the best choice for this sentence (reproduced below)?

Therefore, the animal's chances to mate are increased and these useful (8) genes are passed into their offspring.

a. NO CHANGE
b. genes are passed onto their offspring.
c. genes are passed on to their offspring.
d. genes are passed within their offspring.

9. Which of the following would be the best choice for this sentence (reproduced below)?

(9) For example, Bloodhounds have broad snouts and droopy ears that fall to the ground when they smell.

a. NO CHANGE
b. For example, Bloodhounds,
c. For example Bloodhounds
d. For example, bloodhounds

230

Questions 10–18 are based on the following passage:

I'm not alone when I say that it's hard to pay attention sometimes. I can't count how many times I've sat in a classroom, lecture, speech, or workshop and (10) been bored to tears or rather sleep. (11) Usually I turn to doodling in order to keep awake. This never really helps; I'm not much of an artist. Therefore, after giving up on drawing a masterpiece, I would just concentrate on keeping my eyes open and trying to be attentive. This didn't always work because I wasn't engaged in what was going on.

(12) Sometimes in particularly dull seminars, I'd imagine comical things going on in the room or with the people trapped in the room with me. Why? (13) Because I wasn't invested in what was going on I wasn't motivated to listen. I'm not going to write about how I conquered the difficult task of actually paying attention in a difficult or unappealing class—it can be done, sure. I have sat through the very epitome of boredom (in my view at least) several times and come away learning something. (14) Everyone probably has had to at one time do this. What I want to talk about is that profound moment when curiosity is sparked (15) in another person drawing them to pay attention to what is before them and expand their knowledge.

What really makes people pay attention? (16) Easy it's interest. This doesn't necessarily mean (17) embellishing subject matter drawing people's attention. This won't always work. However, an individual can present material in a way that is clear to understand and actually engages the audience. Asking questions to the audience or class will make them a part of the topic at hand. Discussions that make people think about the content and (18) how it applies to there lives world and future is key. If math is being discussed, an instructor can explain the purpose behind the equations or perhaps use real-world applications to show how relevant the topic is. When discussing history, a lecturer can prompt students to imagine themselves in the place of key figures and ask how they might respond. The bottom line is to explore the ideas rather than just lecture. Give people the chance to explore material from multiple angles, and they'll be hungry to keep paying attention for more information.

10. Which of the following would be the best choice for this sentence (reproduced below)?

I can't count how many times I've sat in a classroom, lecture, speech, or workshop and (10) been bored to tears or rather sleep.

a. NO CHANGE
b. been bored to, tears, or rather sleep.
c. been bored, to tears or rather sleep.
d. been bored to tears or, rather, sleep.

11. Which of the following would be the best choice for this sentence (reproduced below)?

(11) Usually I turn to doodling in order to keep awake.

a. NO CHANGE
b. Usually, I turn to doodling in order to keep awake.
c. Usually I turn to doodling, in order, to keep awake.
d. Usually I turned to doodling in order to keep awake.

12. Which of the following would be the best choice for this sentence (reproduced below)?
(12) <u>Sometimes in particularly dull seminars,</u> I'd imagine comical things going on in the room or with the people trapped in the room with me.

a. NO CHANGE
b. Sometimes, in particularly, dull seminars,
c. Sometimes in particularly dull seminars
d. Sometimes in particularly, dull seminars,

13. Which of the following would be the best choice for this sentence (reproduced below)?

(13) <u>Because I wasn't invested in what was going on I wasn't motivated to listen.</u>

a. NO CHANGE
b. Because I wasn't invested, in what was going on, I wasn't motivated to listen.
c. Because I wasn't invested in what was going on. I wasn't motivated to listen.
d. I wasn't motivated to listen because I wasn't invested in what was going on.

14. Which of the following would be the best choice for this sentence (reproduced below)?

(14) <u>Everyone probably has had to at one time do this.</u>

a. NO CHANGE
b. Everyone probably has had to, at one time. Do this.
c. Everyone's probably had to do this at some time.
d. At one time everyone probably has had to do this.

15. Which of the following would be the best choice for this sentence (reproduced below)?

What I want to talk about is that profound moment when curiosity is sparked (15) <u>in another person drawing them to pay attention to what is before them</u> and expand their knowledge.

a. NO CHANGE
b. in another person, drawing them to pay attention
c. in another person; drawing them to pay attention to what is before them.
d. in another person, drawing them to pay attention to what is before them.

16. Which of the following would be the best choice for this sentence (reproduced below)?

(16) <u>Easy it's interest.</u>

a. NO CHANGE
b. Easy it is interest.
c. Easy. It's interest.
d. Easy—it's interest.

232

17. Which of the following would be the best choice for this sentence (reproduced below)?

This doesn't necessarily mean (17) embellishing subject matter drawing people's attention.

    a. NO CHANGE
    b. embellishing subject matter which draws people's attention.
    c. embellishing subject matter to draw people's attention.
    d. embellishing subject matter for the purpose of drawing people's attention.

18. Which of the following would be the best choice for this sentence (reproduced below)?

Discussions that make people think about the content and (18) how it applies to there lives world and future is key.

    a. NO CHANGE
    b. how it applies to their lives, world, and future is key.
    c. how it applied to there lives world and future is key.
    d. how it applies to their lives, world and future is key.

19. My favorite teacher gave _____ and _____ extra credit on our project.
    a. me, him
    b. he, I
    c. him, I
    d. him, me

20. Which of these sentences uses correct punctuation?
    a. We traveled through six states on our road trip; Texas, New Mexico, Colorado, Wyoming, Utah, and Montana.
    b. We traveled through six states on our road trip: Texas, New Mexico, Colorado, Wyoming, Utah, and Montana.
    c. We traveled through six states on our road trip -- Texas, New Mexico, Colorado, Wyoming, Utah, and Montana.
    d. We traveled through six states on our road trip, Texas, New Mexico, Colorado, Wyoming, Utah, and Montana.

21. Which of the following sentences employs correct usage?
    a. You're going to need to go there to get your backpack from their house.
    b. Your going to need to go there to get you're backpack from their house.
    c. You're going to need to go their to get your backpack from there house.
    d. Your going to need to go their to get you're backpack from there house.

22. The following sentence contains what kind of error?
    Forgetting that he was supposed to meet his girlfriend for dinner, Anita was mad when Fred showed up late.

    a. Parallelism
    b. Run-on sentence
    c. Misplaced modifier
    d. Subject-verb agreement

233

23. The following sentence contains what kind of error?

Some workers use all their sick leave, other workers cash out their leave.

a. Parallelism
b. Comma splice
c. Sentence fragment
d. Subject-verb agreement

24. A student writes the following in an essay:

Protestors filled the streets of the city. Because they were dissatisfied with the government's leadership.

Which of the following is an appropriately punctuated correction for this sentence?

a. Protestors filled the streets of the city, because they were dissatisfied with the government's leadership.
b. Protesters, filled the streets of the city, because they were dissatisfied with the government's leadership.
c. Because they were dissatisfied with the government's leadership protestors filled the streets of the city.
d. Protestors filled the streets of the city because they were dissatisfied with the government's leadership.

25. Which word choices will correctly complete the sentence?

Increasing the price of bus fares has had a greater [affect / effect] on ridership [then / than] expected.

a. affect; then
b. affect; than
c. effect; then
d. effect; than

26. Which of the following would be a good topic sentence if you were writing a paragraph about the effects of education on crime rates?

a. Crime statistics are difficult to verify for a number of reasons.
b. Educated people do not commit crimes.
c. Education is an important factor in lowering crime rates.
d. Education has been proven to lower crime rates by as much as 20% in some urban areas.

27. Which of the following is not an example of a good thesis statement for an essay?

a. Animals in danger of becoming extinct come from a wide range of countries.
b. Effective leadership requires specific qualities that anyone can develop.
c. Industrial waste poured into Lake Michigan has killed 27 percent of marine life in the past decade.
d. In order to fully explore the wreck of the Titanic, scientists must address several problems.

234

28. Each patient, having gone through rehabilitative therapy, needed _____ file returned to the nursing station.
    a. their
    b. there
    c. his or her
    d. the people's

29. A man decided not to take his family to the zoo after hearing about a bomb threat on the news. The man believed the threat to be real and _____ .
    a. eminent
    b. imminent
    c. emanate
    d. amanita

30. Which of the following passages best displays clarity, fluency, and parallelism?
    a. Ernest Hemingway is probably the most noteworthy of expatriate authors. Hemingway's concise writing style, void of emotion and stream of consciousness, had a lasting impact, one which resonates to this very day. In Hemingway's novels, much like in American cinema, the hero acts without thinking, is living in the moment, and is repressing physical and emotional pain.
    b. Ernest Hemingway is probably the most noteworthy of expatriate authors since his concise writing style is void of emotion and stream of consciousness and has had a lasting impact on Americans which has resonated to this very day, and Hemingway's novels are much like in American cinema. The hero acts. He doesn't think. He lives in the moment. He represses physical and emotional pain.
    c. Ernest Hemingway is probably the most noteworthy of authors. His concise writing style, void of emotion and consciousness, had a lasting impact, one which resonates to this very day. In Hemingway's novels, much like in American cinema, the hero acts without thinking, lives in the moment, and represses physical and emotional pain.
    d. Ernest Hemingway is probably the most noteworthy of expatriate authors. His concise writing style, void of emotion and stream of consciousness, had a lasting impact, one which resonates to this very day. In Hemingway's novels, much like in American cinema, the hero acts without thinking, lives in the moment, and represses physical and emotional pain.

Answer Explanations #2

Math

1. B: To be directly proportional means that $y = kx$. If x is changed from 5 to 20, the value of x is multiplied by 4. Applying the same rule to the y-value, also multiply the value of y by 4. Therefore:

$$y = 12$$

2. A: Each bag contributes $4x + 1$ treats. The total treats will be in the form $4nx + n$ where n is the total number of bags. The total is in the form $60x + 15$, from which it is known $n = 15$.

3. D: Let a be the number of apples and b be the number of bananas. Then, the total cost is $2a + 3b = 22$, while it also known that $a + b = 10$. Using the knowledge of systems of equations, cancel the b variables by multiplying the second equation by -3. This makes the equation $-3a - 3b = -30$. Adding this to the first equation, the values cancel to get $-a = -8$, which simplifies to $a = 8$.

4. A: Lining up the given scores provides the following list: 60, 75, 80, 85, and one unknown. Because the median needs to be 80, it means 80 must be the middle data point out of these five. Therefore, the unknown data point must be the fourth or fifth data point, meaning it must be greater than or equal to 80. The only answer that fails to meet this condition is 60.

5. A: Let the unknown score be x. The average will be:

$$\frac{5 \times 50 + 4 \times 70 + x}{10} = \frac{530 + x}{10} = 55$$

Multiply both sides by 10 to get $530 + x = 550$, or $x = 20$.

6. D: For manufacturing costs, there is a linear relationship between the cost to the company and the number produced, with a y-intercept given by the base cost of acquiring the means of production and a slope given by the cost to produce one unit. In this case, that base cost is $50,000, while the cost per unit is $40. So, $y = 40x + 50,000$.

7. D: This problem can be solved by using unit conversion. The initial units are miles per minute. The final units need to be feet per second. Converting miles to feet uses the equivalence statement 1 mi = 5,280 ft. Converting minutes to seconds uses the equivalence statement 1 min = 60 s. Setting up the ratios to convert the units is shown in the following equation:

$$\frac{72 \text{ mi}}{90 \text{ min}} \times \frac{1 \text{ min}}{60 \text{ s}} \times \frac{5{,}280 \text{ ft}}{1 \text{ mi}} = 70.4 \frac{\text{ft}}{\text{s}}$$

The initial units cancel out, and the new units are left.

8. D: First, the train's journey in the real word is $3 \times 50 = 150$ miles. On the map, 1 inch corresponds to 10 miles, so that is equivalent to $150 \div 10 = 15$ inches on the map.

9. D: This problem involves a composition function, where one function is plugged into the other function. In this case, the $f(x)$ function is plugged into the $g(x)$ function for each x-value. The composition equation becomes:

$$g(f(x)) = (2)^3 - 3(2)^2 - 2(2) + 6$$

Simplifying the equation gives the answer:

$$g(f(x)) = 8 - 3(4) - 2(2) + 6$$

$$8 - 12 - 4 + 6 = -2$$

10. B: The formula can be manipulated by dividing both sides by the length, l, and the width, w. The length and width will cancel on the right, leaving height by itself.

11. D: The slope from this equation is 50, and it is interpreted as the cost per gigabyte used. Since the g-value represents number of gigabytes and the equation is set equal to the cost in dollars, the slope relates these two values. For every gigabyte used on the phone, the bill goes up 50 dollars.

12. D: The slope is given by the change in y divided by the change in x. Specifically, it's:

$$slope = \frac{y_2 - y_1}{x_2 - x_1}$$

The first point is $(-5, -3)$, and the second point is $(0, -1)$. Work from left to right when identifying coordinates. Thus, the point on the left is point 1 $(-5, -3)$ and the point on the right is point 2 $(0, -1)$.

Now we need to just plug those numbers into the equation:

$$slope = \frac{-1 - (-3)}{0 - (-5)}$$

It can be simplified to:

$$slope = \frac{-1 + 3}{0 + 5}$$

$$slope = \frac{2}{5}$$

13. C: $40N$ would be 4,000% of N. All of the other coefficients are equivalent to $\frac{40}{100}$ or 40%.

14. B: 180 miles. The rate, 60 miles per hour, and time, 3 hours, are given for the scenario. To determine the distance traveled, the given values for the rate (r) and time (t) are substituted into the distance formula and evaluated:

$$d = r \times t$$

$$d = \left(\frac{60 \text{ mi}}{1 \text{ h}}\right) \times (3 \text{ h}) \rightarrow d = 180 \text{ mi}$$

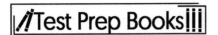

15. B: Since $850 is the price *after* a 20% discount, $850 represents 80% of the original price. To determine the original price, set up a proportion with the ratio of the sale price (850) to the original price (unknown) equal to the ratio of the sale percentage (where x represents the unknown original price):

$$\frac{850}{x} = \frac{80}{100}$$

To solve a proportion, cross multiply and set the products equal to each other:

$$(850)(100) = (80)(x)$$

Multiplying each side results in the equation:

$$85,000 = 80x$$

To solve for x, divide both sides by 80:

$$\frac{85,000}{80} = \frac{80x}{80}$$

$$x = 1,062.5$$

Remember that x represents the original price. Subtracting the sale price from the original price ($1,062.50 − $850) indicates that Frank saved $212.50.

16. A: The tip is not taxed, so he pays 5% tax only on the $10. 5% of $10 is $0.05 \times 10 = \$0.50$. Add up $10 + $2 + $0.50 to get $12.50.

17. C: The equation $x = 3$ is not a function because it does not pass the vertical line test. This test is made from the definition of a function, where each x-value must be mapped to one and only one y-value. This equation is a vertical line, so the x-value of 3 is mapped with an infinite number of y-values.

18. B: The answer choice that contains equivalent fractions is B, $\frac{7}{3}$ and $2\frac{1}{3}$. $\frac{7}{3}$ is the improper fraction for the mixed number $2\frac{1}{3}$. Recall that to convert a mixed number to an improper fraction, multiply the denominator by the whole number then add the numerator and place this sum over the denominator (as your new numerator). In this case:

$$2\frac{1}{3} \rightarrow 3 \times 2 + 1 \rightarrow \frac{7}{3}$$

19. D: Three girls for every two boys can be expressed as a ratio: 3:2. This can be visualized as splitting the school into 5 groups: 3 girl groups and 2 boy groups. The number of students that are in each group can be found by dividing the total number of students by 5:

$$\frac{650 \text{ students}}{5 \text{ groups}} = \frac{130 \text{ students}}{\text{group}}$$

To find the total number of girls, multiply the number of students per group (130) by the number of girl groups in the school (3). This equals 390, Choice *D*.

20. B: If 60% of 50 workers are women, then there are 30 women working in the office. If half of them are wearing skirts, then that means 15 women wear skirts. Since none of the men wear skirts, this means there are 15 people wearing skirts.

21. A: 66 cookies. If the sixth graders bought 45% of the cookies, the number they bought is found by multiplying 0.45 by 500. They bought 225 cookies. The number of cookies left is $500 - 225 = 275$. During the second lunch, the seventh graders bought 40% of the cookies, which is found by multiplying 0.40 by the remaining 275 cookies. The seventh graders bought 110 cookies. This leaves 165 cookies to sell to the eighth graders. If they bought 60% of the remaining cookies, then they bought 99 cookies. Subtracting 99 from 165 cookies leaves Kelly with 66 cookies remaining after the three lunches.

22. C: $\frac{1}{3}$ of the shirts sold were patterned. Therefore, $1 - \frac{1}{3} = \frac{2}{3}$ of the shirts sold were solid. Anytime "of" a quantity appears in a word problem, multiplication needs to be used. Therefore:

$$192 \times \frac{2}{3} = 192 \times \frac{2}{3} = \frac{384}{3} = 128 \text{ solid shirts were sold}$$

The entire expression is $192 \times \left(1 - \frac{1}{3}\right)$.

23. C: 80 min. To solve the problem, a proportion is written consisting of ratios comparing distance and time. One way to set up the proportion is:

$$\frac{3}{48} = \frac{5}{x} \left(\frac{distance}{time} = \frac{distance}{time} \right)$$

To solve a proportion, the ratios are cross-multiplied:

$$(3)(x) = (5)(48) \rightarrow 3x = 240$$

The equation is solved by isolating the variable, or dividing by 3 on both sides, to produce $x = 80$.

24. D: By grouping the four numbers in the answer into factors of the two numbers of the question (6 and 12), it can be determined that:

$$(3 \times 2) \times (4 \times 3) = 6 \times 12$$

Alternatively, you could find the prime factorization of each answer choices and compare it to the original value. The product of 6×12 is 72 and has a prime factorization of $2^3 \times 3^2$. The answer choices respectively have values of 64, 84, 108, 72, and 144 and prime factorizations of 2^6, $2^2 \times 3 \times 7$, $2^2 \times 3^3$, $2^3 \times 3^2$, and $2^4 \times 3^2$, so Choice *D* is the correct choice.

25. C: To solve for the value of b, isolate the variable b on one side of the equation.

Start by moving the lower value of -4 to the other side by adding 4 to both sides:

$$5b - 4 = 2b + 17$$

$$5b - 4 + 4 = 2b + 17 + 4$$

$$5b = 2b + 21$$

239

Then subtract $2b$ from both sides:

$$5b - 2b = 2b + 21 - 2b$$

$$3b = 21$$

Then divide both sides by 3 to get the value of b:

$$\frac{3b}{3} = \frac{21}{3}$$

$$b = 7$$

26. D: The total faculty is:

$$15 + 20 = 35$$

So, the ratio is $35 : 200$. Then, divide both of these numbers by 5, since 5 is a common factor to both, with a result of $7 : 40$.

27. C: 85% of a number means that number should be multiplied by 0.85: $0.85 \times 20 = \frac{85}{100} \times \frac{20}{1}$, which can be simplified to $\frac{17}{20} \times \frac{20}{1} = 17$. The answer is C.

28. D: This problem can be solved by setting up a proportion involving the given information and the unknown value. The proportion is:

$$\frac{21 \text{ pages}}{4 \text{ nights}} = \frac{140 \text{ pages}}{x \text{ nights}}$$

Solving the proportion by cross-multiplying, the equation becomes $21x = 4 \times 140$, where $x = 26.67$. Since it is not an exact number of nights, the answer is rounded up to 27 nights. 26 nights would not give Sarah enough time.

29. D: First, subtract \$1,437 from \$2,334.50 to find Johnny's monthly savings; this equals \$897.50. Then, multiply this amount by 3 to find out how much he will have (in three months) before he pays for his vacation: this equals \$2,692.50. Finally, subtract the cost of the vacation (\$1,750) from this amount to find how much Johnny will have left: \$942.50.

30. A: To solve this correctly, keep in mind the order of operations with the mnemonic PEMDAS (Please Excuse My Dear Aunt Sally). This stands for Parentheses, Exponents, Multiplication, Division, Addition, Subtraction. Taking it step by step, solve inside the parentheses first:

$$3 \times 8 - (3)^2 + 8$$

Then, apply the exponent:

$$3 \times 8 - 9 + 8$$

Multiplication is performed next:

$$24 - 9 + 8$$

240

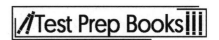

Subtraction and addition are performed after that:

$$15 + 8 = 23$$

Addition and subtraction are done last. The solution is 23.

Reading

1. C: All the details in this paragraph suggest that Brookside is a great place to live, plus the last sentence states that it is an *idyllic neighborhood*, meaning it is perfect, happy, and blissful. Choices *A* and *B* are incorrect, because although they do contain specific details from the paragraph that support the main idea, they are not the main idea. Choice *D* is incorrect because there is no reference in the paragraph to the crime rate in Brookside.

2. B: A passage like this one would likely appear in some sort of community profile, highlighting the benefits of living or working there. Choice *A* is incorrect because nothing in this passage suggests that it is fictional. It reads as non-fiction, if anything. Choice *C* is incorrect because it does not report anything particularly newsworthy, and Choice *D* is incorrect because it has absolutely nothing to do with a movie review.

3. D: In the first sentence, it states very clearly that the Brookside neighborhood is *one of the nation's first planned communities*. This makes it unique, as many other neighborhoods are old, many other neighborhoods exist in Kansas City, and many other neighborhoods have shopping areas. For these reasons, all the other answer choices are incorrect.

4. B: Choice *B* is correct because a *simile* is a comparison between two unlike things using the words *like* or *as*. Choice *A* is incorrect because *hyperbole* is an exaggeration for affect. Choice *C* is incorrect because *personification* attributes human characteristics to an inanimate object. Choice *D* is incorrect because *alliteration* is a poetic device in which several words begin with the same letter or letters. It is used to add emphasis or affect.

5. A: Choice *A* is correct because there is evidence in the passage to support it, specifically when he mentions catching "a mess of black-fish, which you couldn't buy in New York for a dollar—large fat fellows, with meat on their bones that it takes a pretty long fork to stick through." There is no evidence to support the other answer choices.

6. B: Prodigious means *great in extent, size, or degree*. In this passage, Whitman is comparing the easternmost part of Long Island to a very large alligator. Therefore, the other answer choices are incorrect.

7. B: The author clearly states that education is crucial to the survival of the human race, and it can be easily inferred that if this is true, then improvements to our educational system are certainly worth fighting for. Choices *A* and *C* are incorrect because there is nothing in the passage that relates to these statements. Choice *D* is incorrect because it directly contradicts what the author states about all children's ability to learn.

8. A: Clearly, this author feels passionately about the importance of education. This is evident especially in the word choices. For this reason, all the other answer choices are incorrect.

9. C: Based on the author's passionate stance about the importance of education for all children, this answer choice makes the most sense. For this reason, all the other answer choices are incorrect.

10. D: The author mentions the importance of parent involvement and communication between school and home. He also devotes one full paragraph to the impact of technology on education. Nowhere in the passage does the author mention the cost of textbooks, so Choice *D* is correct.

11. B: The correct answer is *personification* because Dickinson gives death characteristics of a human person. In addition, by capitalizing the word, she has made "Death" a proper noun or name. Choice *A* is incorrect because *hyperbole* is an exaggeration for affect. Choice *C* is incorrect because an *allusion* is a brief or indirect reference to a person, place, or thing from history, culture, literature, or politics. Choice *D* is incorrect because *alliteration* is a poetic device in which several words begin with the same letter or letters. It is used to add emphasis or affect.

12. C: This is the correct answer because the slash mark represents the break between the first line of this poem and the second. A slash mark would not be used to indicate any of the other answer choices.

13. A: This is the correct answer because he makes it clear that sometimes conflict must happen, and that it can even be a good thing.

14. C: Analogy is the correct answer because an analogy is a comparison between two seemingly unlike things, used to help clarify meaning. In this case, Jefferson is comparing what it takes to keep the ideal of liberty alive to a tree. Choice *A* is incorrect because *personification* attributes human traits or characteristics to an inanimate object. Choice *B* is incorrect because an *allusion* is a brief or indirect reference to a person, place, or thing from history, culture, literature, or politics. Choice *D* is incorrect because an *idiom* is an expression whose meaning is not to be taken literally.

15. B: Persuasive is the correct answer because the author is clearly trying to convey the point that history education is very important. Choice *A* is incorrect because expository writing is more informational and less emotional. Choice *C* is incorrect because narrative writing involves story telling. Choice *D* is incorrect because this is a piece of prose, not poetry.

16. C: This is the correct answer because boldface type is often used to indicate emphasis. Choice *A* is incorrect because quotation marks are used to indicate dialogue. Choice *B* is incorrect because volume is typically indicated by the use of capital letters. Choice *D* is incorrect because there is no way to indicate misspelling by altering the text.

17. C: This answer choice is correct because *one of the most intelligent* is a matter of opinion, not a quantifiable fact. All the other answer choices are factual statements.

18. A: This answer choice is correct because it is the only statement that is not based on opinion. Nutritionists' belief in one certain diet *might* be a matter of opinion, but the statement that many do believe in the health benefits of this particular diet is a fact.

19. A: This is the correct answer choice because there is evidence to the contrary that Martin Luther King Jr. refused to believe that mankind would be bound to the darkness of racism.

20. B: This is the correct answer choice because Martin Luther King Jr. is using an analogy, comparing the evil of racism to the darkness one would experience on a starless night. He is also making the point that just as one cannot see in the dark, racism blinds one to the truth.

21. D: This is the correct answer choice because expository writing involves straightforward, factual information and analysis. It is unbiased and does not rely on the writer's personal feelings or opinions. Choice *A* is incorrect because narrative writing tells a story. Choice *B* is incorrect because persuasive writing is intended to change the reader's mind or position on a topic. Choice *C* is incorrect because technical writing attempts to outline a complex object or process.

22. B: This is the correct answer choice because the passage begins by describing Carver's childhood fascination with painting and later returns to this point when it states that at the end of his career "Carver returned to his first love of art." For this reason, all the other answer choices are incorrect.

23. A: This is the correct answer choice because the passage contains a definition of the term, *agricultural monoculture*, which is very similar to this answer.

24. C: This is the correct answer choice because there is ample evidence in the passage that refers to Carver's brilliance and the fact that his discoveries had a far-reaching impact both then and now. There is no evidence in the passage to support any of the other answer choices.

25. A: It introduces certain insects that transition from water to air. Choice *B* is incorrect because although the passage talks about gills, it is not the central idea of the passage. Choices *C* and *D* are incorrect because the passage does not "define" or "invite," but only serves as an introduction to stoneflies, dragonflies, and mayflies and their transition from water to air.

26. C: The act of shedding part or all of the outer shell. Choices *A*, *B*, and *D* are incorrect.

27. B: The first paragraph serves as a contrast to the second. Notice how the first paragraph goes into detail describing how insects are able to breathe air. The second paragraph acts as a contrast to the first by stating "[i]t is of great interest to find that, nevertheless, a number of insects spend much of their time under water." Watch for transition words such as "nevertheless" to help find what type of passage you're dealing with.

28: C: The stage of preparation in between molting is acted out in the water, while the last stage is in the air. Instars are the phases between two periods of molting, and the text explains when these transitions occur. The preparatory stages are acted out in the water while the last stage is in the air. Choices A, B, and D are all incorrect.

29. C: The author's tone is informative and exhibits interest in the subject of the study. Overall, the author presents us with information on the subject. One moment where personal interest is depicted is when the author states, "It is of great interest to find that, nevertheless, a number of insects spend much of their time under water."

30. C: Italics are often used to indicate emphasis. Choice *A* is incorrect because quotation marks, not italics, are used to indicate dialogue. Choice *B* is incorrect because although italics can also indicate someone's interior thoughts, in this case, it would not make sense for the word *any* to be a thought rather than spoken aloud. Choice *D* is incorrect because volume is typically indicated by capital letters.

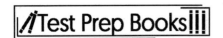

Writing

1. C: Choice *C* correctly uses *from* to describe the fact that dogs are related to wolves. The word *through* is incorrectly used here, so Choice *A* is incorrect. Choice *B* makes no sense. Choice *D* unnecessarily changes the verb tense in addition to incorrectly using *through*.

2. B: Choice *B* is correct because the Oxford comma is applied, clearly separating the specific terms. Choice *A* lacks this clarity. Choice *C* is correct but too wordy since commas can be easily applied. Choice *D* doesn't flow with the sentence's structure.

3. D: Choice *D* correctly uses the question mark, fixing the sentence's main issue. Thus, Choice *A* is incorrect because questions do not end with periods. Choice *B*, although correctly written, changes the meaning of the original sentence. Choice *C* is incorrect because it completely changes the direction of the sentence, disrupts the flow of the paragraph, and lacks the crucial question mark.

4. A: Choice *A* is correct since there are no errors in the sentence. Choices *B* and *C* both have extraneous commas, disrupting the flow of the sentence. Choice *D* unnecessarily rearranges the sentence.

5. D: Choice *D* is correct because the commas serve to distinguish that *artificial selection* is just another term for *selective breeding* before the sentence continues. The structure is preserved, and the sentence can flow with more clarity. Choice *A* is incorrect because the sentence needs commas to avoid being a run-on. Choice *B* is close but still lacks the required comma after *selection*, so this is incorrect. Choice *C* is incorrect because the comma to set off the aside should be placed after *breeding* instead of *called*.

6. B: Choice *B* is correct because the sentence is talking about a continuing process. Therefore, the best modification is to add the word *to* in front of *increase*. Choice *A* is incorrect because this modifier is missing. Choice *C* is incorrect because with the additional comma, the present tense of *increase* is inappropriate. Choice *D* makes more sense, but the tense is still not the best to use.

7. A: The sentence has no errors, so Choice *A* is correct. Choice *B* is incorrect because it adds an unnecessary comma. Choice *C* is incorrect because *advantage* should not be plural in this sentence without the removal of the singular *an*. Choice *D* is very tempting. While this would make the sentence more concise, this would ultimately alter the context of the sentence, which would be incorrect.

8. C: Choice *C* correctly uses *on to*, describing the way genes are passed generationally. The use of *into* is inappropriate for this context, which makes Choice *A* incorrect. Choice *B* is close, but *onto* refers to something being placed on a surface. Choice *D* doesn't make logical sense.

9. D: Choice *D* is correct, since only proper names should be capitalized. Because the name of a dog breed is not a proper name, Choice *A* is incorrect. In terms of punctuation, only one comma after *example* is needed, so Choices *B* and *C* are incorrect.

10. D: Choice *D* is the correct answer because "rather" acts as an interrupting word here and thus should be separated by commas. Choices *B* and *C* use commas unwisely, breaking the flow of the sentence.

11. B: Since the sentence can stand on its own without *Usually*, separating it from the rest of the sentence with a comma is correct. Choice *A* needs the comma after *Usually*, while Choice *C* uses

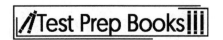

commas incorrectly. Choice *D* is tempting, but changing *turn* to past tense goes against the rest of the paragraph.

12. A: In Choice *A*, the dependent clause *Sometimes in particularly dull seminars* is seamlessly attached with a single comma after *seminars*. Choice *B* contains too many commas. Choice *C* does not correctly combine the dependent clause with the independent clause. Choice *D* introduces too many unnecessary commas.

13. D: Choice *D* rearranges the sentence to be more direct and straightforward, so it is correct. Choice *A* needs a comma after *on*. Choice *B* introduces unnecessary commas. Choice *C* creates an incomplete sentence, since *Because I wasn't invested in what was going on* is a dependent clause.

14. C: Choice *C* is fluid and direct, making it the best revision. Choice *A* is incorrect because the construction is awkward and lacks parallel structure. Choice *B* is incorrect because of the unnecessary comma and period. Choice *D* is close, but its sequence is still awkward and overly complicated.

15. B: Choice *B* correctly adds a comma after *person* and cuts out the extraneous writing, making the sentence more streamlined. Choice *A* is poorly constructed, lacking proper grammar to connect the sections of the sentence correctly. Choice *C* inserts an unnecessary semicolon and doesn't enable this section to flow well with the rest of the sentence. Choice *D* is better but still unnecessarily long.

16. D: This sentence, though short, is a complete sentence. The only thing the sentence needs is an em-dash after "Easy." In this sentence the em-dash works to add emphasis to the word "Easy" and also acts in place of a colon, but in a less formal way. Therefore, Choice *D* is correct. Choices *A* and *B* lack the crucial comma, while Choice *C* unnecessarily breaks the sentence apart.

17. C: Choice *C* successfully fixes the construction of the sentence, changing *drawing* into *to draw*. Keeping the original sentence disrupts the flow, so Choice *A* is incorrect. Choice *B*'s use of *which* offsets the whole sentence. Choice *D* is incorrect because it unnecessarily expands the sentence content and makes it more confusing.

18. B: Choice *B* fixes the homophone issue. Because the author is talking about people, *their* must be used instead of *there*. This revision also appropriately uses the Oxford comma, separating and distinguishing *lives, world, and future*. Choice *A* uses the wrong homophone and is missing commas. Choice *C* neglects to fix these problems and unnecessarily changes the tense of *applies*. Choice *D* fixes the homophone but fails to properly separate *world* and *future*.

19. D: This is the correct answer because the pronouns *him* and *me* are in the objective case. *Him* and *me* are the indirect objects of the verb *gave*. Choice *A* is incorrect because the personal pronoun in this case, *me*, should always go last. Choices *B* and *C* are incorrect because they contain at least one subjective pronoun.

20. B: In this sentence, a colon is correctly used to introduce a series of items. Choice *A* incorrectly uses a semicolon to introduce the series of states. Choice *C* incorrectly uses a dash to introduce the series. Choice *D* is incorrect because it incorrectly uses a comma to introduce the series.

21. A: This sentence uses the correct form of the contraction *you are* as the subject of the sentence, and it uses the correct form of the possessive pronoun *your* to indicate ownership of the backpack. It also uses the correct form of the adverb *there,* indicating place and the possessive pronoun *their* indicating

245

ownership. Choice *B* is incorrect because it reverses the possessive pronoun *your* and the contraction *you are*. Choice *C* is incorrect because it reverses the adverb *there* and the possessive pronoun *their*. Choice *D* is incorrect because it reverses the contraction *you are* and the possessive pronoun *your* and the possessive pronoun *their* and the adverb *there*.

22. C: In this sentence, the modifier is the phrase "Forgetting that he was supposed to meet his girlfriend for dinner." This phrase offers information about Fred's actions, but the noun that immediately follows it is Anita, creating some confusion about the "do-er" of the phrase. A more appropriate sentence arrangement would be "Forgetting that he was supposed to meet his girlfriend for dinner, Fred made Anita mad when he showed up late." Choice *A* is incorrect as parallelism refers to the consistent use of sentence structure and verb tense, and this sentence is appropriately consistent. Choice *B* is incorrect as this sentence contains appropriate punctuation for the number of independent clauses presented; it is not a run-on sentence. Choice *D* is incorrect because subject-verb agreement refers to the appropriate conjugation of a verb relative to the subject, and all verbs have been properly conjugated.

23. B: A comma splice occurs when a comma is used to join two independent clauses together without the additional use of an appropriate conjunction. One way to remedy this problem is to replace the comma with a semicolon. Another solution is to add a conjunction: "Some workers use all their sick leave, but other workers cash out their leave." Choice *A* is incorrect as parallelism refers to the consistent use of sentence structure and verb tense; all tenses and structures in this sentence are consistent. Choice *C* is incorrect because a sentence fragment is a phrase or clause that cannot stand alone—this sentence contains two independent clauses. Choice *D* is incorrect because subject-verb agreement refers to the proper conjugation of a verb relative to the subject, and all verbs have been properly conjugated.

24. D: The problem in the original passage is that the second sentence is a dependent clause that cannot stand alone as a sentence; it must be attached to the main clause found in the first sentence. Because the main clause comes first, it does not need to be separated by a comma. However, if the dependent clause came first, then a comma would be necessary, which is why Choice *C* is incorrect. *A* and *B* also insert unnecessary commas into the sentence.

25. D: In this sentence, the first answer choice requires a noun meaning *impact* or *influence*, so *effect* is the correct answer. For the second answer choice, the sentence is drawing a comparison. *Than* shows a comparative relationship whereas *then* shows sequence or consequence. Choices *A* and *C* can be eliminated because they contain the choice *then*. Choice *B* is incorrect because *affect* is a verb while this sentence requires a noun.

26. C: Choice *C* is correct because it states the fact that education has a positive impact on lowering crime rates, and it tells your reader what you will cover in that paragraph without providing specific details yet. That's what the remainder of the paragraph is for. Choice *A* is incorrect because the paragraph is about the verification of crime statistics. Choice *B* is incorrect because it is a broad generalization that is simply not true. Choice *D*, while it is on topic, is too specific to be a topic sentence but would be an excellent supporting detail.

27. C: This sentence would not be a good thesis statement because it conveys one very specific detail. All the other answer choices would be good thesis statements because they are general enough for an entire essay but specific enough so that the reader knows exactly what the essay will cover.

28. C: *His* or *her* is correct. *Each* indicates the need for a singular pronoun, and because the charts belong to the patients, they must be possessive as well. To indicate that the group of patients could include males and females, *his* and *her* must be included. For Choice *A*, *their* is plural. For Choice *B*, *there* is an adverb, not a pronoun. For Choice *D*, *the people's* is collective plural, not singular.

29. B: *Imminent* means impending or happening soon. The man fears going to the zoo because a bomb might soon be detonated. For Choice *A*, *eminent* means of a high rank or status. For Choice *C*, *emanate* means to originate from. For Choice *D*, *amanita* is a type of fungus.

30. D: This passage displays clarity (the author states precisely what he or she intended), fluency (the sentences run smoothly together), and parallelism (words are used in a similar fashion to help provide rhythm). Choice *A* lacks parallelism. When the author states, "the hero acts without thinking, is living in the moment, and is repressing physical and emotional pain," the words *acts*, *is living* and *is repressing* are in different tenses. Choice *B* runs on endlessly in the first half ("Ernest Hemingway is probably the most noteworthy of expatriate authors since his concise writing style is void of emotion and stream of consciousness and has had a lasting impact on Americans which has resonated to this very day, and Hemingway's novels are much like in American cinema.")

It demands some type of pause and strains the readers' eyes. The second half of the passage is choppy: "The hero acts. He doesn't think. He lives in the moment. He represses physical and emotional pain." For Choice *C*, leaving out *expatriate* is, first, vague, and second, alters the meaning. The correct version claims that Hemingway was the most notable of the expatriate authors while the second version claims he's the most notable of any author *ever*, a very bold claim indeed. Also, leaving out *stream of* in "stream of consciousness" no longer references the non-sequential manner in which most people think. Instead, this version sounds like all the characters in the novel are in a coma!

Practice Test #3

Math

1. Solve the following:

$$\left(\sqrt{36} \times \sqrt{16}\right) - 3^2$$

    a. 30
    b. 21
    c. 15
    d. 13

2. A closet is filled with red, blue, and green shirts. If there are 54 shirts total, and 12 are green and 28 are red, which equation below could be used to calculate the number of blue shirts?

    a. $54 - 12 - 28 = \Box$
    b. $54 = 28 - 12 + \Box$
    c. $54 - \Box = 28 - 12$
    d. $54 + 12 + 28 = \Box$

3. What is the solution to $4 \times 7 + (25 - 21)^2 \div 2$?

    a. 512
    b. 36
    c. 60.5
    d. 22

4. Kimberley earns $10 an hour babysitting, and after 10 p.m., she earns $12 an hour, with the amount paid being rounded to the nearest hour accordingly. On her last job, she worked from 5:30 p.m. to 11 p.m. In total, how much did Kimberley earn on her last job?

    a. $45
    b. $57
    c. $62
    d. $42

5. What value of x would solve the following equation?

$$9x + x - 7 = 16 + 2x$$

    a. $x = -4$

    b. $x = 3$

    c. $x = \dfrac{9}{8}$

    d. $x = \dfrac{23}{8}$

6. Keith's bakery had 252 customers go through its doors last week. This week, that number increased to 378. Express this increase as a percentage.

    a. 26%

    b. 50%

    c. 35%

    d. 12%

7. Simplify the following fraction:

$$\frac{\frac{5}{7}}{\frac{9}{11}}$$

    a. $\dfrac{55}{63}$

    b. $\dfrac{7}{1,000}$

    c. $\dfrac{13}{15}$

    d. $\dfrac{5}{11}$

8. Bernard can make $80 per day. If he needs to make $300 and only works full days, how many days will this take?

    a. 2

    b. 3

    c. 4

    d. 5

9. Express the solution to the following problem in decimal form:

$$\frac{3}{5} \times \frac{7}{10} \div \frac{1}{2}$$

    a. 0.042

    b. 84%

    c. 0.84

    d. 0.42

10. A National Hockey League store in the state of Michigan advertises 50% off all items. Sales tax in Michigan is 6%. How much would a hat originally priced at $32.99 and a jersey originally priced at $64.99 cost during this sale? Round to the nearest penny.

    a. $97.98

    b. $103.86

    c. $51.93

    d. $48.99

11. Store brand coffee beans cost $1.23 per pound. A local coffee bean roaster charges $1.98 per 1 ½ pounds. How much more would 5 pounds from the local roaster cost than 5 pounds of the store brand?
    a. $0.55
    b. $1.55
    c. $1.45
    d. $0.45

12. An equation for the line passing through the origin and the point $(2, 1)$ is
    a. $y = 2x$
    b. $y = \frac{1}{2}x$
    c. $y = x - 2$
    d. $2y = x + 1$

13. What are the zeros of $f(x) = x^2 + 4$?
    a. $x = -4$
    b. $x = \pm 2i$
    c. $x = \pm 2$
    d. $x = \pm 4i$

14. Karen gets paid a weekly salary and a commission for every sale that she makes. The table below shows the number of sales and her pay for different weeks.

Sales	2	7	4	8
Pay	$380	$580	$460	$620

Which of the following equations represents Karen's weekly pay?
    a. $y = 90x + 200$
    b. $y = 90x - 200$
    c. $y = 40x + 300$
    d. $y = 40x - 300$

15. If $-3(x + 4) \geq x + 8$, what is the value of x?
    a. $x = 4$
    b. $x \geq 2$
    c. $x \geq -5$
    d. $x \leq -5$

16. Which of the ordered pairs below is a solution to the following system of inequalities?
$$y > 2x - 3$$
$$y < -4x + 8$$
    a. $(4, 5)$
    b. $(-3, -2)$
    c. $(3, -1)$
    d. $(5, 2)$

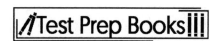

17. The graph of which function has an x-intercept of -2?
    a. $y = 2x - 3$
    b. $y = 4x + 2$
    c. $y = x^2 + 5x + 6$
    d. $y = -\frac{1}{2} \times 2^x$

18. How will the following algebraic expression be simplified: $(5x^2 - 3x + 4) - (2x^2 - 7)$?
    a. x^5
    b. $3x^2 - 3x + 11$
    c. $3x^2 - 3x - 3$
    d. $x - 3$

19. A traveler takes an hour to drive to a museum, spends 3 hours and 30 minutes there, and takes half an hour to drive home. What percentage of their time was spent driving?
    a. 15%
    b. 30%
    c. 40%
    d. 60%

20. Marty wishes to save $150 over a 4-day period. How much must Marty save each day on average?
    a. $37.50
    b. $35
    c. $45.50
    d. $41

21. A family purchases a vehicle in 2005 for $20,000. In 2010, they decide to sell it for a newer model. They are able to sell the car for $8,000. By what percentage did the value of the family's car drop?
    a. 40%
    b. 68%
    c. 60%
    d. 33%

22. At the beginning of the day, Xavier has 20 apples. At lunch, he meets his sister Emma and gives her half of his apples. After lunch, he stops by his neighbor Jim's house and gives him 6 of his apples. He then uses $\frac{3}{4}$ of his remaining apples to make an apple pie for dessert at dinner. At the end of the day, how many apples does Xavier have left?
    a. 4
    b. 6
    c. 2
    d. 1

23. If $6t + 4 = 16$, what is t?
    a. 1
    b. 2
    c. 3
    d. 4

24. A line passes through the point $(1, 2)$ and crosses the y-axis at $y = 1$. Which of the following is an equation for this line?

   a. $y = 2x$
   b. $y = x + 1$
   c. $x + y = 1$
   d. $y = \frac{x}{2} - 2$

25. What are the polynomial roots of $x^2 + x - 2$?

   a. 1 and -2
   b. -1 and 2
   c. 2 and -2
   d. 9 and 13

26. $(4x^2 y^4)^{\frac{3}{2}}$ can be simplified to which of the following?

   a. $8x^3 y^6$

   b. $4x^{\frac{5}{2}} y$

   c. $4xy$

   d. $32x^{\frac{7}{2}} y^{\frac{11}{2}}$

27. Suppose $\frac{x+2}{x} = 2$. What is x?

   a. -1
   b. 0
   c. 2
   d. 4

28. A solution needs 5 mL of saline for every 8 mL of medicine given. How much saline is needed for 45 mL of medicine?

   a. $\frac{225}{8}$ mL
   b. 72 mL
   c. 28 mL
   d. $\frac{45}{8}$ mL

29. How will the following number be written in standard form:
$$(1 \times 10^4) + (3 \times 10^3) + (7 \times 10^1) + (8 \times 10^0)$$

   a. 137
   b. 13,078
   c. 1,378
   d. 8,731

30. A piggy bank contains 12 dollars' worth of nickels. A nickel weighs 5 grams, and the empty piggy bank weighs 1,050 grams. What is the total weight of the full piggy bank?
   a. 1,110 grams
   b. 1,200 grams
   c. 2,250 grams
   d. 2,200 grams

Reading

Questions 1–4 are based on the following passage:

Science fiction has been a part of the American fabric for a long time. During the Great Depression, many Americans were looking for an escape from dismal circumstances, and their escape often took the form of reading. Outlandish stories of aliens and superheroes were printed on cheap, disposable paper stock, hence the name *pulp* (as in paper) *fiction*. Iconic heroes like Buck Rogers, the Shadow, and Doc Rogers got their start in throwaway magazines and pulp novels.

As time went on, science fiction evolved, presenting better plots and more sophisticated questions, and, consequently, it garnered more respect. Authors like Kurt Vonnegut and Ray Bradbury, now household names and respected American authors, emerged from the science fiction fringe. Thanks to works like Vonnegut's 1961 short story "Harrison Bergeron," in which mediocrity is the law and exceptional ability is punished, and Bradbury's 1953 novel *Fahrenheit 451*, in which books are illegal and burned on sight, science fiction rose to a serious genre.

In the late 1970s, the genre that begun in the medium of pulp fiction and crossed into serious literature had a resurgence in the medium of film. The new prominence of science fiction film was spearheaded by the first *Star Wars* movie, which harkened to pulp fiction roots. The tide of science fiction films hasn't really slowed since. *Blade Runner, Jurassic Park, The Matrix, I Am Legend*, even Disney's *Wall-E* all continue the tradition of unrealized futures and alternate realities. Modern science fiction movies can trace their roots back to the pulp fiction published during the Great Depression.

1. The main purpose of this passage is to:
   a. Describe
   b. Inform
   c. Persuade
   d. Entertain

2. This passage was written with a _____ structure.
   a. Compare/contrast
   b. Sequential
   c. Cause/effect
   d. Problem/solution

Practice Test #3 | Reading

3. Which of the following passages from the above text best summarizes the main idea?
   a. "Science fiction has been a part of the American fabric for a long time."
   b. "As time went on, science fiction evolved, posing better plots and more sophisticated questions."
   c. "Outlandish stories of aliens and superheroes were printed on cheap, disposable paper stock, hence the name *pulp* (as in paper) *fiction*."
   d. "Modern science fiction movies can trace their roots back to the pulp fiction published during the Great Depression."

4. "These outlandish stories of aliens and superheroes were printed on cheap, disposable paper stock, hence the name *pulp* (as in paper) *fiction*." The author most likely wrote this sentence because:
   a. He or she wants the reader to understand that science fiction was not always taken seriously.
   b. He or she wants the reader to understand that science fiction is not a new medium.
   c. He or she wants to demonstrate that science fiction was constrained by the technology of the time.
   d. He or she wants to demonstrate that even those in the past imagined what the future might hold.

5. After applying for a job multiple times, Bob was finally granted an interview. During the interview, he fumbled several questions, mispronounced his potential supervisor's name, and forgot the name of the company. Soon it was clear he knew he wouldn't be working there. At the end of the interview, he stood up and, with *spurious* confidence, shook the interviewer's hand firmly.

Based on the context of the word *spurious*, a good substitution might be:
   a. Extreme
   b. Mild
   c. Fake
   d. Genuine

254

Questions 6–9 are based on the following passage:

The more immediately after the commission of a crime a punishment is inflicted, the more just and useful it will be. It will be more just, because it spares the criminal the cruel and superfluous torment of uncertainty, which increases in proportion to the strength of his imagination and the sense of his weakness; and because the privation of liberty, being a punishment, ought to be inflicted before condemnation, but for as short a time as possible. Imprisonments, I say, being only the means of securing the person of the accused, until he be tried, condemned, or acquitted, ought not only to be of as short duration, but attended with as little severity as possible. The time should be determined by the necessary preparation for the trial, and the right of priority in the oldest prisoners. The confinement ought not to be closer than is requisite to prevent his flight, or his concealing the proofs of the crime; and the trial should be conducted with all possible expedition. Can there be a more cruel contrast than that between the indolence of a judge, and the painful anxiety of the accused; the comforts and pleasures of an insensible magistrate, and the filth and misery of the prisoner? In general, as I have before observed, *the degree of the punishment, and the consequences of a crime, ought to be so contrived, as to have the greatest possible effect on others, with the least possible pain to the delinquent.* If there be any society in which this is not a fundamental principle, it is an unlawful society; for mankind, by their union, originally intended to subject themselves to the least evils possible.

An immediate punishment is more useful; because the smaller the interval of time between the punishment and the crime, the stronger and more lasting will be the association of the two ideas of *Crime* and *Punishment;* so that they may be considered, one as the cause, and the other as the unavoidable and necessary effect. It is demonstrated, that the association of ideas is the cement which unites the fabric of the human intellect; without which, pleasure and pain would be simple and ineffectual sensations. The vulgar, that is, all men who have no general ideas or universal principles, act in consequence of the most immediate and familiar associations; but the more remote and complex only present themselves to the minds of those who are passionately attached to a single object, or to those of greater understanding, who have acquired an habit of rapidly comparing together a number of objects, and of forming a conclusion; and the result, that is, the action in consequence, by these means, becomes less dangerous and uncertain.

It is, then, of the greatest importance, that the punishment should succeed the crime as immediately as possible, if we intend, that, in the rude minds of the multitude, the seducing picture of the advantage arising from the crime, should instantly awake the attendant idea of punishment. Delaying the punishment serves only to separate these two ideas; and thus affects the minds of the spectators rather as being a terrible sight than the necessary consequence of a crime; the horror of which should contribute to heighten the idea of the punishment.

There is another excellent method of strengthening this important connexion between the ideas of crime and punishment; that is, to make the punishment as analogous as possible to the nature of the crime; in order that the punishment may lead the mind to consider the crime in a different point of view, from that in which it was placed by the flattering idea of promised advantages.

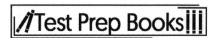

Crimes of less importance are commonly punished, either in the obscurity of a prison, or the criminal is *transported*, to give, by his slavery, an example to societies which he never offended; an example absolutely useless, because distant from the place where the crime was committed. Men do not, in general, commit great crimes deliberately, but rather in a sudden gust of passion; and they commonly look on the punishment due to a great crime as remote and improbable. The public punishment, therefore, of small crimes will make a greater impression, and, by deterring men from the smaller, will effectually prevent the greater.

This excerpt is from Cesare Beccaria, "Punishments, Advantages of Immediate," *The Criminal Recorder*, 1810.

6. What is the main purpose of this passage?
   a. To describe
   b. To inform
   c. To persuade
   d. To entertain

7. What text structure is this passage using?
   a. Compare/contrast
   b. Sequential
   c. Cause/effect
   d. Problem-solution

8. Which of the following excerpts best exemplifies the main idea of this passage?
   a. "The vulgar, that is, all men who have no general ideas or universal principles, act in consequence of the most immediate and familiar associations."
   b. "Crimes of less importance are commonly punished, either in the obscurity of a prison, or the criminal is *transported*, to give, by his slavery, an example to societies which he never offended."
   c. "Men do not, in general, commit great crimes deliberately, but rather in a sudden gust of passion; and they commonly look on the punishment due to a great crime as remote and improbable."
   d. "The more immediately after the commission of a crime a punishment is inflicted, the more just and useful it will be."

9. With which of the following statements would the author most likely disagree?
   a. Criminals are incapable of connecting crime and punishment.
   b. A punishment should quickly follow the crime.
   c. Most criminals do not think about the consequences of their actions.
   d. Where a criminal is punished is just as important as when.

10. Carl's chore for the day was to clean out a little-used storage shed. When he unlocked the door and walked through it, he got a mouthful of spider web. Brushing his mouth and sputtering, he reached for the light's pull chain. As soon as the bulb went on, a mouse ran between his legs and out the door. *This place is worse than a zoo*, thought Carl as he reached *reluctantly* for a box.

The best replacement for *reluctantly* would be which of the following?
- a. Angrily
- b. Suspiciously
- c. Fearfully
- d. Hesitantly

Questions 11–14 are based on the following two passages:

Passage 1

In the modern classroom, cell phones have become indispensable. Cell phones, which are essentially handheld computers, allow students to take notes, connect to the web, perform complex computations, teleconference, and participate in surveys. Most importantly, though, due to their mobility and excellent reception, cell phones are necessary in emergencies. Unlike tablets, laptops, or computers, cell phones are a readily available and free resource—most school district budgets are already strained to begin with—and since today's student is already strongly rooted in technology, when teachers incorporate cell phones, they're "speaking" the student's language, which increases the chance of higher engagement.

Passage 2

As with most forms of technology, there is an appropriate time and place for the use of cell phones. Students are comfortable with cell phones, so it makes sense when teachers allow cell phone use at their discretion. Allowing cell phone use can prove advantageous if done correctly. Unfortunately, if that's not the case—and often it isn't—then a sizable percentage of students pretend to pay attention while *surreptitiously* playing on their phones. This type of disrespectful behavior is often justified by the argument that cell phones are not only a privilege but also a right. Under this logic, confiscating phones is akin to rummaging through students' backpacks. This is in stark contrast to several decades ago when teachers regulated where and when students accessed information.

11. With which of the following statements would both the authors of Passages 1 and 2 agree?
- a. Teachers should incorporate cell phones into curriculum whenever possible.
- b. Cell phones are useful only when an experienced teacher uses them properly.
- c. Cell phones and, moreover, technology, are a strong part of today's culture.
- d. Despite a good lesson plan, cell phone disruptions are impossible to avoid.

12. Which of the following reasons is NOT listed in Passage 1 as a reason for students to have cell phones?
- a. Cell phones are a free, readily available resource.
- b. Cell phones incorporate others forms of technology.
- c. Due to their mobility, cell phones are excellent in an emergency.
- d. Cell phones allow teachers to "speak" clearly with students.

13. Passage 2 includes the statement, "confiscating phones is akin to rummaging through students' backpacks." The author most likely included this statement to do which of the following?
   a. Indicate how unlikely students are to change their minds.
   b. Exemplify how strongly students believe this is a right.
   c. Exemplify how easily the modern student is offended.
   d. Demonstrate how illogical most students' beliefs are.

14. Based on the context of Passage 2, the best substitute for *surreptitiously* would most likely be which of the following?
   a. Privately
   b. Slyly
   c. Obstinately
   d. Defiantly

15. Which of the following statements least supports the argument that the American economy is healthy?
   a. The United States' Gross Domestic Product (GDP), which is the measure of all the goods and services produced in a country, increased by two percent last year.
   b. Unemployment is the lowest it's been in over a decade due to a spike in job creation.
   c. Average household income just hit a historical high point for the twentieth consecutive quarter.
   d. Last year, the output of the United States' manufacturing sector decreased despite repeated massive investments by both the private and public sectors.

The next question is based on the following passage:

> Annabelle Rice started having trouble sleeping. Her biological clock was suddenly amiss and she began to lead a nocturnal schedule. She thought her insomnia was due to spending nights writing a horror story, but then she realized that even the idea of going outside into the bright world scared her to bits. She concluded she was now suffering from heliophobia.

16. Which of the following most accurately describes the meaning of the underlined word in the sentence above?
   a. Fear of dreams
   b. Fear of sunlight
   c. Fear of strangers
   d. Anxiety spectrum disorder

The next question is based on the following passage:

> A famous children's author recently published a historical fiction novel under a pseudonym; however, it did not sell as many copies as her children's books. In her earlier years, she had majored in history and earned a graduate degree in Antebellum American History, which is the time frame of her new novel. Critics praised this newest work far more than the children's series that made her famous. In fact, her new novel was nominated for the prestigious Albert J. Beveridge Award but still isn't selling like her children's books, which fly off the shelves because of her name alone.

17. Which one of the following statements might be accurately inferred based on the above passage?
    a. The famous children's author produced an inferior book under her pseudonym.
    b. The famous children's author is the foremost expert on Antebellum America.
    c. The famous children's author did not receive the bump in publicity for her historical novel that it would have received if it were written under her given name.
    d. People generally prefer to read children's series than historical fiction.

The next four questions are based on the following passage:

Smoking tobacco products is terribly destructive. A single cigarette contains over 4,000 chemicals, including 43 known carcinogens and 400 deadly toxins. Some of the most dangerous ingredients include tar, carbon monoxide, formaldehyde, ammonia, arsenic, and DDT. Smoking can cause numerous types of cancer including throat, mouth, nasal cavity, esophageal, gastric, pancreatic, renal, bladder, and cervical cancer.

Cigarettes contain a drug called nicotine, one of the most addictive substances known to man. Addiction is defined as a compulsion to seek the substance despite negative consequences. According to the National Institute of Drug Abuse, nearly 35 million smokers expressed a desire to quit smoking in 2015; however, more than 85 percent of those who struggle with addiction will not achieve their goal. Almost all smokers regret picking up that first cigarette. You would be wise to learn from their mistake if you have not yet started smoking.

According to the U.S. Department of Health and Human Services, 16 million people in the United States presently suffer from a smoking-related condition and nearly nine million suffer from a serious smoking-related illness. According to the Centers for Disease Control and Prevention (CDC), tobacco products cause nearly six million deaths per year. This number is projected to rise to over eight million deaths by 2030. Smokers, on average, die ten years earlier than their nonsmoking peers.

In the United States, local, state, and federal governments typically tax tobacco products, which leads to high prices. Nicotine users who struggle with addiction sometimes pay more for a pack of cigarettes than for a few gallons of gas. Additionally, smokers tend to stink. The smell of smoke is all-consuming and creates a pervasive nastiness. Smokers also risk staining their teeth and fingers with yellow residue from the tar.

Smoking is deadly, expensive, and socially unappealing. Clearly, smoking is not worth the risks.

18. Which of the following best describes the passage?
    a. Narrative
    b. Persuasive
    c. Expository
    d. Technical

259

19. Which of the following statements most accurately summarizes the passage?
a. Tobacco is less healthy than many alternatives.
b. Tobacco is deadly, expensive, and socially unappealing, and smokers would be much better off kicking the addiction.
c. In the United States, local, state, and federal governments typically tax tobacco products, which leads to high prices.
d. Tobacco products shorten smokers' lives by ten years and kill more than six million people per year.

20. The author would be most likely to agree with which of the following statements?
a. Smokers should only quit cold turkey and avoid all nicotine cessation devices.
b. Other substances are more addictive than tobacco.
c. Smokers should quit for whatever reason that gets them to stop smoking.
d. People who want to continue smoking should advocate for a reduction in tobacco product taxes.

21. Which of the following represents an opinion statement on the part of the author?
a. According to the Centers for Disease Control and Prevention (CDC), tobacco products cause nearly six million deaths per year.
b. Nicotine users who struggle with addiction sometimes pay more for a pack of cigarettes than a few gallons of gas.
c. They also risk staining their teeth and fingers with yellow residue from the tar.
d. Additionally, smokers tend to stink. The smell of smoke is all-consuming and creates a pervasive nastiness.

The next question is based on the following passage:

In 2015, 28 countries, including Estonia, Portugal, Slovenia, and Latvia, scored significantly higher than the United States on standardized high school math tests. In the 1960s, the United States consistently ranked first in the world. Today, the United States spends more than $800 billion dollars on education, which exceeds the next highest country by more than $600 billion dollars. The United States also leads the world in spending per school-aged child by an enormous margin.

22. If these statements above are factual, which of the following statements must be correct?
a. Outspending other countries on education has benefits beyond standardized math tests.
b. The United States' education system is corrupt and broken.
c. The standardized math tests are not representative of American academic prowess.
d. Spending more money does not guarantee success on standardized math tests.

The next three questions are based on the following passage:

George Washington emerged out of the American Revolution as an unlikely champion of liberty. On June 14, 1775, the Second Continental Congress created the Continental Army, and John Adams, serving in the Congress, nominated Washington to be its first commander. Washington fought under the British during the French and Indian War, and his experience and prestige proved instrumental to the American war effort. Washington provided invaluable leadership, training, and strategy during the Revolutionary War. He emerged from the war as the embodiment of liberty and freedom from tyranny.

After vanquishing the heavily favored British forces, Washington could have pronounced himself as the autocratic leader of the former colonies without any opposition, but he famously refused and returned to his Mount Vernon plantation. His restraint proved his commitment to the fledgling state's republicanism. Washington was later unanimously elected as the first American president. But it is Washington's farewell address that cemented his legacy as a visionary worthy of study.

In 1796, President Washington issued his farewell address by public letter. Washington enlisted his good friend, Alexander Hamilton, in drafting his most famous address. The letter expressed Washington's faith in the Constitution and rule of law. He encouraged his fellow Americans to put aside partisan differences and establish a national union. Washington warned Americans against meddling in foreign affairs and entering military alliances. Additionally, he stated his opposition to national political parties, which he considered partisan and counterproductive.

Americans would be wise to remember Washington's farewell, especially during presidential elections when politics hits a fever pitch. They might want to question the political institutions that were not planned by the Founding Fathers, such as the nomination process and political parties themselves.

23. Which of the following statements is logically based on the information contained in the passage above?
   a. George Washington's background as a wealthy landholder directly led to his faith in equality, liberty, and democracy.
   b. George Washington would have opposed America's involvement in the Second World War.
   c. George Washington would not have been able to write as great a farewell address without the assistance of Alexander Hamilton.
   d. George Washington would probably not approve of modern political parties.

24. Which of the following statements is the best description of the author's purpose in writing this passage about George Washington?
   a. To inform American voters about a Founding Father's sage advice on a contemporary issue and explain its applicability to modern times
   b. To introduce George Washington to readers as a historical figure worthy of study
   c. To note that George Washington was more than a famous military hero
   d. To convince readers that George Washington is a hero of republicanism and liberty

25. In which of the following materials would the author be the most likely to include this passage?
   a. A history textbook
   b. An obituary
   c. A fictional story
   d. A newspaper editorial

Questions 26-30 are based upon the following passage:

Christopher Columbus is often credited for discovering America. This is incorrect. First, it is impossible to "discover" something where people already live; however, Christopher Columbus did explore places in the New World that were previously untouched by Europe, so the term "explorer" would be more accurate. Another correction must be made, as well: Christopher

261

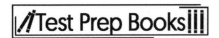

Columbus was not the first European explorer to reach the present day Americas! Rather, it was Leif Erikson who first came to the New World and contacted the natives, nearly five hundred years before Christopher Columbus.

Leif Erikson, the son of Erik the Red (a famous Viking outlaw and explorer in his own right), was born in either 970 or 980, depending on which historian you read. His own family, though, did not raise Leif, which was a Viking tradition. Instead, one of Erik's prisoners taught Leif reading and writing, languages, sailing, and weaponry. At age 12, Leif was considered a man and returned to his family. He killed a man during a dispute shortly after his return, and the council banished the Erikson clan to Greenland.

In 999, Leif left Greenland and traveled to Norway where he would serve as a guard to King Olaf Tryggvason. It was there that he became a convert to Christianity. Leif later tried to return home with the intention of taking supplies and spreading Christianity to Greenland, however his ship was blown off course and he arrived in a strange new land: present day Newfoundland, Canada.

When he finally returned to his adopted homeland Greenland, Leif consulted with a merchant who had also seen the shores of this previously unknown land we now know as Canada. The son of the legendary Viking explorer then gathered a crew of 35 men and set sail. Leif became the first European to touch foot in the New World as he explored present-day Baffin Island and Labrador, Canada. His crew called the land Vinland since it was plentiful with grapes.

During their time in present-day Newfoundland, Leif's expedition made contact with the natives whom they referred to as Skraelings (which translates to "wretched ones" in Norse). There are several secondhand accounts of their meetings. Some contemporaries described trade between the peoples. Other accounts describe clashes where the Skraelings defeated the Viking explorers with long spears, while still others claim the Vikings dominated the natives. Regardless of the circumstances, it seems that the Vikings made contact of some kind. This happened around 1000, nearly five hundred years before Columbus famously sailed the ocean blue.

Eventually, in 1003, Leif set sail for home and arrived at Greenland with a ship full of timber.

In 1020, seventeen years later, the legendary Viking died. Many believe that Leif Erikson should receive more credit for his contributions in exploring the New World.

26. Which of the following best describes how the author generally presents the information?
    a. Chronological order
    b. Comparison-contrast
    c. Cause-effect
    d. Conclusion-premises

27. Which of the following is an opinion, rather than historical fact, expressed by the author?
    a. Leif Erikson was definitely the son of Erik the Red; however, historians debate the year of his birth.
    b. Leif Erikson's crew called the land Vinland since it was plentiful with grapes.
    c. Leif Erikson deserves more credit for his contributions in exploring the New World.
    d. Leif Erikson explored the Americas nearly five hundred years before Christopher Columbus.

28. Which of the following most accurately describes the author's main conclusion?
    a. Leif Erikson is a legendary Viking explorer.
    b. Leif Erikson deserves more credit for exploring America hundreds of years before Columbus.
    c. Spreading Christianity motivated Leif Erikson's expeditions more than any other factor.
    d. Leif Erikson contacted the natives nearly five hundred years before Columbus.

29. Which of the following best describes the author's intent in the passage?
    a. To entertain
    b. To inform
    c. To alert
    d. To suggest

30. Which of the following can be logically inferred from the passage?
    a. The Vikings disliked exploring the New World.
    b. Leif Erikson's banishment from Iceland led to his exploration of present-day Canada.
    c. Leif Erikson never shared his stories of exploration with the King of Norway.
    d. Historians have difficulty definitively pinpointing events in the Vikings' history.

Writing

Questions 1–9 are based on the following passage:

Since the first discovery of dinosaur bones, (19) <u>scientists has made strides in technological development and methodologies used to investigate</u> these extinct animals. We know more about dinosaurs than ever before and are still learning fascinating new things about how they looked and lived. However, one has to ask, (20) <u>how if earlier perceptions of dinosaurs</u> continue to influence people's understanding of these creatures? Can these perceptions inhibit progress towards further understanding of dinosaurs?

(21) <u>The biggest problem with studying dinosaurs is simply that there are no living dinosaurs to observe.</u> All discoveries associated with these animals are based on physical remains. To gauge behavioral characteristics, scientists cross-examine these (22) <u>finds with living animals that seem similar in order to gain understanding.</u> While this method is effective, these are still deductions. Some ideas about dinosaurs can't be tested and confirmed simply because humans can't replicate a living dinosaur. For example, a Spinosaurus has a large sail, or a finlike structure that grows from its back. Paleontologists know this sail exists and have ideas for the function of (23) <u>the sail however they are uncertain of which idea is the true function.</u> Some scientists believe (24) <u>the sail serves to regulate the Spinosaurus' body temperature and yet others believe its used to attract mates.</u> Still, other scientists think the sail is used to intimidate other predatory dinosaurs for self-defense. These are all viable explanations, but they are also influenced by what scientists know about modern animals. (25) <u>Yet, it's quite possible</u> that the sail could hold a completely unique function.

While it's (26) <u>plausible, even likely that dinosaurs share many</u> traits with modern animals, there is the danger of overattributing these qualities to a unique, extinct species. For much of the early nineteenth century, when people first started studying dinosaur bones, the assumption was that they were simply giant lizards. (27) <u>For the longest time this image was the prevailing</u>

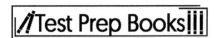

view on dinosaurs, until evidence indicated that they were more likely warm blooded. Scientists have also discovered that many dinosaurs had feathers and actually share many traits with modern birds.

1. Which of the following would be the best choice for this sentence (reproduced below)?

Since the first discovery of dinosaur bones, (19) scientists has made strides in technological development and methodologies used to investigate these extinct animals.

a. NO CHANGE
b. scientists has made strides in technological development, and methodologies, used to investigate
c. scientists have made strides in technological development and methodologies used to investigate
d. scientists, have made strides in technological development and methodologies used, to investigate

2. Which of the following would be the best choice for this sentence (reproduced below)?

However, one has to ask, (20) how if earlier perceptions of dinosaurs continue to influence people's understanding of these creatures?

a. NO CHANGE
b. how perceptions of dinosaurs
c. how, if, earlier perceptions of dinosaurs
d. whether earlier perceptions of dinosaurs

3. Which of the following would be the best choice for this sentence (reproduced below)?

(21) The biggest problem with studying dinosaurs is simply that there are no living dinosaurs to observe.

a. NO CHANGE
b. The biggest problem with studying dinosaurs is simple, that there are no living dinosaurs to observe.
c. The biggest problem with studying dinosaurs is simple. There are no living dinosaurs to observe.
d. The biggest problem with studying dinosaurs, is simply that there are no living dinosaurs to observe.

4. Which of the following would be the best choice for this sentence (reproduced below)?

To gauge behavioral characteristics, scientists cross-examine these (22) finds with living animals that seem similar in order to gain understanding.

a. NO CHANGE
b. finds with living animals to explore potential similarities.
c. finds with living animals to gain understanding of similarities.
d. finds with living animals that seem similar, in order, to gain understanding.

5. Which of the following would be the best choice for this sentence (reproduced below)?

Paleontologists know this sail exists and have ideas for the function of (23) <u>the sail however they are uncertain of which idea is the true function.</u>

a. NO CHANGE
b. the sail however, they are uncertain of which idea is the true function.
c. the sail however they are, uncertain, of which idea is the true function.
d. the sail; however, they are uncertain of which idea is the true function.

6. Which of the following would be the best choice for this sentence (reproduced below)?

Some scientists believe (24) <u>the sail serves to regulate the Spinosaurus' body temperature and yet others believe its used to attract mates.</u>

a. NO CHANGE
b. the sail serves to regulate the Spinosaurus' body temperature, yet others believe it's used to attract mates.
c. the sail serves to regulate the Spinosaurus' body temperature and yet others believe it's used to attract mates.
d. the sail serves to regulate the Spinosaurus' body temperature however others believe it's used to attract mates.

7. Which of the following would be the best choice for this sentence (reproduced below)?

(25) <u>Yet, it's quite possible</u> that the sail could hold a completely unique function.

a. NO CHANGE
b. Yet, it's quite possible,
c. It's quite possible,
d. Its quite possible

8. Which of the following would be the best choice for this sentence (reproduced below)?

While it's (26) <u>plausible, even likely that dinosaurs share many</u> traits with modern animals, there is the danger of over attributing these qualities to a unique, extinct species.

a. NO CHANGE
b. plausible, even likely that, dinosaurs share many
c. plausible, even likely, that dinosaurs share many
d. plausible even likely that dinosaurs share many

265

9. Which of the following would be the best choice for this sentence (reproduced below)?

(27) <u>For the longest time this image was the prevailing view on dinosaurs</u>, until evidence indicated that they were more likely warm blooded.

a. NO CHANGE
b. For the longest time this was the prevailing view on dinosaurs
c. For the longest time, this image, was the prevailing view on dinosaurs
d. For the longest time this was the prevailing image of dinosaurs

Questions 10–18 are based on the following passage:

Everyone has heard the (28) <u>idea of the end justifying the means; that would be Weston's philosophy</u>. Weston is willing to cross any line, commit any act no matter how heinous, to achieve success in his goal. (29) <u>Ransom is reviled by this fact, seeing total evil in Weston's plan.</u> To do an evil act in order (30) <u>to gain a result that's supposedly good would ultimately warp the final act.</u> (31) <u>This opposing viewpoints immediately distinguishes Ransom as the hero.</u> In the conflict with Un-man, Ransom remains true to his moral principles, someone who refuses to be compromised by power. Instead, Ransom makes it clear that by allowing such processes as murder and lying dictate how one attains a positive outcome, (32) <u>the righteous goal becomes corrupted.</u> The good end would not be truly good, but a twisted end that conceals corrupt deeds.

(33) <u>This idea of allowing necessary evils to happen, is very tempting, it is what Weston fell prey to.</u> (34) <u>The temptation of the evil spirit Un-man ultimately takes over Weston and he is possessed.</u> However, Ransom does not give into temptation. He remains faithful to the truth of what is right and incorrect. This leads him to directly face Un-man for the fate of Perelandra and its inhabitants.

Just as Weston was corrupted by the Un-man, (35) <u>Un-man after this seeks to tempt the Queen of Perelandra</u> to darkness. Ransom must literally (36) <u>show her the right path, to accomplish this, he does this based on the same principle as the "means to an end" argument</u>—that good follows good, and evil follows evil. Later in the plot, Weston/Un-man seeks to use deceptive reasoning to turn the queen to sin, pushing the queen to essentially ignore Melildil's rule to satisfy her own curiosity. In this sense, Un-man takes on the role of a false prophet, a tempter. Ransom must shed light on the truth, but this is difficult; his adversary is very clever and uses brilliant language. Ransom's lack of refinement heightens the weight of Un-man's corrupted logic, and so the Queen herself is intrigued by his logic.

Based on an excerpt from *Perelandra* by C.S. Lewis

10. Which of the following would be the best choice for this sentence (reproduced below)?

Everyone has heard the (28) <u>idea of the end justifying the means; that would be Weston's philosophy.</u>

a. NO CHANGE
b. idea of the end justifying the means; this is Weston's philosophy.
c. idea of the end justifying the means, this is the philosophy of Weston
d. idea of the end justifying the means. That would be Weston's philosophy.

11. Which of the following would be the best choice for this sentence (reproduced below)?

(29) <u>Ransom is reviled by this fact, seeing total evil in Weston's plan.</u>

a. NO CHANGE
b. Ransom is reviled by this fact; seeing total evil in Weston's plan.
c. Ransom, is reviled by this fact, seeing total evil in Weston's plan.
d. Ransom reviled by this, sees total evil in Weston's plan.

12. Which of the following would be the best choice for this sentence (reproduced below)?

To do an evil act in order (30) <u>to gain a result that's supposedly good would ultimately warp the final act.</u>

a. NO CHANGE
b. for an outcome that's for a greater good would ultimately warp the final act.
c. to gain a final act would warp its goodness.
d. to achieve a positive outcome would ultimately warp the goodness of the final act.

13. Which of the following would be the best choice for this sentence (reproduced below)?

(31) <u>This opposing viewpoints immediately distinguishes Ransom as the hero.</u>

a. NO CHANGE
b. This opposing viewpoints immediately distinguishes Ransom, as the hero.
c. This opposing viewpoint immediately distinguishes Ransom as the hero.
d. Those opposing viewpoints immediately distinguishes Ransom as the hero.

14. Which of the following would be the best choice for this sentence (reproduced below)?

Instead, Ransom makes it clear that by allowing such processes as murder and lying dictate how one attains a positive outcome, (32) <u>the righteous goal becomes corrupted.</u>

a. NO CHANGE
b. the goal becomes corrupted and no longer righteous.
c. the righteous goal becomes, corrupted.
d. the goal becomes corrupted, when once it was righteous.

267

15. Which of the following would be the best choice for this sentence (reproduced below)?
    (33) <u>This idea of allowing necessary evils to happen, is very tempting, it is what Weston fell prey to.</u>

   a. NO CHANGE
   b. This idea of allowing necessary evils to happen, is very tempting. This is what Weston fell prey to.
   c. This idea, allowing necessary evils to happen, is very tempting, it is what Weston fell prey to.
   d. This tempting idea of allowing necessary evils to happen is what Weston fell prey to.

16. Which of the following would be the best choice for this sentence (reproduced below)?

    (34) <u>The temptation of the evil spirit Un-man ultimately takes over Weston and he is possessed.</u>

   a. NO CHANGE
   b. The temptation of the evil spirit Un-man ultimately takes over and possesses Weston.
   c. Weston is possessed as a result of the temptation of the evil spirit Un-man ultimately, who takes over.
   d. The temptation of the evil spirit Un-man takes over Weston and he is possessed ultimately.

17. Which of the following would be the best choice for this sentence (reproduced below)?

    Just as Weston was corrupted by the Un-man, (35) <u>Un-man after this seeks to tempt the Queen of Perelandra</u> to darkness.

   a. NO CHANGE
   b. Un-man, after this, would tempt the Queen of Perelandra
   c. Un-man, after this, seeks to tempt the Queen of Perelandra
   d. Un-man then seeks to tempt the Queen of Perelandra

18. Which of the following would be the best choice for this sentence (reproduced below)?

    Ransom must literally (36) <u>show her the right path, to accomplish this, he does this based on the same principle as the "means to an end" argument</u>—that good follows good, and evil follows evil.

   a. NO CHANGE
   b. show her the right path. To accomplish this, he uses the same principle as the "means to an end" argument
   c. show her the right path; to accomplish this he uses the same principle as the "means to an end" argument
   d. show her the right path, to accomplish this, the same principle as the "means to an end" argument is applied

268

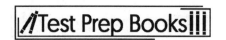

19. Which of the following is punctuated correctly?

a. After reading *Frankenstein*, Daisy turned to her sister and said, "You told me this book wasn't 'all that bad.' You scare me as much as the book!"

b. After reading "Frankenstein," Daisy turned to her sister and said, "You told me this book wasn't 'all that bad.' You scare me as much as the book!"

c. After reading *Frankenstein*, Daisy turned to her sister and said, 'You told me this book wasn't "all that bad." You scare me as much as the book!'

d. After reading *Frankenstein*, Daisy turned to her sister, and said "You told me this book wasn't 'all that bad'. You scare me as much as the book!"

20. Even though Ralph knew it was wrong to steal, he had still taken a grape from the vegetable stand. He stood there, befuddled, wrestling with his _____ , trying decide whether to put it back or pop it in his mouth.

a. Conscious

b. Conscience

c. Consensus

d. Census

21. Which of the following statements would make the best conclusion to an essay about civil rights activist Rosa Parks?

a. On December 1, 1955, Rosa Parks refused to give up her bus seat to a white passenger, setting in motion the Montgomery bus boycott.

b. Rosa Parks was a hero to many and came to symbolize the way that ordinary people could bring about real change in the Civil Rights Movement.

c. Rosa Parks died in 2005 in Detroit, having moved from Montgomery shortly after the bus boycott.

d. Rosa Parks' arrest was an early part of the Civil Rights Movement and helped lead to the passage of the Civil Rights Act of 1964.

22. Read the following passage:

Last week, we adopted a dog from the local animal shelter, after looking for our perfect pet for several months. We wanted a dog that was not too old, but also past the puppy stage, so that training would be less time-intensive and to give an older animal a home. Robin, as she's called, was a perfect match, and we filled out our application and, upon approval, were permitted to bring her home. Her physical exam and lab work all confirmed she was healthy. We went to the pet store and bought all sorts of bedding, food, toys, and treats to outfit our house as a dog-friendly and fun place. The shelter told us she liked dry food only, which is a relief because wet food is expensive and pretty off-putting. We even got fencing and installed a dog run in the backyard for Robin to roam unattended. Then we took her to the vet to make sure she was healthy. Next week, she starts the dog obedience class that we enrolled her in with a discount coupon from the shelter. It will be a good opportunity to bond with her and establish commands and dominance. When we took her to the park the afternoon after we adopted her, it was clear that she is a sociable and friendly dog, easily playing cohesively with dogs of all sizes and dispositions.

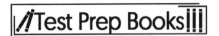
Which of the following is out of sequence in the story?
a. Last week, we adopted a dog from the local animal shelter, after looking for our perfect pet for several months.
b. Robin, as she's called, was a perfect match, and we filled out our application and, upon approval, were permitted to bring her home.
c. Her physical exam and lab work all confirmed she was healthy.
d. Next week, she starts the dog obedience class that we enrolled her in with a discount coupon from the shelter.

23. Which of these examples shows incorrect use of subject-verb agreement?
a. Neither of the cars are parked on the street.
b. Both of my kids are going to camp this summer.
c. Any of your friends are welcome to join us on the trip in November.
d. Each of the clothing options is appropriate for the job interview.

24. When it gets warm in the spring, _____ and _____ like to go fishing at Cobbs Creek.
Which of the following word pairs should be used in the blanks above?
a. me, him
b. he, I
c. him, I
d. he, me

25. Which of the following sentences shows correct word usage?
a. It's often been said that work is better then rest.
b. Its often been said that work is better then rest.
c. It's often been said that work is better than rest.
d. Its often been said that work is better than rest.

26. Which of the following sentences uses correct subject-verb agreement?
a. There is two constellations that can be seen from the back of the house.
b. At least four of the sheep needs to be sheared before the end of summer.
c. Lots of people were auditioning for the singing competition on Saturday.
d. Everyone in the group have completed the assignment on time.

27. The realtor showed _____ and _____ a house on Wednesday afternoon.
Which of the following pronoun pairs should be used in the blanks above?
a. she, I
b. she, me
c. me, her
d. her, me

28. Which of the following sentences uses second person point of view?
a. I don't want to make plans for the weekend before I see my work schedule.
b. She had to miss the last three yoga classes due to illness.
c. Pluto is no longer considered a planet because it is not gravitationally dominant.
d. Be sure to turn off all of the lights before locking up for the night.

29. Which of the following sentences shows correct word usage?
    a. Your going to have to put you're jacket over their.
    b. You're going to have to put your jacket over there.
    c. Your going to have to put you're jacket over they're.
    d. You're going to have to put you're jacket over their.

30. Every week, Cindy volunteers time at the local shelter. She always has a smile on her face, and she always talks to others with kindness and patience. Considering that her current job is very taxing, that two of her three children are still in diapers, and that her husband, Steve, the old curmudgeon, is the opposite of her in temperament, it's amazing that no one has ever seen her angry.

Based on the context in this passage, the best substitute for *curmudgeon* would be:
    a. Stingy
    b. Surly
    c. Scared
    d. Shy

Answer Explanations #3

Math

1. C: Follow the order of operations in order to solve this problem. Solve the parentheses first, being sure to follow the order of operations inside the parentheses as well. First, simplify the square roots:

$$(6 \times 4) - 3^2$$

Then, multiply inside the parentheses:

$$24 - 3^2$$

Next, simplify the exponents:

$$24 - 9$$

Finally, subtract to get 15, Choice *C*.

2. A: The sum of the shirts is 54. So, we know that the number of green shirts, plus the number of red shirts, plus the number of blue shirts is 54. By subtracting the number of green shirts (12) and the number of red shirts (28) from the total number of shirts (54), we can calculate the number of blue shirts, which make up the remaining portion of the total.

3. B: To solve this correctly, keep in mind the order of operations with the mnemonic PEMDAS (Please Excuse My Dear Aunt Sally). This stands for Parentheses, Exponents, Multiplication, Division, Addition, Subtraction. Taking it step by step, solve inside the parentheses first:

$$4 \times 7 + (4)^2 \div 2$$

Then, apply the exponent:

$$4 \times 7 + 16 \div 2$$

Multiplication and division are both performed next:

$$28 + 8$$

And then finally, addition:

$$28 + 8 = 36$$

4. C: Kimberley worked 4.5 hours at the rate of $10/h and 1 hour at the rate of $12/h. The problem states that her pay is rounded to the nearest hour, so the 4.5 hours would round up to 5 hours at the rate of $10/h.

$$(5h) \times \left(\frac{\$10}{h}\right) + (1h) \times \left(\frac{\$12}{h}\right) = \$50 + \$12 = \$62$$

5. D:

$$9x + x - 7 = 16 + 2x \qquad \text{Combine } 9x \text{ and } x.$$

$$10x - 7 = 16 + 2x$$

$$10x - 7 + 7 = 16 + 2x + 7 \qquad \text{Add 7 to both sides to remove } (-7).$$

$$10x = 23 + 2x$$

$$10x - 2x = 23 + 2x - 2x \qquad \text{Subtract } 2x \text{ from both sides to move it to the other side of the equation.}$$

$$8x = 23$$

$$\frac{8x}{8} = \frac{23}{8} \qquad \text{Divide by 8 to get } x \text{ by itself.}$$

$$x = \frac{23}{8}$$

6. B: First, calculate the difference between the larger value and the smaller value.

$$378 - 252 = 126$$

To calculate this difference as a percentage of the original value, and thus calculate the percentage *increase*, divide 126 by 252, then multiply by 100 to reach the percentage 50%, Choice *B*.

7. A: First, simplify the larger fraction by separating it into two fractions. When dividing one fraction by another, remember to *invert* the second fraction and multiply the two as follows:

$$\frac{5}{7} \times \frac{11}{9}$$

The resulting fraction $\frac{55}{63}$ cannot be simplified further, so this is the answer to the problem.

8. C: The number of days can be found by taking the total amount Bernard needs to make and dividing it by the amount he earns per day:

$$\frac{300}{80} = \frac{30}{8} = \frac{15}{4} = 3.75$$

But Bernard is only working full days, so he will need to work 4 days, since 3 days is not a sufficient amount of time.

9. C: The first step in solving this problem is expressing the result in fraction form. Multiplication and division are typically performed in order from left to right but they can be performed in any order. For this problem, let's start by solving the division operation of the last two fractions. When dividing one fraction by another, invert or flip the second fraction and then multiply the numerator and denominator.

$$\frac{7}{10} \times \frac{2}{1} = \frac{14}{10}$$

273

Next, multiply the first fraction with this value:

$$\frac{3}{5} \times \frac{14}{10} = \frac{42}{50}$$

In this instance, you can find the decimal form by converting the fraction into $\frac{x}{100}$, where x is the number from which the final decimal is found. Multiply both the numerator and denominator by 2 to get the fraction as an expression of $\frac{x}{100}$.

$$\frac{42}{50} \times \frac{2}{2} = \frac{84}{100}$$

In decimal form, this would be expressed as 0.84.

10. C: $51.93

List the givens.

$$Tax = 6.0\% = 0.06$$

$$Sale = 50\% = 0.5$$

$$Hat = \$32.99$$

$$Jersey = \$64.99$$

Calculate the sales prices.

$$Hat\ Sale = 0.5(32.99) = 16.495$$

$$Jersey\ Sale = 0.5(64.99) = 32.495$$

Total the sales prices.

$$Hat\ sale + jersey\ sale = 16.495 + 32.495 = 48.99$$

Calculate the tax and add it to the total sales prices.

$$Total\ after\ tax = 48.99 + (48.99 \times 0.06) = \$51.93$$

11. D: $0.45

List the givens.

$$Store\ coffee = \$1.23/lbs$$

$$Local\ roaster\ coffee = \$1.98/1.5\ lbs$$

Calculate the cost for 5 lbs of store brand.

$$\frac{\$1.23}{1\ lbs} \times 5\ lbs = \$6.15$$

Calculate the cost for 5 lbs of the local roaster.

$$\frac{\$1.98}{1.5\ lbs} \times 5\ lbs = \$6.60$$

Subtract to find the difference in price for 5 lbs.

$$\begin{array}{r} \$6.60 \\ - \$6.15 \\ \hline \$0.45 \end{array}$$

12. B: The slope will be given by $m = \frac{y_2 - y_1}{x_2 - x_1}$, and $\frac{1-0}{2-0} = \frac{1}{2}$. The y-intercept will be 0, since it passes through the origin. Using slope-intercept form, the equation for this line is $y = \frac{1}{2}x$.

13. B: The zeros of this function can be found by using the quadratic formula:

$$x = \frac{-b \pm \sqrt{b^2 - 4ac}}{2a}$$

Identifying a, b, and c can also be done from the equation because it is in standard form. The formula becomes:

$$x = \frac{0 \pm \sqrt{0^2 - 4(1)(4)}}{2(1)} = \frac{\sqrt{-16}}{2}$$

Since there is a negative underneath the radical, the answer is a complex number:

$$x = \pm 2i$$

14. C: $y = 40x + 300$. In this scenario, the variables are the number of sales and Karen's weekly pay. The weekly pay depends on the number of sales. Therefore, weekly pay is the dependent variable (y), and the number of sales is the independent variable (x). Each pair of values from the table can be written as an ordered pair (x, y): $(2, 380)$, $(7, 580)$, $(4, 460)$, $(8, 620)$. The ordered pairs can be substituted into the equations to see which creates true statements (both sides equal) for each pair. Even if one ordered pair produces equal values for a given equation, the other three ordered pairs must be checked.

The only equation which is true for all four ordered pairs is $y = 40x + 300$:

$$380 = 40(2) + 300 \rightarrow 380 = 380$$

$$580 = 40(7) + 300 \rightarrow 580 = 580$$

$$460 = 40(4) + 300 \rightarrow 460 = 460$$

$$620 = 40(8) + 300 \rightarrow 620 = 620$$

Test Prep Books!!!

21. C: In order to find the percentage by which the value of the car has been reduced, the current cash value should be subtracted from the initial value and then the difference divided by the initial value. The result should be multiplied by 100 to find the percentage decrease.

$$\frac{20,000 - 8,000}{20,000} = 0.6$$

$$(0.60) \times 100 = 60\%$$

22. D: This problem can be solved using basic arithmetic. Xavier starts with 20 apples, then gives his sister half, so 20 divided by 2.

$$\frac{20}{2} = 10$$

He then gives his neighbor 6, so 6 is subtracted from 10.

$$10 - 6 = 4$$

Lastly, he uses $\frac{3}{4}$ of his apples to make an apple pie, so to find remaining apples, the first step is to subtract $\frac{3}{4}$ from one and then multiply the difference by 4.

$$\left(1 - \frac{3}{4}\right) \times 4 = ?$$

$$\left(\frac{4}{4} - \frac{3}{4}\right) \times 4 = ?$$

$$\left(\frac{1}{4}\right) \times 4 = 1$$

23. B: First, subtract 4 from each side. This yields $6t = 12$. Now, divide both sides by 6 to obtain $t = 2$.

24. B: From the slope-intercept form, $y = mx + b$, it is known that b is the y-intercept, which is 1. Compute the slope as $\frac{2-1}{1-0} = 1$, so the equation is $y = x + 1$.

25. A: Finding the roots means finding the values of x when y is zero. The quadratic formula could be used, but in this case, it is possible to factor by hand, since the numbers -1 and 2 add to 1 and multiply to -2. So, factor $x^2 + x - 2 = (x-1)(x+2) = 0$, then set each factor equal to zero. Solving for each value gives the values $x = 1$ and $x = -2$.

26. A: Simplify this to:

$$(4x^2y^4)^{\frac{3}{2}} = 4^{\frac{3}{2}}(x^2)^{\frac{3}{2}}(y^4)^{\frac{3}{2}}$$

Now:

$$4^{\frac{3}{2}} = (\sqrt{4})^3 = 2^3 = 8$$

277

For the other, recall that the exponents must be multiplied, so this yields:

$$8x^{2 \cdot \frac{3}{2}} y^{4 \cdot \frac{3}{2}} = 8x^3 y^6$$

27. C: Multiply both sides by x to get $x + 2 = 2x$, which simplifies to $x = 2$.

28. A: Every 8 mL of medicine requires 5 mL. The 45 mL first needs to be split into portions of 8 mL. This results in $\frac{45}{8}$ portions. Each portion requires 5 mL. Therefore,

$$\frac{45}{8} \times 5 = \frac{45 \times 5}{8} = \frac{225}{8} \text{ mL is necessary}$$

29. B: 13,078. The power of 10 by which a digit is multiplied corresponds with the number of zeros following the digit when expressing its value in standard form. Therefore:

$$(1 \times 10^4) + (3 \times 10^3) + (7 \times 10^1) + (8 \times 10^0)$$

$$10,000 + 3,000 + 70 + 8 = 13,078$$

30. C: A dollar contains 20 nickels. Therefore, if there are 12 dollars' worth of nickels, there are:

$$12 \times 20 = 240 \text{ nickels}$$

Each nickel weighs 5 grams. Therefore, the weight of the nickels is:

$$240 \times 5 = 1,200 \text{ grams}$$

Adding in the weight of the empty piggy bank, the filled bank weighs 2,250 grams.

Reading

1. B: The main purpose of this passage was to inform. It wants the reader to understand how American science fiction evolved. Choice A is incorrect because the passage is not very descriptive; there is not an abundance of adjectives and adverbs painting a picture in the reader's mind. The passage is not persuasive Choice C; the author is not asking the reader to adopt a stance or argument. For Choice D, it might be mildly entertaining, but the entertainment aspect of the passage takes a back seat to its informative aspects.

2. B: This passage begins with the oldest (the pulp fiction magazines of the Great Depression), moves forward to the science fiction of the fifties and sixties via names like Ray Bradbury and Kurt Vonnegut, and ends with a discussion of modern science fiction movies—*Jurassic Park*, *The Matrix*, *I am Legend*. It follows a sequential timeline of American science fiction.

3. A: All other concepts discussed throughout this passage connect to the main idea: "Science fiction has been a part of the American fabric for a long time." Choice B states: "As time went on, science fiction evolved, posing better plots and more sophisticated questions." This is only a portion of the entire history of American science fiction. The same is true of Choice C: "These outlandish stories of aliens and superheroes were printed on cheap, disposable paper stock, hence the name *pulp* (as in paper) *fiction*." Choice D, though it ties together the Great Depression and modern American cinema, doesn't touch on the period in between.

4. A: There are several clues that support Choice *A*. First, the fact that the stories were printed on *disposable paper* proves that these stories were, at the time, not considered serious literature. Furthermore, it's noted later in the passage that science fiction *was taken seriously* as authors like Kurt Vonnegut and Ray Bradbury gained prominence. This further reinforces the notion that at the beginning it was considered only fanciful and for children. Choice *B* is incorrect. Even though the statement is true of the passage, it's not supported by the individual sentence. Choice *C* is incorrect because the sentence never states directly or hints at this, and, in addition, movies and radio were available during this time period. Choice *D* is incorrect. The premise of the whole passage is that the medium of science fiction is not new. It doesn't spend any time discussing *how* science fiction was written and *what* those authors believed.

5. C: To arrive at the correct answer, find the best synonym for *spurious*. *Fake* makes the most sense because Bob is trying to hide his true emotions. Based on his horrible performance, he understands that he didn't get the job, so the reader can infer that his confidence is not at an all-time high. Therefore, *fake* would make just as much sense in this case as *spurious*. *Extreme* would indicate that Bob is euphoric and the interview went well. *Mild* would indicate that Bob thought he had a slight chance at getting hired. In this instance, *genuine* would be an antonym; i.e., the exact opposite of what Bob is feeling.

6. C: Throughout the entire text, the author maintains a persuasive tone. He argues that punishment should quickly follow the crime and gives a host of reasons why: it's more humane; it helps the prisoner to understand the nature of their crimes; it makes a better example for society. To confirm it's a persuasive stance, try reversing the argument. If the position cannot be reversed, then it's not persuasive. In this instance, the reader could argue in rebuttal that the punishment does not have to quickly follow the crime. Regardless of the veracity of this argument, simply creating it proves that the passage is persuasive.

7. C: This passage was written with a cause/effect structure. The cause is that the length between incarceration and trial should be as short as possible. The author, then, lists multiple effects of this cause. There are several key words that indicate this is a cause/effect argument. For instance, the author states, "The degree of the punishment, and the consequences of a crime, ought to be so contrived, as to have the greatest possible effect on others, with the least possible pain to the delinquent." The key words *as to have* indicate that changing the manner of punishment will change the outcome. Similarly, the authors states, "An immediate punishment is more useful; because the smaller the interval of time between the punishment and the crime, the stronger and more lasting will be the association of the two ideas of Crime and Punishment." Similar to *as to have* in the previous excerpt, *because* shows causation. In this instance, the author argues that the shorter the duration between crime and punishment, the more criminals will grasp the consequences of their actions. In general, for cause-effect passages, keep a lookout for words like *because*, *since*, *consequently*, *so*, and *as a result*.

8. D: "The more immediately after the commission of a crime a punishment is inflicted, the more just and useful it will be," best exemplifies the main idea of this passage. All subsequent discussion links back to this main idea and plays the role of supporting details. "The vulgar, that is, all men who have no general ideas or universal principles, act in consequence of the most immediate and familiar associations," supports this idea because the "vulgar," criminals, in other words, are used to making quick associations and are not used to delaying gratification or ignoring their impulses.

"Crimes of less importance are commonly punished, either in the obscurity of a prison, or the criminal is transported, to give, by his slavery, an example to societies which he never offended," supports the main idea because the author argues that this is the wrong way to punish because if the punishment occurs in the same area the crime was committed, then the punishment will have more effect, since criminals will associate the areas with their crimes. Furthermore, transferring a prisoner takes time and delays punishment. Lastly, the author states, "Men do not, in general, commit great crimes deliberately, but rather in a sudden gust of passion; and they commonly look on the punishment due to a great crime as remote and improbable." To reduce the sense of punishments being remote and improbable, criminals must, according to the author, receive an immediate punishment. Therefore, by removing a lengthy gap between crime and punishment, a criminal's punishment will be close and probable, which the author argues is the most humane way to punish and the mark of a civilized society.

9. A: The author would disagree most strongly with the statement *criminals are incapable of connecting crime and punishment*. Though the author states that criminals are often passionate and consider punishment unlikely in the heat of the crime, the entire premise of the passage is that reducing the time between crime and punishment increases the likelihood of an association. He also argues that if a society does this consistently, the probability that individuals will consider the consequences of their actions increases. *A punishment should quickly follow the crime* is a restatement of the main idea, supported by evidence throughout the passage. *Most criminals do not think about the consequences of their actions*. Though the author makes this clear, he goes on to say that, in general, reducing the time between crime and punishment will have the most positive effect on the prisoner and on society. *Where a criminal is being punished is just as important as when*. The author argues in the passage that a punishment should be immediate and near where the crime originally occurred.

10. D: Based on what Carl has encountered—a spider web and a mouse—he would be hesitant, lest he encounter another critter. *Fearfully* is too strong a word (unless Carl has a phobia) and would indicate something more serious, like mortal danger. Nowhere in the passage does it indicate Carl is angry, and for Carl to be suspicious, he would have to assume that someone in his life was trying to deceive him. There's no evidence of deception here.

11. C: Despite the opposite stances in Passages 1 and 2, both authors establish that cell phones are a strong part of culture. In Passage 1 the author states, "Today's student is already strongly rooted in technology." In Passage 2 the author states, "Students are comfortable with cell phones." The author of Passage 2 states that cell phones have a "time and place." The author of Passage 2 would disagree with the statement that *teachers should incorporate cell phones into curriculum whenever possible*. *Cell phones are useful only when an experienced teacher uses them properly*—this statement is implied in Passage 2, but the author in Passage 1 says cell phones are "indispensable." In other words, no teacher can do without them. *Despite a good lesson plan, cell phone disruptions are impossible to avoid*. This is not supported by either passage. Even though the author in the second passage is more cautionary, the author states, "This can prove advantageous if done correctly." Therefore, there is a possibility that a classroom can run properly with cell phones.

12. D: Here, "speaking" has nothing to do with communication. The original quotation from Passage 1 reads, *Since today's student is already strongly rooted in technology, when teachers incorporate cell phones, they're 'speaking' the student's language*. The first dependent clause makes reference to technology, then uses the word "speaking" as an analogy. The "language" the author refers to is culture. The author never intended the word "speak" to imply actual communication. *Cell phones are a free,* *readily available resource*; *cell phones incorporate other forms of technology*; and *due to their mobility, cell phones are excellent in an emergency* are all listed as reasons in Passage 1 to have cell phones.

13. B: The author states in Passage 2, "Confiscating phones is akin to rummaging through students' backpacks." The author most likely included this passage to exemplify how strongly students believe this is a right. This quotation is the evidence or example, and it ties to the previous sentence: "This type of disrespectful behavior is often justified by the argument that cell phones are not only a privilege but also a right." The backpack example illustrates how students believe it's a right. *Indicate how unlikely students are to change their minds*; *exemplify how easily the modern student is offended* and *demonstrate how illogical most students' beliefs are* are not supported by Passage 2.

14. B: The best substitute for *surreptitiously* would be *slyly*. Let's look at the context of the sentence: "a sizable percentage of a classroom pretends to pay attention while surreptitiously playing on their phones." The key word here is *pretends*. The students in the classroom, therefore, want to use their cell phones but are afraid of getting caught. *Privately* doesn't work because it leaves out the connotation of hiding a wrong act or ulterior motive. *Obstinately* and *defiantly* are also incorrect since students are hiding their disobedience.

15. D: We are looking for the claim that is least supportive of the argument that the American economy is healthy. Choice *A* says that the GDP increased by 2% last year, which supports a claim of health. Choice *B* relays that unemployment is the lowest it's been in over a decade, a sign of a strong economy. Choice *C* states that average household income is at a historical high point. In contrast, the final choice draws a negative conclusion about the economy—a decrease in output even after investments— therefore, a declining manufacturing sector is least supportive that the economy is healthy. Choice *D* is the correct answer.

16. B: The passage indicates that Annabelle has a fear of going outside into the daylight. Thus *heliophobia* must refer to a fear of bright lights or sunlight. Choice *B* is the only answer that describes this.

17. C: We are looking for an inference—a conclusion that is reached on the basis of evidence and reasoning—from the passage that will likely explain why the famous children's author did not achieve her usual success with the new genre (despite the book's acclaim). Choice *A* is wrong because the statement is false according to the passage. Choice *B* is wrong because, although the passage says the author has a graduate degree on the subject, it would be an unrealistic leap to infer that she is the foremost expert on Antebellum America. Choice *D* is wrong because there is nothing in the passage to lead us to infer that people generally prefer a children's series to historical fiction. In contrast, Choice *C* can be logically inferred since the passage speaks of the great success of the children's series and the declaration that the fame of the author's name causes the children's books to "fly off the shelves." Thus, she did not receive any bump from her name since she published the historical novel under a pseudonym, which makes Choice *C* correct.

18. B: Narrative, Choice *A*, means a written account of connected events. Think of narrative writing as a story. Choice *C*, expository writing, generally seeks to explain or describe some phenomena, whereas Choice *D*, technical writing, includes directions, instructions, and/or explanations. This passage is persuasive writing, which hopes to change someone's beliefs based on an appeal to reason or emotion. The author is aiming to convince the reader that smoking is terrible. They use health, price, and beauty in their argument against smoking, so Choice *B*, persuasive, is the correct answer.

281

19. B: The author is opposed to tobacco. He cites disease and deaths associated with smoking. He points to the monetary expense and aesthetic costs. Choice *A* is wrong because alternatives to smoking are not addressed in the passage. Choice *C* is wrong because it does not summarize the passage but rather is just a premise. Choice *D* is wrong because, while these statistics are a premise in the argument, they do not represent a summary of the piece. Choice *B* is the correct answer because it states the three critiques offered against tobacco and expresses the author's conclusion.

20. C: We are looking for something the author would agree with, so it should be anti-smoking or an argument in favor of quitting smoking. Choice *A* is wrong because the author does not speak against means of cessation. Choice *B* is wrong because the author does not reference other substances but does speak of how addictive nicotine, a drug in tobacco, is. Choice *D* is wrong because the author would not encourage reducing taxes to encourage a reduction of smoking costs, thereby helping smokers to continue the habit. Choice *C* is correct because the author is attempting to persuade smokers to quit smoking.

21. D: Here, we are looking for an opinion of the author rather than a fact or statistic. Choice *D* is correct as an opinion because smell is subjective. Some people might like the smell of smoke, they might not have working olfactory senses, and they might not find the smell of smoke akin to "pervasive nastiness," so this is the expression of an opinion. Thus, Choice *D* is the correct answer. Choice *A* is incorrect because quoting statistics from the Centers of Disease Control and Prevention is stating facts, not opinions. Choice *B* is incorrect because it expresses the fact that cigarettes sometimes cost more than a few gallons of gas. It would be an opinion if the author said that cigarettes were not affordable. Choice *C* is incorrect because yellow stains are a known possible adverse effect of smoking.

22. D: Outspending other countries on education could have other benefits, but there is no reference to this in the passage, so Choice *A* is incorrect. Choice *B* is incorrect because the author does not mention corruption. Choice *C* is incorrect because there is nothing in the passage stating that the tests are not genuinely representative. Choice *D* is accurate because spending more money has not brought success. The United States already spends the most money, and the country is not excelling on these tests. Choice *D* is the correct answer.

23. D: Although Washington was from a wealthy background, the passage does not say that his wealth led to his republican ideals, so Choice *A* is not supported. Choice *B* also does not follow from the passage. Washington's warning against meddling in foreign affairs does not mean that he would oppose wars of every kind, so Choice *B* is wrong. Choice *C* is also unjustified since the author does not indicate that Alexander Hamilton's assistance was absolutely necessary. Choice *D* is correct because the farewell address clearly opposes political parties and partisanship. The author then notes that presidential elections often hit a fever pitch of partisanship. Thus, it follows that George Washington would not approve of modern political parties and their involvement in presidential elections.

24. A: The author finishes the passage by applying Washington's farewell address to modern politics, so the purpose probably includes this application. Choice *B* is wrong because George Washington is already a well-established historical figure; furthermore, the passage does not seek to introduce him. Choice *C* is wrong because the author is not fighting a common perception that Washington was merely a military hero. Choice *D* is wrong because the author is not convincing readers. Persuasion does not correspond to the passage. Choice *A* states the primary purpose.

25. D: Choice *A* is wrong because the last paragraph is not appropriate for a history textbook. Choice *B* is false because the piece is not a notice or announcement of Washington's death. Choice *C* is clearly false because it is not fiction, but a historical writing. Choice *D* is correct. The passage is most likely to appear in a newspaper editorial because it cites information relevant and applicable to the present day, a popular format in editorials.

26. D: The passage does not proceed in chronological order since it begins by pointing out Christopher Columbus's explorations in America so Choice *A* does not work. Although the author compares and contrasts Erikson with Christopher Columbus, this is not the main way the information is presented; therefore, Choice *B* does not work. Neither does Choice *C* because there is no mention of or reference to cause and effect in the passage. However, the passage does offer a conclusion (Leif Erikson deserves more credit) and premises (first European to set foot in the New World and first to contact the natives) to substantiate Erikson's historical importance. Thus, Choice *D* is correct.

27. C: Choice *A* is wrong because it describes facts: Leif Erikson was the son of Erik the Red and historians debate Leif's date of birth. These are not opinions. Choice *B* is wrong; that Erikson called the land Vinland is a verifiable fact as is Choice *D* because he did contact the natives almost 500 years before Columbus. Choice *C* is the correct answer because it is the author's opinion that Erikson deserves more credit. That, in fact, is his conclusion in the piece, but another person could argue that Columbus or another explorer deserves more credit for opening up the New World to exploration. Rather than being an incontrovertible fact, it is a subjective value claim.

28. B: Choice *A* is wrong because the author aims to go beyond describing Erikson as merely a legendary Viking. Choice *C* is wrong because the author does not focus on Erikson's motivations, let alone name the spreading of Christianity as his primary objective. Choice *D* is wrong because it is a premise that Erikson contacted the natives 500 years before Columbus, which is simply a part of supporting the author's conclusion. Choice *B* is correct because, as stated in the previous answer, it accurately identifies the author's statement that Erikson deserves more credit than he has received for being the first European to explore the New World.

29. B: Choice *A* is wrong because the author is not in any way trying to entertain the reader. Choice *D* is wrong because he goes beyond merely a suggestion; "suggest" is too vague. Although the author is certainly trying to alert the readers of Leif Erikson's unheralded accomplishments, the word alert carries a sense of urgency or warning that is not found in this passage Choice *C*. Rather, the author would want the reader to be informed about it, which is more substantial and academic Choice *B*.

30. D: Choice *A* is wrong because the author never addresses the Vikings' state of mind or emotions. Choice *B* is wrong because the author does not elaborate on Erikson's exile and whether he would have become an explorer if not for his banishment. Choice *C* is wrong because there is not enough information to support this premise. It is unclear whether Erikson informed the King of Norway of his finding. Although it is true that the King did not send a follow-up expedition, he could have simply chosen not to expend the resources after receiving Erikson's news. It is not possible to logically infer whether Erikson told him. Choice *D* is correct because there are two examples—Leif Erikson's date of birth and what happened during the encounter with the natives—of historians having trouble pinning down important details in Viking history.

Writing

1. C: Choice *C* is correct because it fixes the core issue with this sentence: the singular *has* should not describe the plural *scientists*. Thus, Choice *A* is incorrect. Choices *B* and *D* add unnecessary commas.

2. D: Choice *D* correctly conveys the writer's intention of asking if, or *whether*, early perceptions of dinosaurs are still influencing people. Choice *A* makes no sense as worded. Choice *B* is better, but *how* doesn't coincide with the context. Choice *C* adds unnecessary commas.

3. A: Choice *A* is correct, as the sentence does not require modification. Choices *B* and *C* implement extra punctuation unnecessarily, disrupting the flow of the sentence. Choice *D* incorrectly adds a comma in an awkward location.

4. B: Choice *B* is the strongest revision, as adding *to explore* is very effective in both shortening the sentence and maintaining, even enhancing, the point of the writer. To explore is to seek understanding in order to gain knowledge and insight, which coincides with the focus of the overall sentence. Choice *A* is not technically incorrect, but it is overcomplicated. Choice *C* is a decent revision, but the sentence could still be more condensed and sharpened. Choice *D* fails to make the sentence more concise and inserts unnecessary commas.

5. D: Choice *D* correctly applies a semicolon to introduce a new line of thought while remaining in a single sentence. The comma after *however* is also appropriately placed. Choice *A* is a run-on sentence. Choice *B* is also incorrect because the single comma is not enough to fix the sentence. Choice *C* adds commas around *uncertain* which are unnecessary.

6. B: Choice *B* not only fixes the homophone issue from *its*, which is possessive, to *it's*, which is a contraction of *it is*, but also streamlines the sentence by adding a comma and eliminating *and*. Choice *A* is incorrect because of these errors. Choices *C* and *D* only fix the homophone issue.

7. A: Choice *A* is correct, as the sentence is fine the way it is. Choices *B* and *C* add unnecessary commas, while Choice *D* uses the possessive *its* instead of the contraction *it's*.

8. C: Choice *C* is correct because the phrase *even likely* is flanked by commas, creating a kind of aside, which allows the reader to see this separate thought while acknowledging it as part of the overall sentence and subject at hand. Choice *A* is incorrect because it seems to ramble after *even* due to a missing comma after *likely*. Choice *B* is better but inserting a comma after *that* warps the flow of the writing. Choice *D* is incorrect because there must be a comma after *plausible*.

9. D: Choice *D* strengthens the overall sentence structure while condensing the words. This makes the subject of the sentence, and the emphasis of the writer, much clearer to the reader. Thus, while Choice *A* is technically correct, the language is choppy and over-complicated. Choice *B* is better but lacks the reference to a specific image of dinosaurs. Choice *C* introduces unnecessary commas.

10. B: Choice *B* correctly joins the two independent clauses. Choice *A* is decent, but "that would be" is too verbose for the sentence. Choice *C* incorrectly changes the semicolon to a comma. Choice *D* splits the clauses effectively but is not concise enough.

11. A: Choice *A* is correct, as the original sentence has no error. Choices *B* and *C* employ unnecessary semicolons and commas. Choice *D* would be an ideal revision, but it lacks the comma after *Ransom* that would enable the sentence structure to flow.

12. D: By reorganizing the sentence, the context becomes clearer with Choice *D*. Choice *A* has an awkward sentence structure. Choice *B* offers a revision that doesn't correspond well with the original sentence's intent. Choice *C* cuts out too much of the original content, losing the full meaning.

13. C: Choice *C* fixes the disagreement between the singular *this* and the plural *viewpoints*. Choice *A*, therefore, is incorrect. Choice *B* introduces an unnecessary comma. In Choice *D*, *those* agrees with *viewpoints*, but neither agrees with *distinguishes*.

14. A: Choice *A* is direct and clear, without any punctuation errors. Choice *B* is well-written but too wordy. Choice *C* adds an unnecessary comma. Choice *D* is also well-written but much less concise than Choice *A*.

15. D: Choice *D* rearranges the sentence to improve clarity and impact, with *tempting* directly describing *idea*. On its own, Choice *A* is a run-on. Choice *B* is better because it separates the clauses, but it keeps an unnecessary comma. Choice *C* is also an improvement but still a run-on.

16. B: Choice *B* is the best answer simply because the sentence makes it clear that Un-man takes over and possesses Weston. In Choice *A*, these events sounded like two different things, instead of an action and result. Choices *C* and *D* make this relationship clearer, but the revisions don't flow very well grammatically.

17. D: Changing the phrase *after this* to *then* makes the sentence less complicated and captures the writer's intent, making Choice *D* correct. Choice *A* is awkwardly constructed. Choices *B* and *C* misuse their commas and do not adequately improve the clarity.

18. B: By starting a new sentence, the run-on issue is eliminated, and a new line of reasoning can be seamlessly introduced, making Choice *B* correct. Choice *A* is thus incorrect. While Choice *C* fixes the run-on via a semicolon, a comma is still needed after *this*. Choice *D* contains a comma splice. The independent clauses must be separated by more than just a comma, even with the rearrangement of the second half of the sentence.

19. A: Books are italicized, like *Frankenstein*, and smaller works are put in quotation marks. A direct quotation takes a single set of quotation marks (" ") and a quote within a quote takes a single set (' '). Choice *B* is incorrect because *Frankenstein* should be italicized, not put in quotation marks. In Choice *C*, the double and single-set quotation marks should be reversed. In Choice *D*, the comma is missing before the first quotation mark, and the period for the quote within a quote is on the outside of the quotation mark, not the inside. Punctuation belongs inside the quotation marks, regardless of whether it a single or double set.

20. B: The word *conscience* means a sense of right and wrong. *Conscious* Choice *A* refers to a state of being awake and alert. *Consensus* Choice *C* means an opinion shared by many, and a *census* Choice *D* is a count of an area's population.

21. B: Choice *A*, Choice *C*, and Choice *D* all relate facts but do not present the kind of general statement that would serve as an effective summary or conclusion. Choice *B* is correct.

285

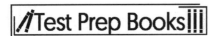

22. C: The passage is told in chronological order, detailing the steps the family took to adopt their dog. The narrator mentions that Robin's physical exam and lab work confirmed she was healthy before discussing that they brought her to the vet to evaluate her health. It is illogical that lab work would confirm good health prior to an appointment with the vet, when, presumably, the lab work would be collected.

23. A: Choice A uses incorrect subject-verb agreement because the indefinite pronoun *neither* is singular and must use the singular verb form *is*. The pronoun *both* is plural and uses the plural verb form of *are*. The pronoun *any* can be either singular or plural. In this example, it is used as a plural, so the plural verb form *are* is used. The pronoun *each* is singular and uses the singular verb form *is*.

24. B: Choice B is correct because the pronouns *he* and *I* are in the subjective case. *He* and *I* are the subjects of the verb *like* in the independent clause of the sentence. Choices A, C, and D are incorrect because they all contain at least one objective pronoun (*me* and *him*). Objective pronouns should not be used as the subject of the sentence, but rather, they should come as an object of a verb. To test for correct pronoun usage, try reading the pronouns as if they were the only pronoun in the sentence. For example, *he* and *me* may appear to be the correct answer choices, but try reading them as the only pronoun.

He like[s] to go fishing…

Me like to go fishing…

When looked at that way, *me* is an obviously incorrect choice.

25. C: This question focuses on the correct usage of the commonly confused word pairs of *it's/its* and *then/than*. *It's* is a contraction for *it is* or *it has*. *Its* is a possessive pronoun. The word *than* shows comparison between two things. *Then* is an adverb that conveys time. Choice C correctly uses *it's* and *than*. *It's* is a contraction for *it has* in this sentence, and *than* shows comparison between *work* and *rest*. None of the other answer choices use both of the correct words.

26. C: The simple subject of this sentence, the word *lots*, is plural. It agrees with the plural verb form *were*. Choice A is incorrect, because the simple subject *there*, referring to the two constellations, is considered plural. It does not agree with the singular verb form *is*. In Choice B, the singular subject *four*, does not agree with the plural verb form *needs*. In Choice D, the plural subject *everyone* does not agree with the singular verb form *have*.

27. D: The object pronouns *her* and *me* act as the indirect objects of the sentence. If *me* is in a series of object pronouns, it should always come last in the series. Choice A is incorrect because it uses subject pronouns *she* and *I*. Choice B is incorrect because it uses the subject pronoun *she*. Choice C uses the correct object pronouns, but they are in the wrong order.

28. D: Choice D directly addresses the reader, so it is in second person point of view. This is an imperative sentence since it issues a command; imperative sentences have an *understood you* as the subject. Choice A uses first person pronouns *I* and *my*. Choices B and C are incorrect because they use third person point of view.

29. B: Choice B correctly uses the contraction for *you are* as the subject of the sentence, and it correctly uses the possessive pronoun *your* to indicate ownership of the jacket. It also correctly uses the adverb

286

there, indicating place. Choice *A* is incorrect because it reverses the possessive pronoun *your* and the contraction for *you are*. It also uses the possessive pronoun *their* instead of the adverb *there*. Choice *C* is incorrect because it reverses *your* and *you're* and uses the contraction for *they are* in place of the adverb *there*. Choice *D* incorrectly uses the possessive pronoun *their* instead of the adverb *there*.

30. B: To arrive at the best answer (*surly*), all the character traits for Cindy must be analyzed. She's described as *happy* ("always has a smile on her face"), *kind* ("volunteers at the local shelter"), and *patient* ("no one has ever seen her angry"). Since Cindy's husband is the *opposite* of her, these adjectives must be converted to antonyms. Someone who is *surly* is *unhappy*, *rude*, and *impatient*. Choice *A* (*stingy*) is too narrow of a word. Someone could be *happy* and *kind*, for instance, but still be *stingy*. For Choice *C*, *scared*, to be plausible, the rest of the passage would need instances of Cindy being *bold* or *courageous*. Though she's certainly *kind* and *helpful*, none of those traits are modeled. Choice *D* (*shy*) also doesn't match. Someone who is *shy* could still be *happy*, *kind*, and *patient*.

Index

Contractions, 82, 139, 158, 169, 174, 175
Contrasting, 81, 103, 104, 106, 107
Coordinate Plane, 12, 21, 27, 47, 55, 58, 59, 61
Coordinating Conjunction, 121, 122, 131, 163
Coordinating Conjunctions, 121, 163
Cosecant, 51
Cosine, 49, 50, 51, 53
Cotangent, 51
Countable, 119, 132
Counterargument, 94, 98, 112, 113
Credible, 76, 98, 101, 109, 110, 111, 113, 141, 142, 214
Cube Root, 20, 43
Cubic Function, 47
Dangling Modifiers, 124
Declarative, 165, 166
Degree of the Polynomial, 47
Demonstratives, 121
Denominator, 19, 20, 23, 28, 29, 36, 44, 46, 202, 204, 206, 207, 238, 273, 274, 276
Denotation, 100, 101, 136, 137
Dependent Clauses, 121, 122, 128, 131, 167, 211
Dependent Variable, 25, 275
Descriptive Writing, 89, 100, 146
Determinant, 45, 46
Determiner, 120
Diction, 88, 96, 100, 106, 107, 144, 145
Diction/Tone, 144
Difference of Squares, 27, 33, 35, 38
Discriminant of the Parabola, 47
Distributive Property, 29, 35, 36
Domain, 25, 26, 46, 47, 48, 49, 53, 181, 206
Double Inequalities, 15
Dynamic Characters, 103
Effect, 77, 89, 92, 97, 99, 100, 101, 102, 110, 123, 128, 153, 157, 160, 166, 169, 190, 191, 213, 214, 227, 234, 246, 253, 255, 256, 262, 279, 280, 282
Ellipse, 57
Ellipsis (...), 171
Em-Dash (—), 174
Emotional Writing, 94
Equation, 12, 13, 14, 15, 16, 17, 18, 20, 21, 22, 25, 27, 28, 29, 36, 37, 38, 41, 42, 46, 48, 49, 51, 55, 56, 57, 60, 61, 62, 63, 64, 65, 66, 67, 69, 70, 181, 182, 202, 203, 204, 205, 206,

216, 218, 219, 236, 237, 238, 239, 240, 248, 250, 252, 273, 275, 276, 277
Essential Clauses, 129, 130
Ethical Appeal, 110
Ethos, 96, 110, 192
Etymology, 134
Even, 1, 3, 4, 5, 23, 25, 26, 41, 42, 47, 56, 71, 80, 81, 83, 93, 99, 112, 113, 130, 131, 137, 139, 140, 143, 153, 158, 159, 162, 166, 167, 173, 174, 185, 211, 226, 242, 253, 254, 258, 263, 265, 269, 275, 279, 280, 281, 284, 285
Even Function, 26
Exaggeration, 85, 138, 155, 156, 208, 241, 242
Exclamatory, 166
Exponential Function, 47, 48, 49
Exponents, 18, 28, 35, 36, 37, 39, 43, 44, 48, 204, 240, 272, 276, 278
Fact, 3, 41, 49, 53, 78, 90, 91, 93, 96, 98, 105, 109, 110, 111, 112, 120, 135, 142, 156, 167, 168, 185, 208, 210, 213, 222, 242, 243, 244, 246, 258, 262, 266, 267, 279, 282, 283
Factors, 15, 23, 27, 32, 33, 34, 37, 42, 98, 167, 203, 205, 239
Fallacy, 111, 112, 156
False Analogy, 111
False Dichotomy, 108, 111, 112
Figurative Language, 84, 85, 145, 146
Figure of Speech, 137, 138, 155
Figures of Speech, 137, 138, 155
First Outer Inner Last (FOIL), 31, 35, 36, 70, 202, 207
First Person Point of View, 108
First Quadrant, 52, 55
First-Person Point of View, 83, 103, 107
Flat Character, 103
Fourth Quadrant, 55
Fraction, 19, 23, 28, 29, 37, 44, 70, 183, 204, 206, 207, 238, 249, 273, 274, 276
Function, 7, 14, 25, 26, 27, 28, 37, 38, 46, 47, 48, 49, 50, 51, 52, 53, 103, 111, 118, 119, 120, 128, 130, 131, 132, 136, 145, 162, 169, 175, 180, 181, 205, 211, 212, 215, 218, 237, 238, 251, 263, 265, 275
General Order, 91
Graph of a Function, 25
Greater Than, 12, 16, 35, 41, 47, 48, 68, 206, 236

Greatest Common Factor, 42, 43

Hasty Generalization, 111, 112

Horizontal Asymptote, 48

Hyperbola, 57

Hyperbole, 85, 138, 146, 187, 189, 208, 209, 221, 223, 241, 242

Hyphen (-), 173

Identity Function, 25

Imperative, 95, 122, 165, 166, 286

Inconsistent, 66, 124

Indefinite Pronouns, 120

Independent Clause, 91, 122, 123, 126, 128, 129, 131, 132, 164, 167, 171, 172, 173, 177, 211, 212, 213, 245, 246, 284, 285, 286

Independent Variable, 25, 37, 275

Index of the Radical, 18, 43

Inequality, 12, 14, 15, 16, 47, 68, 203, 276

Inference, 98, 99, 281

Infinitive Form, 123, 124

Inflection, 132

Infographics, 143, 144

Informative Writing, 87, 94, 96, 99, 100, 146

Integers, 19, 32, 42, 43, 44, 45, 47

Intercept Form, 57

Interjection, 121

Interrogative, 166

Irony, 137, 155, 187

Irregular Plurals, 169

Juxtaposition, 105, 187, 208

Least Common Multiple, 19, 42

Least Common Multiple (LCM), 19

Less Than, 12, 16, 30, 37, 47, 48, 68, 85, 179

Like Terms, 31, 35, 36, 39, 205, 276

Line Graphs, 144

Linear, 13, 14, 16, 30, 47, 56, 57, 62, 63, 64, 65, 66, 67, 68, 205, 236, 276

Linear Equations, 13, 14, 56, 57, 63, 66

Linear System of Two Equations, 62, 64

Logarithmic Function, 49

Logical Fallacy, 111, 112

Logical Sequencing, 153

Logos, 96, 111

Lowest Terms, 23

Main Clauses, 121, 129

Main Idea, 71, 72, 73, 74, 75, 76, 96, 117, 138, 139, 144, 146, 151, 152, 153, 210, 221, 241, 254, 256, 278, 279, 280

Main Point of a Paragraph, 92

Matrix, 45, 46, 63, 204, 253, 278

Message, 73, 85, 95, 97, 100, 106, 107, 111, 130, 144, 190

Metonymy, 138

Midpoint, 57

MLA Style Citation, 147

Modifiers, 123, 125, 130

Monomial, 30, 33, 36

Monotone, 26

Mood, 81, 83, 137, 139, 140

Multiplication Principle, 20

Narratives, 94, 95, 100, 174

Narrator, 83, 103, 108, 150, 286

Natural Logarithm, 49

Nonessential Clauses, 129, 130

Non-Restrictive Clauses, 129

Noun Phrase, 119, 120, 125, 130, 136, 165

Nouns, 119, 121, 132, 162, 169, 213

Numerator, 19, 23, 28, 29, 31, 36, 44, 202, 206, 238, 273, 274, 276

Numerical Order/Order of Importance, 91

Object Pronouns, 119, 286

Odd, 27, 41, 47

Odd Function, 27

Onomatopoeia, 84, 85

Opinion, 95, 100, 109, 110, 112, 113, 154, 184, 191, 224, 225, 242, 260, 262, 282, 283, 285

Order of Operations, 24, 29, 39, 43, 44, 240, 272

Ordered Pair, 46, 56, 58, 66, 68, 250, 275, 276

Outline, 72, 73, 74, 243

Overgeneralization, 108, 111, 112

Parabola, 21, 37, 47, 48, 57, 63, 67, 206

Parallel Lines, 57

Parallel Structure, 123, 164, 211, 213, 245

Paraphrasing, 72, 73, 74, 75

Parentheses, 22, 35, 39, 40, 44, 49, 173, 174, 240, 272, 276

Past Tense, 124, 127, 132, 211, 212, 213, 245

Pathetic or Emotional Appeal, 110

Pathos, 96, 110, 192

Perfect Square, 33, 43

Perpendicular or Orthogonal Lines, 57

Personal Pronouns, 83, 103, 119

Persuasive Writing, 94, 100, 243, 281

Dear PERT Test Taker,

We would like to start by thanking you for purchasing this study guide for your PERT exam. We hope that we exceeded your expectations.

Our goal in creating this study guide was to cover all of the topics that you will see on the test. We also strove to make our practice questions as similar as possible to what you will encounter on test day. With that being said, if you found something that you feel was not up to your standards, please send us an email and let us know.

We would also like to let you know about other books in our catalog that may interest you.

SAT

This can be found on Amazon: amazon.com/dp/1637759878

ACT

amazon.com/dp/163775583X

ACCUPLACER

amazon.com/dp/1637750250

We have study guides in a wide variety of fields. If the one you are looking for isn't listed above, then try searching for it on Amazon or send us an email.

Thanks Again and Happy Testing!
Product Development Team
info@studyguideteam.com

FREE Test Taking Tips Video/DVD Offer

To better serve you, we created videos covering test taking tips that we want to give you for FREE. **These videos cover world-class tips that will help you succeed on your test.**

We just ask that you send us feedback about this product. Please let us know what you thought about it—whether good, bad, or indifferent.

To get your **FREE videos**, you can use the QR code below or email freevideos@studyguideteam.com with "Free Videos" in the subject line and the following information in the body of the email:

 a. The title of your product

 b. Your product rating on a scale of 1-5, with 5 being the highest

 c. Your feedback about the product

If you have any questions or concerns, please don't hesitate to contact us at info@studyguideteam.com.

Thank you!

Made in United States
Orlando, FL
21 April 2024